Nature Is Nurture

Nature Is Nurture
Counseling and the Natural World

Megan E. Delaney, PhD, LPC

OXFORD
UNIVERSITY PRESS

Oxford University Press is a department of the University of Oxford. It furthers
the University's objective of excellence in research, scholarship, and education
by publishing worldwide. Oxford is a registered trade mark of Oxford University
Press in the UK and certain other countries.

Published in the United States of America by Oxford University Press
198 Madison Avenue, New York, NY 10016, United States of America.

© Oxford University Press 2020

All rights reserved. No part of this publication may be reproduced, stored in
a retrieval system, or transmitted, in any form or by any means, without the
prior permission in writing of Oxford University Press, or as expressly permitted
by law, by license, or under terms agreed with the appropriate reproduction
rights organization. Inquiries concerning reproduction outside the scope of the
above should be sent to the Rights Department, Oxford University Press, at the
address above.

You must not circulate this work in any other form
and you must impose this same condition on any acquirer.

CIP data is on file at the Library of Congress
ISBN 978-0-19-084976-4

9 8 7 6 5 4 3 2 1

Printed by Marquis, Canada

To my daughters Fiona and Maeve, for lighting the way with your adventurous spirits, and Mother Nature for always taking such good care of me.

CONTENTS

Preface　ix
Acknowledgments　xiii
Contributors　xv

PART I: Counseling With Nature: An Overview
1. Our Connection With Nature　3
   Megan E. Delaney
2. Ecotherapy: Applied Ecopsychology　17
   Megan E. Delaney

PART II: Counseling and Nature: Interventions for Counselors in Everyday Practice
3. Nature and Play: Ecotherapy With Children　31
   Megan E. Delaney
3A. Counseling With Nature: A Reflection　47
   Daniel G. Zebrowski
4. Ecotherapy With Adults: Reclaiming Relationships and Reconnecting to the Natural World　50
   Megan E. Delaney
4A. Nature's Expressway　67
   Rashmi Kamath Talpady
5. Group Work in the Natural World　72
   Sarah I. Springer, Emmi McCauley, and Mallory Sheklian
5A. Skipping Stones　94
   Bethany Sheridan
6. Incorporating Nature in Schools　99
   Jason T. Duffy and Miranda Brumber
6A. The Joy of Exploration: Ecotherapy With Middle School Children　113
   Cory Brosch

7. Nature-Based Interventions for the Military/Veteran Population   119
   Nicole M. Arcuri Sanders and Kellie Forziat-Pytel
7A. From Combat to Calm: Equine Therapy With Veterans   150
   Brooke Lichter
8. Ecospirituality   154
   Joanne Jodry and Merritt Reid
8A. From the Delaware to the Ganges River   175
   Jessica Colucci
9. Ecotherapy Interventions   180
   Maeve Hogan and Megan E. Delaney
9A. The Cycle of the Garden   195
   Jonathan Yellowhair
9B. The Human–Animal Connection   201
   Jill Elizabeth Schwarz
10. Integrating Ecotherapy Into Counselor Education   206
   Megan E. Delaney
10A. Ecotherapist in Training   225
   Emmi McCauley
11. Becoming an Ecotherapist   232
   Megan E. Delaney
11A. On Being an Ecotherapist   245
   Kristen Huber

Index   251

PREFACE

It is midnight, and it is dark and cold. Despite their tough exteriors, the 10 adolescent boys and 2 girls are scared. They know they voluntarily signed up for this program to reduce their time at the juvenile detention center, but they are not sure now if it was a good idea. We are in a small room in a nondescript building in the outskirts of southern Utah. Outside, the sky is pitch dark and eerily silent—very different from the cities and towns these kids grew up in. It is quiet in the room as well, despite it being filled with teens and staff. One side of the room is filled with tarps, seat belt straps, boots, pants, shirts, socks, sweaters, and T-shirts. The other side has a long table covered in sandwiches, chips, cookies, fruit, water, and juice. The instructors, myself included, remind the teens to eat as much as they can, as it will be their last "civilized" meal for months. We help them with their new-issued clothes, help them put on warm socks and hiking boots, and teach them how to fold their tarps just right, so when they wrap the bundle with the seat belt straps, they create backpacks. When everyone is settled, a van takes us all out into the wilderness where we will spend the next 60 days pushing our physical and emotional limits.

Our hike on the first night is in silence. We start slow and steady as the kids get used to their boots, the surroundings, and each other. The days to follow usually result in a spectrum of emotions: sadness, anger, fear, and resistance, to start. Most of the kids are used to tough situations, as the homes and streets from which they came were full of challenges forcing them to be resilient and tough. The wilderness, however, brings a new type of challenge. It does not talk or push back; it does not make any demands or force anyone to do anything. It is just there in front of you. Wide-open and silent, it beckons you forward, further into its depths. The teens blindly trudge forward, their minds cloudy with thoughts of what they left behind, but now also of what lies ahead. Being in the wilderness, out in the elements and without the help (or distraction) of any modern convenience forces you to think strategically about what to do in each moment. Over time, we instructors lead less and follow more. The kids learn to work together and make decisions as a team. Do we cross the river here or follow it downstream to a place less treacherous? Are those storm clouds on the horizon heading this way, and do we need to find shelter? Which spot on the horizon looks good for stopping for the night? How do we, as a group, interact with each other in order to get along? What seemed impossible on day one gradually evolves: The group becomes cohesive, both with each other and with the surrounding environment.

The participants grow physically stronger every day. We hike farther, we become more efficient in our camp setups and breakdowns, and we find a rhythm to the daily life of picking up and moving on. Yet what is more remarkable is the emotional transformation that happens. Throughout the day, the teens, lulled into the rhythm of placing one foot in front of the other, find the time to have real conversations. They have hours to talk and listen without distraction. Intimate, deep, painful conversations and confessions occur. The shared narratives of lost childhoods, broken families, missing parents, bullies, gang violence, and survival are spoken in each mile walked. At night, we sit around a fire and as a group, share, connect, cry, laugh, support, and console. By the end of the 60-day program, the group is cohesive and connected. They know each other intimately, having shared honest and raw emotions. Some have learned to trust for the first time.

With the physical and emotional transformation, the participants also experience a connection to the surrounding environment. They learn about the natural ecosystems, including the local plants and wildlife. They get to know the rhythms of the land, how to read the contours in the ridgelines and river beds, the plants to avoid, the ones to admire, the animals and bugs that visit at different times of the day and night. In time, they appreciate the best places to find shelter from the elements as well as the perfect spots to watch the sunset. After hiking, they wander off by themselves to sit among the juniper trees or near a riverbed. They relax and breathe, the most freely that they have in years. The desert of Utah is a spectacular place of natural beauty. You can see for miles in the wide-open skies. There are unexpected pops of color everywhere—vibrant wildflowers and bright berries. Night skies are magnificent and seemingly endless. You can spend days, weeks, in the Utah backcountry and not see any sign of the modern world.

It is hard not to have deep, reflective, profound experiences in this type of immersive wilderness experience. Time and the vast openness of the surroundings awaken a sensory awareness and heighten all of your sensations. The students thrived in it. They experienced deep changes in their bodies, physically and mentally. They lost fat, gained muscle, gained a deeper shade of their skin tone. Their hair got wild and untamed. They moved more freely and were visibly relaxed and at peace. The students also were happier, more alive, connected with each other and the surrounding area in profound ways. They talked about how they felt, with a deep sense of wonder and awe for their own capabilities. Every student I worked with expressed pride and often surprise at their own capacity to do the work on a physical and emotional level. After the 60-day period was complete, we had a closing ceremony. Those who had parents and guardians saw them for the first time in months. The reunions were remarkable to watch. Parents and children were filled with joy and hope. Many tears were shed.

Each time a group left, I was filled with hope too, but also with fear. Would the lessons the kids learned out in the wild translate back home? Would they be able to carry their new confidence and ability into their old neighborhoods and environments? How long would the nature high last? Would they be able to resist old habits now that they were drug/alcohol free and healthy? How did the lessons learned in the wilderness translate to their urban landscapes? These were the questions that weighed on my mind for many years.

It has been over 20 years since I worked as a wilderness instructor, but the memories are some of my sharpest. The impact of these experiences has had a tremendous influence on my own development. However, it is the unanswered questions that have brought me full circle. It is with humility and gratefulness that I write this book and dedicate it to the natural world and the humans I met along the way. I hope it answers some questions, sparks some ideas, and creates new relationships.

ACKNOWLEDGMENTS

I would like to acknowledge several people who have supported me with this and so many other journeys. First are my parents Eileen and Peter, who raised me with nature in so many ways and always support, encourage, and appreciate all of my endeavors. Their guidance, love, and unwavering belief in me allows me to live fully. To my husband, Chris, and my daughters, Fiona and Maeve, who are now a part of my adventures—thank you for being my greatest loves of all. I would also like to acknowledge my professor at Montclair State University, Dr. Gloria Pierce, who first opened my eyes to ecopsychology, which answered so many questions for me. To Dr. Dana Levitt for her unwavering support and her connection to the Oxford University Press team. Thank you to my colleagues, students, and friends and Monmouth University for supporting my passion, especially my department chair, Dr. Stephanie Hall—when I asked to teach an ecotherapy class she without hesitation said yes. Finally, a big shout-out to my ecotherapy graduate students who are on this path in nature with me, and especially to Emmi McCauley, my nature soul sister and ecotherapy partner now and in the future: thank you for everything you did for our class and for this book, keeping me laughing and sane. Finally, I want to thank my dean at Monmouth University, Dr. Kenneth Womack. During my interview, after all the questions were answered and pleasantries were done, he asked "What do you *really* want to do" and I replied, "Write a book about ecotherapy." He said, "Go do that."

So I did.

CONTRIBUTORS

Cory Brosch, MS, is an adjunct instructor at SUNY Oswego as well as a mental health counselor at the college's counseling services center. She is currently a part of a school-based mental health counseling research project. Before becoming a mental health counselor, Cory earned bachelor's and master's degrees in elementary education. She has an interest in enhancing a student's achievement through hands-on learning and exposure to the natural world. After being a stay-at-home mom for 10 years, Cory returned to school to earn a master's degree in mental health counseling as well as a certificate in trauma studies. Cory has research and advocacy interests in ecotherapy and school-based mental health. Cory weaves a connection to nature in most aspects of her and her family's life and is energized by improving others' connections to the natural world.

Miranda Brumber, MS candidate, is a master's-level student at Oswego State University in Upstate New York. She is studying mental health counseling and has a background in psychology and neuroscience. With extensive experience in the field, Miranda has worked with researchers in the United Kingdom, involved herself in mental health based internships, and worked in schools as a mental health provider. Miranda is a large proponent of the health benefits of nature, as much of her free time is spent appreciating and exploring the green spaces of Upstate New York.

Jessica Colucci, MS, LAC, NCC, holds a master's degree in clinical mental health counseling from Monmouth University with a specialization in spirituality. During her time at Monmouth, Jessica traveled to India to further her passion of serving others. Jessica volunteered with One Life to Love Orphanage while in India and serves as the events manager on the board of directors for One Life to Love. Jessica works as a mental health clinician at a nonprofit organization that works primarily with children and families who have experienced abuse and neglect. Jessica is driven to continue working with vulnerable populations to provide mental health services to those in need.

Megan E. Delaney, PhD, LPC, is an assistant professor in the Department of Professional Counseling at Monmouth University. Her research explores the influence of the natural world and mental health and the use of ecotherapy in clinical practice and the counselor education classroom. Trained in outdoor education through the National Outdoor Leadership School, Megan spent several years as a wilderness instructor for organizations including the National Wildlife Federation and Outward Bound. As a wilderness therapist Megan had immersive experiences in nature throughout the United States including North Carolina, Colorado, Utah, and the boundary waters of Minnesota. Currently her favorite places to explore include the Adirondacks and the wonderful parks of Monmouth County, New Jersey. She infuses ecotherapy in her private practice with children and adults as well as teaches Ecotherapy: Counseling with Nature at Monmouth University.

Jason T. Duffy, PhD, LMHC, NCC, ACS, is an assistant professor at Oswego State University, where he teaches clinical and content classes to mental health counselors, school counselors, and school psychologists. Jason's research revolves around creative approaches to pedagogy, counseling, and supervision, and he has published, presented, and led many workshops on this topic. Having spent much of his childhood and adulthood enjoying the benefits of the natural world, he has a keen interest in how engaging the natural world affects wellness and promotes development.

Kellie Forziat-Pytel, MS, NCC, is a current doctoral candidate in counselor education and supervision at The Pennsylvania State University. She has researched, authored, and presented numerous works related to addressing needs of the military-connected population in a counseling setting, and she continues to engage in scholarly work surrounding this population. Kellie currently works at the Clearinghouse for Military Family Readiness at The Pennsylvania State University implementing and evaluating evidence-informed programs and practices for the Department of Defense.

Maeve Hogan, MS, LAC, NCC, graduated from Monmouth University with a master of science in clinical mental health counseling and is currently pursuing licensure as a professional counselor. She spent a majority of her childhood either on the sandy beaches of the Jersey Shore or in the glacier lakes of the Adirondack Mountains. Maeve is a strong proponent of the notion that modern society is in need of a radical reconnection to the natural world. Currently, she enjoys starting her days off by watching the sunrise with a loved one, usually her younger brother. Maeve plans to incorporate her natural outlook into practice, as she believes the connection to nature to be essential for the overall wellness of the human person.

Kristen Huber, MS, LPC, is a licensed professional counselor in the state of New Jersey with a master's in psychological counseling and a post master's certificate in professional mental health counseling from Monmouth University. She has been working as a counselor for 19 years after getting her start in the Pacific Northwest. Kristen is uniquely specialized in ecotherapy and owns and operates the first practice of its kind on the East Coast, Jersey Shore Ecotherapy. For over five years she's has been hiking, paddling, and sailing with her clients in the direction of the personal, mental health, and well-being goals. Kristen is fluent in American Sign Language and is a certified yoga teacher who integrates gentle and complimentary practices like mindfulness in her work wherever possible. You can usually find her opting outside and teaching others how to think outside the couch.

Joanne Jodry, EdD, DMH, LPC, LCADC, is an assistant professor at Monmouth University in West Long Branch, New Jersey. She has been a counselor educator for 12 years with a focus on mental health. In addition to her counselor education and supervision doctorate, she has a doctorate of medical humanities from Drew University in Madison, New Jersey, where she focused her studies on the interactions of world religions and clinical practice. Joanne's specialties are feminist theory and the integration of spirituality into counseling. In addition, Joanne has a clinical mental health practice where she specializes with integrating spirituality into counseling and uses feminist theory lens.

Brooke Lichter, MSW, LSW, is a licensed social worker who earned both her master's and bachelor's social work degrees from Monmouth University with a concentration in clinical practice with families and children. Her college career included courses in the areas of animal-assisted therapy, veterinary social work, psychology of animal training, play therapy, and positive psychology. Brooke graduated summa cum laude and with numerous community service and leadership awards. She is dually certified through the Professional Association of Therapeutic Horsemanship International as an Equine Specialist in Mental Health and Learning, and through the Equine Assisted Growth and Learning Association. Brooke has always had a deep passion for animals. She helped establish Serenity Stables, From Combat to Calm, a program that provides free equine-assisted therapy to veterans, active duty military personnel, and their family members.

Emmi McCauley, MS, LAC, NCC, holds a master's degree in clinical mental health counseling from Monmouth University and was the first graduate of the program with a specialization in ecotherapy. Emmi has traveled the United States conducting service work with Habitat for Humanity and completed a year of service with AmeriCorps in New Orleans, Louisiana. While a student in Monmouth, Emmi continued her love of service abroad, volunteering in both Haiti and India. Emmi's passion is group work within the natural world, emerging from her diverse experiences throughout the world. Emmi plans to continue to raise awareness of the positive mental health benefits of connecting with nature through her work as a counselor.

Merritt Reid, MS, has a master's in clinical mental health counseling from Monmouth University. Merritt Reid has been a professional actor for the past 10 years and owns his own production company called Last Straw Films. He studied for the extent of his career under Ann Ratray in New York. Merritt is currently working on creating a documentary while simultaneously co-conducting research on a service-learning trip to India sponsored through Monmouth University revolving around topics of spirituality, empathy, expanding ego boundaries, and multicultural awareness.

Nicole M. Arcuri Sanders, PhD, ACS, LPC, NCC, BC-TMH, SAC, is core faculty at Capella University within the School of Counseling and Human Services. Clinically, Dr. Arcuri Sanders engages in practice with the military-connected population. Within this specific area of focus, she has also completed researched, published, and presented at local, regional, and national conferences with an interest of advocating for effective clinical services to meet this population's needs. In the past, Dr. Arcuri Sanders worked as DODEA district military liaison counselor, substance awareness counselor, school counselor, psychiatric assessment counselor, anti-bullying specialist, and teacher.

Jill Elizabeth Schwarz, PhD, NCC, is an associate professor and school counseling program coordinator in the Department of Counselor Education at the College of New Jersey. In addition to teaching on campus, Jill has taught graduate students internationally in several countries throughout Asia and Europe and is the co-coordinator of a Council for Accreditation of Counseling and Related Educational Programs–accredited international school counseling program offered in Portugal. Prior to being a counselor educator, Jill worked many years in the public schools as a professional school counselor. Jill's scholarly pursuits have included publications, as well as national and regional presentations, focused on school counselor preparation and practice and spirituality and gender issues in counseling. She is the editor of the textbook *Counseling Women across the Lifespan: Empowerment, Advocacy, & Intervention*. Jill currently serves as a research consultant for a counseling agency that provides counseling services to survivors of sexual assault and domestic violence.

Mallory Sheklian, MS, LAC, NCC, holds a master's degree in clinical mental health counseling from Monmouth University. She obtained her undergraduate degree in psychology from Purdue University with a focus on equine-assisted therapy for people with disabilities. Mallory enjoys being outdoors whenever possible and brings nature indoors through her jungle of houseplants. She wholeheartedly believes in the healing properties of nature and hopes to continue expanding the clinical context of mental health with the natural world.

Bethany Sheridan, PhD, NCC, CPC-1, holds a doctoral degree from the University of Nevada, Reno, in counselor education and supervision. She is licensed as both a clinical and school counselor and is currently working at High Desert Montessori, an ecoliterate school and the only school in Nevada to receive a Green Ribbon Award for actively reducing environmental impacts and providing comprehensive environmental education. Bethany's professional work also aligns with her research passion and dissertation, which studied the effects of nature-based guidance lessons on elementary school students' anxiety and connection to nature. Bethany has a strong spiritual connection to nature and has experienced first-hand the many physical and emotional benefits that spending time in the natural world has to offer. She hopes to continue working with children and adolescents in school settings to spread her passion for the outdoors to the next generation.

Sarah I. Springer, PhD, LPC, ACS, is an assistant professor in the Department of Professional Counseling at Monmouth University and has a small private practice working with children, families, and prelicensed clinicians. Prior to becoming a counselor educator, Dr. Springer spent several years as a school counselor. Her scholarly interests include supervision and counselor development in the areas of group work and child and adolescent counseling.

Rashmi Kamath Talpady, MS, LAC, NCC, is a graduate of the professional counseling at Monmouth University. She brings to Monmouth University a multifaceted educational background spanning a major in biology, a degree in the school of Ayurveda, and priceless experiences lived and learned while working in the chaotic and vibrant cities of Delhi and Bangalore, India. She is a proud member of Monmouth University's honor society Chi Sigma Iota and an even prouder creator of her bundle of joy, her daughter Peaches. As a new mama pursuing an exciting and ambitious career, she finds her balance in life by practicing mindfulness, being one with nature, and spending as much time as possible with adorable furballs. When all else fails, she stands by the magic combination of sizzling coffee and a paperback.

Jonathan Yellowhair, MS candidate, is a second-year masters of science student in Georgia State University's Clinical Mental Health Counseling program. After his service in the U.S. Marine Corps and deployments to Iraq and Afghanistan, Jonathan earned a bachelor of arts in international affairs and bachelor of science in applied Indigenous studies at Northern Arizona University in his hometown of Flagstaff, Arizona. Currently in his internship at Decatur High School, Jonathan aims to alleviate anxiety for young men reintegrating into high schools from detention centers, alternative schools, and probation periods while increasing the retention rate of these students through individual counseling initiatives and group therapy. Simultaneously, Jonathan is teaching health classes focused on addictions advocacy and substance abuse prevention through the Pathways2Life foundation at Renfroe Middle School. As a Pat Tillman Foundation Scholar and National Board for Certified Counselors Minority Addictions Fellow, Jonathan advocates for the recognition of Indigenous mental health disparities on a national platform. Upon graduation, Jonathan aspires to develop therapeutic practices and initiatives consolidated toward Indigenous tribal members to combat mental health stigmas on Indigenous reservations.

Daniel G. Zebrowski, MS, LPC, CEC, is a private practitioner and co-owner of Back on Track, LLC. As a counselor, he brings a goal-oriented mindset to the session in order to assist clients of all ages. He believes that developing a strong counseling relationship, accurately assessing challenges, and individualizing treatment plans lead to the desired change and growth of his clients. His approach is humanistic and incorporates cognitive behavioral therapy, positive psychology, as well as other evidence-based treatments. He incorporates nature in his work, especially with children. For over a decade, he has gained experience in various treatment settings that has allowed him to witness first-hand which approaches are most effective for positive change.

PART I

Counseling With Nature

An Overview

CHAPTER 1

Our Connection With Nature

MEGAN E. DELANEY

EARLY INTRODUCTION TO NATURE

My connection to nature began in childhood. My parents, both teachers, dedicated time each summer for adventures. Many of my childhood memories were made at Stokes State Forest, a small piece of northwestern New Jersey that hosts a portion of the Appalachian Trail. Besides the one night we would venture into town for pizza, we would spend the rest of our time digging in the earth, exploring trails, and just being outside. My childhood also involved month-long trips across the United States. In our VW Vanagon, we would camp along the way at the varied and amazing national and state parks. While some of my memories involve using masking tape to partition my section of the van from my brother's, my most vivid memories involve the amazing landscapes, vegetation, wildlife, sunsets, sunrises, rainbows, and night skies experienced along the way.

I have done a lot of reflection about my childhood now that I am a mother. I appreciate these experiences more than I ever could as a child and understand the lasting impact they have made on my own development. The memories I made while traveling with my family are some of the most vivid from my entire childhood. I will never forget looking at Mount Saint Helens just a few years after its 1980 eruption. I will never forget the time when we were exploring a cave in Craters of the Moon National Park when, out of nowhere, hundreds of bats flew out all at once. We all fell flat on the ground in shock. I also have vivid memories of open fields of wildflowers near the mountains in Colorado and the endless sky in South Dakota.

Since childhood, wanderlust has distracted my mostly predictable and steadfast brain. As a typical firstborn, I was a diligent child and a studious young person. As a result of my diligence, I found myself ahead in my studies at the start of my junior year in college and had the opportunity to take time off during the spring semester. I wanted an experience that was adventurous and challenging. One of my friends suggested that I look into exploring the National Outdoor Leadership School (NOLS) based out of Lander, Wyoming. NOLS is an outdoor adventure-based leadership school offering a variety of different immersive wilderness experiences. Their website states, "Our mission is to be the leading source and teacher of wilderness skills and leadership that serve people and the environment" (NOLS, n.d.). Founded in 1965, NOLS has always had a philosophy of training students to become leaders, not only in outdoor and wilderness skills but also in championing the preservation and sustainability of the wild. Outdoor classrooms are the foundation of the NOLS philosophy, allowing students to connect on a deeper level, improve their communication abilities with others, overcome challenges as a group, build abilities and confidence, and think as leaders and as environmental stewards.

I discovered NOLS through college friends who were perceptive enough to know I was longing for life-changing experience. Both of my friends had their own transformative experiences in semester-long NOLS courses in the Rocky Mountains. With the support of my parents, a terrific mentor/coach, and some wild desire to travel, I was able to participate in a semester-long NOLS course in Kenya. This experience was transformative. Long before I understood the concept of privilege, I felt it in my bones when I traveled through parts of rural Africa. Many of the places we visited did not have indoor plumbing or running water or access to most of the basic needs I took for granted at home. But the wild was so wild—raw, untouched, and incredible.

During the semester, we spent a month hiking Mount Kenya, trekking through the Masai Mara, and sailing along the Indian Ocean. Carrying 70-pound packs, we slowly ascended Mount Kenya, starting at sea level and reaching the peak over 17,000 feet high. Along the way, we camped in astonishing landscapes. On more than one occasion, we watched herds of zebra grazing. We called out to warn buffalo of our presence so as not to scare them into charging at us. We saw amazing vegetation and witnessed a landscape that transformed the further we climbed.

I felt a sense of awe and self-pride when we summited Mount Kenya. It took 4 weeks of hiking and climbing for our group to reach the peak.

I cried, swore, hurt, and laughed, pushing myself beyond mental and physical limits. Our journey went beyond Mount Kenya to other parts of the country, but the theme throughout was the same: Respect the natural world and cultures you encounter, attend to the earth, and listen to the people you meet. Trust yourself and your capacities, and know that you are capable of more.

My experience in Kenya inspired many of my next adventures. Postgraduation, I worked for several wilderness-based adventure programs and crisscrossed the United States. I worked with hundreds of students in different wilderness-based settings, ranging from 15-day to 60-day full-immersion wilderness therapy programs. I taught wilderness survival skills, fire-making techniques, shelter building, and meal preparation. Our groups hiked, paddled, swam, climbed, and camped in a wide range of geographic areas. We monitored weather patterns, persisting through snow, rain, freezing cold and boiling hot temperatures, thunderstorms, and, more often, the beautiful sunshine and incredible night sky. Typically ranging in age from 14 to 18, the students came to the different programs with a variety of experiences, strengths, and challenges. More often than not, their family lives were fractured and difficult, and children were suffering. The majority of students I encountered were in juvenile detention facilities or had been in the judicial or family court system in some way. Many abused

Figure 1.1 Author at the summit of Mount Kenya in 1993.

drugs and alcohol, most starting at a young age. They came to our programs wounded and scarred, and they presented their sadness as anger and resentment. A considerable amount of time, as any therapist would know, was initially spent establishing rapport and building trust.

Our natural surroundings ranged from the deep woods of North Carolina to the boundary waters of northern Minnesota, the southern deserts of Utah, and the mountain ranges of Colorado. Regardless of the particular surroundings, these broken children began to heal, first physically. The physical challenges of the routine of everyday life were enough to fill an entire day. Often activities included preparing and making meals; setting up and breaking down camp; packing and repacking backpacks or dry sacks; hiking, paddling, or climbing; as well as navigating terrain, weather, wildlife, bugs, and unexpected obstacles. Taken together, these challenges were enough to make sleeping at night welcome and restorative.

The other parts of the day, we talked. A group of people cannot move through a wilderness setting together unless they are in some semblance of a unified team. Some days were better than others, and, with time, the rhythmic and cyclical patterns of group dynamics surfaced. Natural leaders emerged, but often it was the voices or insights from the quieter group members that provided needed clarity or moments of inspiration. When you have 15 miles of hiking for the day (translating into hours and hours of placing one foot in front of the other), you find much to talk about. At night, we sat in a circle around a fire, a natural conduit for sharing feelings, emotions, and personal stories.

At the time, I was a young adult myself and often only a few years older than those in my care. I had significant responsibility as head instructor, and it was my charge to safely return my students as well as my coleaders. As head instructor, there were a number of situations, still sharply engrained in my memory, where I did not think that would happen. On numerous other occasions I handled very significant emotional situations. Students often shared personal and traumatic life events, and the emotional and physical reactions that accompanied the revelations needed my attention, support, and care. At other times, intense disagreements or arguments needed to be defused and processed. Yet more often, the group was filled with laughter, comradery, a sense of purpose, accomplishment, and pride. Threaded in all of these physical and emotional experiences were our surroundings. With time, the students became much more aware of the natural setting. They marveled at flowers growing in the desert sun, stared in awe at the majesty of a clear night sky, watched in reverence at an early morning sunrise over a misty lake, paddled softly near an impressive

800-pound moose, or just appreciated the silence and tranquility of the natural world.

Physical changes came to the teens in the wild; within days, they could hike/paddle longer and carry more weight, all while complaining less. But the emotional changes were more significant. The tension in shoulders dropped, stressed faces relaxed, smiles and laughter emerged. Even at my age and with my lack of training, it was impossible not to notice. I knew the natural world had some mystical power and influence over me, but I began to realize it also did for the teens as well, young people so different from me in many ways. However, I had yet to understand why or how. This was to come later.

After working as a wilderness instructor for years, I journeyed back home to the East Coast. I spent several years mostly lost in a corporate and urban landscape. Working in New York City, I bounced around from corporate job to corporate job. As you might suspect, I was never satisfied, nor could I sit still. I held jobs in windowless offices under fluorescent lights, where I would spend my days in a desperate attempt to stay awake while endlessly watching the clock. I held other positions in cubicles so small that if I backed up my chair, I hit my neighbor's chair. I spent hours sitting, willing myself to not get up and stare out a conference room window. I rarely went out for lunch because I felt such dread upon returning to the office. I was resentful and frustrated by the confines of the workspace, the computer, and the phone. I say this knowing, of course, that I am privileged. I was college educated and I had a job. So many people sacrifice, or would sacrifice if they could, to have that opportunity. Yet I was not productive, nor was I happy. Then September 11 happened. When I was able to leave New York City the next day, I knew, like so many, that I needed a change. I left the corporate world to pursue a master's degree in mental health counseling.

I chose counseling because of my experiences in wilderness therapy. I felt alive during that time of my life. I knew that while I was untrained and inexperienced, I was making a difference in the lives of others. I missed that feeling of connection and purpose. While pursing my master's degree, I took a class called Ecotherapy: Applied Ecopsychology with Dr. Gloria Pierce. Dr. Pierce, forever a mentor and friend, changed the trajectory of my life. This class explained so many of my unanswered questions. We read Roszak, Gomes, and Kanner's (1995) *Ecopsychology: Restoring the Earth, Healing the Mind,* and Clinebell's (1996) *Ecotherapy: Healing Ourselves, Healing the Earth.* We talked about our growing understanding of the subject and our collective worries for our planet. As a class, we bonded over our love of nature in different forms, and we explored our relationship with the natural world. This relationship with nature is where we will start now.

HUMANS AND NATURE: A RELATIONSHIP

When you think of your connection with nature, how was that formulated? Did you have a favorite place to go outside when you were a child? Did your parents take you to a beloved lake, park, or stream? Did your yard or neighborhood park provide solace to you in some capacity? Perhaps you have a strong memory of your first look at the ocean or of a camping trip. Or maybe you didn't have access to safe places and yearned to go outside. I ask these questions of both my clients and my students. When I first approach the subject, I am less specific. I might ask . . . "Tell me about your favorite place to go to feel at peace. Where do you go to find relaxation and solitude? What are some of your favorite memories as a child? Where do you remember going as a child to have fun and play?" Think about how you might answer these questions. More times than not, people describe a place in nature—whether it is a park or a special place in the neighborhood. Others describe the beach or sitting near a lake or a stream. Still, 9 times out of 10, the description is somewhere in the natural world.

Why are we so drawn to natural spaces? Some say it is in our DNA and goes back to our earliest connections to the earth. As developing mammals, we had to connect with our surroundings in order to survive. Early humans had a deep knowledge of the land, understood the cycles of life in their environments, and used the skills of hunting and gathering. For many thousands of years, humans lived on the earth as nomads, their life depending on direct harmony with their surroundings. The notion that humans and the earth are intrinsically connected has been noted in many different academic, religious, and philosophical disciplines (Louv, 2005). Erich Fromm (1973), a German-born psychologist who fled to American from Nazi Germany, first coined the term *biophilia* to mean one's love of life and living systems. The biophilia hypothesis, brought forward by Edward Wilson in his 1984 book *Biophilia,* proposes that humans naturally affiliate with other life-forms and natural environments in order to survive, overcome stress, and remain physically and mentally stable. Wilson's theory is based on several concepts, including the practical dependence of humans on the natural world for food and water, the positive emotional effect of the natural world when interacting with nature, and the connections humans have to specific places and to other animals. Wilson's call for a deeper understanding of the interconnection and coevolution with other living systems helped lead the environmental movement (Krčmářová, 2009). The movement itself rose in response to humans' growing disconnect and misuse of the planet.

The industrialized world started changing our connection to our surroundings. As industrialization spread, many cultures lost their right to roam the land as they had done for centuries before. As history shows, these cultures were manipulated, deceived, poisoned, and pushed out of the land they knew (LaDuke, 2017). As industrialized societies progressed, so did the theme of control and dominance. The land became something to be owned and, as such, used in any way that would benefit the human occupying it. The term *anthropocentrism* has been used to describe this type of dominance: the belief that humans are the most important living thing on the planet. While scholars have varying understandings and uses of the term, environmentalists have pointed out the impact that this viewpoint has contributed to the current condition of our planet and, consequentially, our relationship with the natural world. Environmentalists, ecologists, and ecopsychologists argue that dominance and control are powerful themes in the history of our relationship with nature (Roszak, Gomes, & Kanner, 1995). For eons, humans lived in harmony with nature, or at least with respect for and a deeper intuition about the natural world. Some have lost this deep connection, respect, and understanding. The shift to anthropocentrism emerged as humans became place bound and reliant on trade and commodities for survival. Most of us no longer grow our own food but rather shop in markets for what we need. Forests, wetlands, and other natural places are cleared out for big farms, factories, shopping malls, and the sprawl of the growing population.

The environmental consequences of the growth of industrialization are beyond the scope of this book, but its impact on the human psyche is important to understand. At the core is the feeling of control. The climates in our buildings and homes are now controlled. Rivers, streams, and lakes are controlled to provide water where and when we need it. Forests and parks are placed within borders and controlled. Wild animals are confined to certain geographical areas and seen as a threat if they wander off these confined lands. This deep need to control our environment has exacerbated our separation from nature. For many, the disconnection with nature has manifested as fear. This fear is termed *biophobia* (White & Heerwagen, 1998). Biophobia has a long evolutionary history for humans. Our ancestors needed to fear certain predatory animals, as well as spiders and snakes, for survival. Humans also needed to fear weather patterns (such as thunder and lightning) in order to take cover. Today most of us do not need to worry about death from a snakebite, yet some of our fears are justified. A consequence of the industrialization of our planet is climate change (Crowley, 2000). As a result of climate change, our storms are bigger, more frequent and devastating. On occasion, they have resulted in the loss of many human (and animal and plant) lives. The droughts on our planet are worse, the flooding more intense, wild fires more frequent and widespread. Creatures such as mosquitoes and ticks have adapted to pesticides and spread disease. Our global society has spread nonindigenous plants and bugs that can overwhelm other ecosystems. Wild animals, searching for food due to dwindling habitats, are forced to come into contact with humans and domesticated pets. News coverage of massive storms, tornados, hurricanes, and encounters with wild animals may accurately cover the consequences of the event but also spread fear and anxiety. These fears have a significant impact on our mental health.

DO WE EVEN GO OUTSIDE ANYMORE?

Humans, in general, have retreated inside, spending less time outdoors than ever. The numbers support this trend: With increasingly sedentary and indoor lifestyles, the average American now spends only 7% of their day outdoors, a significant decrease in the last few decades (Bratman, Hamilton, Hahn, Daily, & Gross, 2015). This is especially true for children. Richard Louv (2005), American journalist and author of *Last Child in the Woods*, reports on the rapidly growing disconnection between children and the outdoors. Louv calls this societal malady *nature-deficit disorder* and links this trend to some of the most pervasive childhood ailments, such as anxiety, depression, attention deficit hyperactivity disorder (ADHD), and obesity. Children are also losing their freedom to roam wild and explore their environments. Children need to be children and have the opportunity to wander free and wild in their surroundings. Nature is an endless mecca for a curious, creative, and imaginative child. If the future generation does not have a connection to, respect for, or understanding of the natural world, this disconnection will continue to expand, which could have a far-reaching impact on the physical and mental health of humans, as well as the health of the planet.

And yet, when I ask my clients, children or adults, to describe their favorite place to go for peace and relaxation, they tell me about somewhere in nature. I ask them to describe that place, the sights and sounds and smells. I ask them about this place and what it does to them physically as well as mentally. They look off, likely envisioning it in their minds. I can see a physical change in their posture when they describe it to me; their shoulders relax and their faces soften. They breathe more slowly. They sigh. They look off into the distance as they describe their place to me and share how they feel when they are there. When I ask, how often do you go there now?

Usually the answer is, not very often. Therefore, despite knowing that a special place can bring peace and calmness, they—we—do not make the time to go. We have lost our relationship with our special places.

For me, my special place is in the woods. I am instantaneously more relaxed as soon as I am under the canopies of trees. The more evergreen the better. The taller the better. The mossier the ground the better. Do the trees muffle the noise of the nearby street? Can I hear nothing that is human-made? Even better. Is there a babbling brook? I am in my heaven. We recently moved to a new town, and everyone is adjusting. I am the reason we moved, so that I could be closer to work and, while at work, closer to my kids. I myself have moved many times (from New Jersey to Connecticut, North Carolina, Utah, Minnesota, Colorado, and back to New Jersey), but I have never moved a family. It is hard work and tough on everyone involved. The other day, I was in the thick of helping my kids adjust to new schools and feeling overwhelmed with worry and guilt. With effort, I got up and took myself to my new local park. There I discovered a half-mile path that provided the perfect walk through the woods. I listened to the birds talking to each other; I could feel the breeze through the trees; the leaves whistled as the winds picked up; a chipmunk scurried in front of the path. I could feel my cares lift a little. I was able to take deeper breaths. I was reassured that everyone was going to be fine. It was worth putting something else (likely unpacking boxes or grocery shopping or writing this book) on the back burner.

WHAT DOES THE RESEARCH SAY?

A growing body of research suggests nature is scientifically *good* for us; the natural world promotes mental and physical health (Bratman et al., 2015; Sweatman & Warner, 2009; Waller, 2009). Research on the effectiveness of spending time outdoors has correlated positive effects on participants, including stress relief, improved mood, and neurological and cardiovascular benefits (Hattie, Marsh, Neill, & Richards, 1997; Maller, Henderson-Wilson, & Townsend, 2009; Thorp, Owen, Neuhaus, & Dunstan, 2011; Wells & Evans, 2003; Wilmot et al., 2012). The research also points to a strong connection between nature and mental well-being (Bratman et al., 2015; Sweatman & Warner, 2009; Waller, 2009). Well-being can mean many different things, including increases in concentration (Faber Taylor & Kuo, 2011), increases in self-concept (Kaplan & Kaplan, 1989), decreases in symptoms of ADHD (Faber Taylor & Kuo, 2011), decreases in stress (Grahn & Stigsdotter, 2003), reduction of symptoms related to depression (Morrison & Gore, 2010), and restoration from mental fatigue (Brymer, Cuddihy, & Sharma-Brymer, 2010). Recent literature has explored outcomes of infusing nature to assist clients struggling with various mental health-related concerns, such as depression, anxiety, ADHD, and conduct-related issues (Berman, Jonides, & Kaplan, 2008; Kahn & Hasbach, 2012; Kaplan, 2008; Louv, 2005, 2012). Research has shown that people who engage in nature feel much more centered and calm, with less anxiety and depression and better focus (Hattie et al., 1997; Maller et al., 2009; Wells & Evans, 2003). This is just a small scraping of the surface on the research that is out there encompassing the human–nature connection. Current researchers are exploring, among other topics, the ways that incorporating nature into different aspects of life and routine can influence achievement gaps, the impacts of greening schoolyards on student performance, the effects of urban green space exposure, and the benefits of park prescriptions for cognitive and brain development.

These findings and the continuation of research are important, as our society is trending toward urbanization, including increased sedentary and indoor lifestyles. Americans spend 87% of time indoors and 6% in cars (Bratman et al., 2015; Klepeis et al., 2001). Ninety-three percent is alarming—that is only *one half of one day per week outdoors*. According to these statistics, the majority of us spend *339 days a year completely indoors*. There are many grassroots organizations trying to reverse this trend. Physicians and pediatricians have been writing prescriptions for the outdoors, called ParksRx (Root, 2017) to help patients and their families get outside. The Children and Nature Network (CN&N) is a movement sparked by Richard Louv's (2005) "Last Child in the Woods" and nature-deficit disorder. The mission of CN&N is to get kids back playing and exploring outside and to ensure access to safe outdoor spaces for all children.

While this increased attention to getting back outdoors is important, little has been addressed within the counseling field about the ways in which we, as therapists, can connect our clients to the healing power of nature. I was recently interviewed for an article in *Counseling Today* (2018) titled "Using Nature as a Therapeutic Partner." It was exciting to have the topic of ecotherapy broadcast to such a wide audience of counselors and counselor educators. But still, ecotherapy remains a little-known modality in our field. The purpose of this book is to start to bridge this gap. Over the past decade of reading and researching many of the concepts of nature and mental health, I noticed that, for the most part, books have been written to explain the theory or discuss the reasons *why* our connection to nature is so good for our mental health. These concepts are important to understand. I outline the theoretical concepts in the next chapter as well as direct readers to seminal texts from scholars and writers researching and exploring the concept for decades. But one of my main goals for this book is to provide the *how* to incorporate the natural world in our work as counselors.

The discipline of counseling provides a unique perspective in the helping professions. Counselors use a developmental, wellness- and strength-based lens to view our clients. Counselors help clients understand emotions and develop strategies, through a culturally sensitive perspective, to cope and work through issues. The American Counseling Association (2019) defines professional counseling as "a professional relationship that empowers diverse individuals, families, and groups to accomplish mental health, wellness, education, and career goals." Because the counselor–client relationship is paramount to success, counselors work to develop trust and mutual respect primarily with their clients. There are over 700,000 mental health counselors in the United States (Data USA, 2016). If our connection to nature is so important to our own mental and physical health, and there are over half a million counselors working with individuals and families every day, there is an untapped conduit to spread this message.

When I give lectures, talks, and presentations on the human–nature connection, many counselors approach me to ask "how"—how can I reach this client? How can I integrate the natural world into my practice? How do I start? How do I learn more? Is what I am doing okay? What are the ways that I can work with clients in urban areas? What techniques do you recommend? The truth is that many counselors are intuitively infusing nature into their practice. One counselor told me she takes walks with her clients rather than sitting in her office. Another described her outdoor office in the middle of lush gardens where she sits with her clients among flowers and birds. Another described a small house she built in her wooded backyard. The little house has a front porch where she sits with her clients on rocking chairs. Still another counselor created a tranquil space by incorporating elements of nature into her office by using earth tones and adding greenery, plants, pictures of nature, and a soothing nature sound machine. Is this what you are talking about in your presentation, they would ask? Yes. Absolutely. All of that and more.

If you are reading this book, you may be incorporating some form of nature into your work, or at least thinking about it. Perhaps you incorporate nature into your self-care. Perhaps you have a particular client in mind, and you are thinking that incorporating nature into your treatment plan might be just what this person needs. Perhaps you are a student, trying to learn as much about different modalities as you can. I hope this book can be a start or a part of your journey to understanding and infusing nature in your practice. Core concepts and theoretical foundations are detailed in the next chapter. The other chapters in this book are devoted to practical application and offer suggestions for how you, as a counselor, can incorporate nature into your work with a range of clients. Embedded in each chapter are vignettes, written by folks inspired by nature. These vignettes are personal experiences, stories, and reflections that help bring the concepts to life and offer other voices in the field doing amazing work in harmony with the environment surrounding them.

My ultimate goal for this book is to inspire you, in whichever ways feel comfortable to you and your clients, to go into the natural world. My hope is that you will be nurtured by nature. My aspiration is that you and your clients will care for nature as it cares for you, thus fulfilling the mutuality of healthy relationships.

REFERENCES

American Counseling Association. (2019). *Our vision and mission: ACA's strategic plan.* Retrieved from https://www.counseling.org/about-us/about-aca/our-mission

Berman, M. G., Jonides, J., & Kaplan, S. (2008). The cognitive benefits of interacting with nature. *Psychological Science, 19*(12), 1207–1212.

Bratman, G. N., Hamilton, J. P., Hahn, K. S., Daily, G. C., & Gross, J. J. (2015). Nature experience reduces rumination and subgenual prefrontal cortex activation. *Proceedings of the National Academy of Sciences of the United States of America, 112,* 8567–8572. doi:10.1073/pnas.1510459112

Brymer, E., Cuddihy, T. F., & Sharma-Brymer, V. (2010). The role of nature-based experiences in the development and maintenance of wellness. *Asia-Pacific Journal of Health, Sport and Physical Education, 1,* 21–27.

Clinebell, H. (1996). *Ecotherapy: Healing ourselves, healing the earth.* Minneapolis, MN: Augsburg Fortress Press.

Crowley, T. J. (2000). Causes of climate change over the past 1000 years. *Science, 289*(5477), 270–277. doi:10.1126/science.289.5477.270

Data USA. (2016). *Counselors.* Retrieved from https://datausa.io/profile/soc/211010/

Faber Taylor, A., & Kuo, F. E. (2011). Could exposure to everyday green spaces help treat ADHD? Evidence from children's play settings. *Applied Psychology: Health and Well-Being, 3*(3), 281–303.

Fromm, E. (1973). *The anatomy of human destructiveness.* New York: Holt, Rinehart and Winston.

Grahn, P., & Stigsdotter, U. A. (2003). Landscape planning and stress. *Urban Forestry & Urban Greening, 2*(1), 1–18.

Hattie, J., Marsh, H. W., Neill, J. T., & Richards, G. E. (1997). Adventure education and Outward Bound: Out-of-class experiences that make a lasting difference. *Review of Educational Research, 67*(1), 43–87.

Kahn, P. H., & Hasbach, P. H. (Eds.). (2012). *Ecopsychology: Science, totems, and the technological species.* Cambridge, MA: MIT Press.

Kaplan, R., & Kapan, S. (1989). *The experience of nature: A psychological perspective.* Cambridge, England: Cambridge University Press.

Kaplan, D. (2008). *Structural equation modeling: Foundations and extensions* (Vol. 10). Thousand Oaks, CA: SAGE.

Klepeis, N. E., Nelson, W. C., Ott, W. R., Robinson, J. P., Tsang, A. M., Switzer, P., . . . Engelmann, W. H. (2001). The national human activity pattern survey: A resource for assessing exposure to environmental pollutants. *Journal of Exposure Analysis and Environmental Epidemiology, 11,* 231–252. doi:10.1038/sj.jea.7500165.

Krčmářová, J. (2009). E.O. Wilson's concept of biophilia and the environmental movement in the USA. *Klaudyán: Internet Journal of Historical Geography and Environmental History, 6*(1–2), 4–17. Retrieved from www.klaudyan.cz

LaDuke, W. (2017). *All our relations: Native struggles for land and life.* Chicago, IL: Haymarket Books.

Louv, R. (2005). *Last child in the woods: Saving our children from nature-deficit disorder.* Chapel Hill, NC: Algonquin Books of Chapel Hill.

Louv, R. (2012). *The nature principle: Reconnecting with life in a virtual age.* Chapel Hill, NC: Algonquin Books of Chapel Hill.

Maller, C., Henderson-Wilson, C., & Townsend, M. (2009). Rediscovering nature in everyday settings: Or how to create healthy environments and healthy people. *EcoHealth, 6*(4), 553–556.

Morrison, C., & Gore, H. (2010). Relationship between excessive Internet use and depression: A questionnaire-based study of 1,319 young people and adults. *Psychopathology, 43,* 121–126.

National Outdoor Leadership School. (n.d.). *About NOLS.* Retrieved from https://www.nols.edu/en/about/

Phillips, L. (2018, April 26). Using nature as a therapeutic partner. *Counseling Today.* Retrieved from https://ct.counseling.org/2018/04/using-nature-as-a-therapeutic-partner/

Root, T. (2017, January 29). The power of parks: Doctors are prescribing park visits to boost patient health. *National Geographic.* Retrieved from https://news.nationalgeographic.com/2017/06/parks-prescribes-doctors-health-environment/

Roszak, T. (1995). Where psyche meets gaia. In T. Roszak, M. E. Gomes, & A. D. Kanner (Eds.), *Ecopsychology: Restoring the earth, healing the mind* (pp. 1–17). Berkeley: University of California Press.

Sweatman, M., & Warner, A. (2009). Integrating nature experiences into early childhood education. *Canadian Children, 34*(2), 4–9.

Thorp, A. A., Owen, N., Neuhaus, M., & Dunstan, D. W. (2011). Sedentary behaviors and subsequent health outcomes in adults: A systematic review of longitudinal studies, 1996–2011. *American Journal of Preventive Medicine, 41*(2), 207–215.

Waller, V. (2009). Information systems "in the wild": Supporting activity in the world. *Behavior and Information Technology, 28*(6), 577–688.

Wells, N. M., & Evans, G. W. (2003). Nearby nature: A buffer of life stress among rural children. *Environment & Behavior, 35*(3), 311.

White, R., & Heerwagen, J. (1998). Nature and mental health: Biophilia and biophobia. In A. Lundberg (Ed.), *The environment and mental health: A guide for clinicians* (pp. 175–192). Mahwah, NJ: Erlbaum.

Wilmot, E. G., Edwardson, C. L., Achana, F. A., Davies, M. J., Gorely, T., Gray, L. J., . . . Biddle, S. J. (2012). Sedentary time in adults and the association with diabetes, cardiovascular disease and death: Systematic review and meta-analysis. *Diabetologia, 55*, 2895–2905.

Wilson, E. O. (1984). *Biophilia*. Cambridge, MA: Harvard University Press.

CHAPTER 2

Ecotherapy

Applied Ecopsychology

MEGAN E. DELANEY

THE ORIGINS OF ECOPSYCHOLOGY

In traditional psychological theories, understanding of human psyche in connection to the natural world is largely unexplored (Hillman, 1995; Kahn & Hasbach, 2012). Carl Jung was an exception. Jung was deeply connected to the natural world, and this connection is reflected throughout much of his writing and correspondence. Jung emphasized this deep, subconscious, primordial connection with nature, which, even in the early 20th century, he noticed was shifting. Jung emphasized that complete regression back to nature was not the direction to take but instead proposed understanding and reconnecting to the subconscious relationship:

> Through scientific understanding, our world has become dehumanized. Man feels himself isolated in the cosmos. He is no longer involved in nature and has lost his emotional participation in natural events, which hitherto had a symbolic meaning for him. Thunder is no longer the voice of a god, nor is lightning his avenging missile. No river contains a spirit, no tree means a man's life, no snake is the embodiment of wisdom, and no mountain still harbors a great demon. Neither do things speak to him nor can he speak to things, like stones, springs, plants and animals. He no longer has bush-soul identifying him with a

wild animal. His immediate communication with nature is gone forever, and the emotional energy it generated has sunk into the unconscious. (Jung, *Collected Works*, as cited in Sabini, 2002, pp. 79–80)

While Jung wove nature throughout his works, most psychologists and early theorists focused on the human as an individual. Furthermore, most early theorists have been criticized for conceptualizing human development in terms of the understanding of affluent, European men only (Worell & Remer, 2003). This narrow viewpoint left gender, culture, ethnicity, and other differences missing from understanding the true lived experiences of different people. Many scholars have expanded on psychological theory to encompass many different aspects of the human experience, but it was not until the early 1990s when, inspired by environmentalism and ecology, scholars to include the influence of the natural world.

Theodore Roszak, a historian by training, is largely credited with coining the term *ecopsychology* in his book *The Voice of the Earth* (Roszak, 2001). The goal of ecopsychology, Roszak stated, "is to bridge our culture's longstanding, historical gulf between the psychological and the ecological, to see the needs of the plant and the person as a continuum" (p. 14). At the same time, other scholars, including psychologists Mary Gomes and Allen Kanner, were discussing similar themes. Together, these three authors edited the anthology *Ecopsychology: Restoring the Earth, Healing the Mind* (Roszak, Gomes, & Kanner, 1995), which gathered thinkers from several disciplines to further expound on the connection of humans and nature. The authors in this anthology aimed to look beyond just the human experience and explore the whole connection of the natural world to human development and psychological wellness. Roszak et al. called for a "greening of psychology," arguing that if human beings are truly to understand themselves, consciously and unconsciously, they cannot ignore that which supports, sustains, and provides for them: the earth.

Roszak et al. (1995) framed ecopsychology with the intersection of two movements, environmentalism and psychotherapy. Environmentalism, of course, is a movement throughout the world that addresses the scientific, political, and societal influences on how we protect and conserve our planet. An environmental impact can have worldwide effects (think of environmental disasters, such as the Deepwater Horizon oil spill, nuclear reactor explosions, and long-term effects of widely used pesticides such as DDT). Psychotherapy, in the traditional sense, is the study of the individual, where a therapist works with a client and explores emotional difficulties or mental illnesses in order to develop a treatment modality that can help the individual feel better. Roszak et al. sought to redefine emotional well-being on a "personal and planetary" level (p. 1).

A critical element of ecopsychology is the concept that humans experience psychological distress from the distress of the earth. Conn (1995) asked, "When the earth hurts, who responds?" (p. 156). She argued that we all hurt in physical and emotional ways, consciously or unconsciously, in response to the current health of the planet. Although it has been over 20 years since Conn wrote this piece, the truth is, the earth hurts more than ever. Forests are dying, species are becoming extinct, storms are becoming stronger, the oceans are rising, and yet there are people in power who still deny that climate change exists and is largely caused by humans. Ecopsychologists believe that our dying planet weighs heavy on our minds, even if we do not think about it directly every day. The uncertainty of the health and future of our planet creates anxiety in us. That feeling of uncertainty—not knowing if the earth, which houses and sustains us, will be able to support our growing numbers and the continued exploitation of resources—weighs heavy (Conn, 1995; Jordan & Hinds, 2016). Ecopsychologists believe that it is critical to conceptualize human health in context of the health of the planet.

Conn (1995) also suggested that the human disconnection to the earth manifests itself in a "materialistic disorder" that develops addictive and compulsive tendencies in people. Conn stated that "the need to consume [is] a serious signal of our culture's disconnection from the Earth" (p. 162). She meant that we, as humans, are far removed from "our roots," the ways in which the earth provides for us our food, water, and shelter. She suggested that hunting and gathering have developed into shopping addiction and the acquisition of merchandise. Certainly the Western world has moved to this bigger and better mentality: keeping up with the Joneses; having the latest and greatest iPhone, computer, car, house, clothing, jewelry, skin and beauty products, designer pet. All of these acquisitions are marketed to us as ways to improve our lives and to make us feel more comfortable, more loved, and more successful. Conn equated this to an inner emptiness from the loss of connection we once had to the earth, a community, or a place. She saw her clients attempting to ease emptiness, loneliness, and disconnection with substances, purchases, things, gossip, and celebrity obsession—the need for something better, even if the thing they have works perfectly well. This hamster wheel of consumption and addiction only brings a temporary high and, when that wears off, leads to deeper despair. Environmentalists and ecopsychologists also point out that our discarded products are filling landfills and the ocean with garbage.

Ecofeminists, a segment of the ecopsychology movement, tie humans' attempt at domination over the environment to harmful consequences to their physical and mental health (Warren , 1997). Ecofeminists discuss how the way the dominant society views and treats women is often parallel to societal views and treatment of the natural world. For example, "Mother Nature" is often depicted in the media and other venues as something unpredictable that needs to be controlled and mastered (Bosson, Vandello, Michniewicz, & Lenes, 2012). This mentality of domination operates through oppression, exploitation, and abuse. Yet Mother Nature can also be a nurturing provider, offering fertility, new growth, warmth, and comfort. Ecofeminists, by valuing ideals such as equality, mutuality, compassion, and coexistence, use these values as a way of reframing power and dominance. Furthermore, ecofeminists connect the healing power of Mother Nature in their work and use it as source of inspiration and strength (Warren, 1997).

ECOTHERAPY

Around the same time that Roszak et al. (1995) published their volume on the topic of ecopsychology, Clinebell (1996) was writing his own book on the subject, titled *Ecotherapy: Healing Ourselves, Healing the Earth*. Clinebell first coined the term *ecotherapy*. He conceptualized ecotherapy as "ecological spirituality" and, very much like Roszak et al. (1995), believed that our relationship with the natural world must be reciprocal. As nature has the ability to heal us, we too have the ability to heal nature. He called this the *ecological circle,* stating, "Experiencing this enlivening energy can enhance people's love for the natural world, deepen positive bonding with the earth, and add an earthly grounding to their spirituality. In other words, it can bring all of life down to earth" (Clinebell, 1996, p. 8). Clinebell posited three dimensions within ecotherapy: *inreach, upreach,* and *outreach.* By inreach, Clinebell meant for humans to open themselves up to being nurtured by nature, or intentionally allowing themselves to experience and appreciate that which the natural world offers. Through upreach, we can develop what he called a spiritual awareness, which in turn allows us to participate in outreach, or engaging in actions that support and sustain the planet.

Buzzell and Chalquist's (2009) text, *Ecotherapy: Health With Nature in Mind,* continued to expand on the concepts introduced in the previous decades. In this text, the contributors conceptualized green psychology in terms of the techniques, questions, and natural curiosities of the therapeutic process. The authors presented ways in which therapists can start working with their clients in different modalities. For example, they explored the clinicians' awakenings of the human–nature connection and how these awakenings started to influence their work as therapists. The authors discussed how that awakening shaped their work in a traditional office, using natural metaphors in a typical client–counselor exchange. They also discussed different modalities of ecotherapy, such as working in the deep wilderness or with animals, as well as how ecotherapy applies to community, children, and spirituality. This text was critical in expanding on the understanding, conceptualization, and application of ecotherapy techniques.

Based on the literature and for purposes of clarification, ecotherapy is defined as contact with the outdoors and nature as a method or element of therapy (Clinebell, 1996) and addresses the critical fact that as humans we are interwoven with the natural world (Buzzell & Chalquist, 2009). Ecopsychology is largely concerned with expanding on the discipline of psychology to understand the human–nature connection, as well as the human distress caused by the damage caused by human beings to the planet. Ecotherapy is sometimes referred as applied ecopsychology and uses different techniques and conceptualizations, with an emphasis on the reciprocal relationship of humans and nature (Jordan & Hinds, 2016). Ecotherapy encompasses a wide range of therapeutic techniques, from walking or sitting in nature during a counseling session to wilderness immersion therapy, horticulture or gardening, animal-assisted therapy such as equine therapy, and adventure-based work such as climbing or ropes courses (Jordan & Hinds, 2016).

Ecotherapy is not just *using* nature in therapy. A deeper understanding of the human–nature connection and the reciprocity of the relationship is critical in becoming an ecotherapist. A therapist wishing to become an ecotherapist must first explore his or her own relationship with nature. As you might ask a client, start by asking yourself these questions:

1. What are your early experiences with nature?
2. What memories of your childhood involve natural places?
3. What are your current favorite places in nature?
4. What feelings do they invoke in you?
5. Why is nature important to you?
6. Think about your own relationship with nature . . . What do you do to reciprocate the health and healing of the natural world?
7. Why are you interested in learning more about ecotherapy in particular?
8. What strengths do you think you possess as an ecotherapist or budding ecotherapist?

Clinebell's (1996) own Ecological Wellness Checkup is much more comprehensive. His intent was a "do-it-yourself tool" for those who want an "ecological check-in" (pp. 173–176). The questionnaire provides a way for individuals to think about what items they feel "excellent" about, "doing OK but there is definitely room for improvement," and "need strengthening" (see questionnaire in appendix). After taking this assessment, Clinebell suggests individuals write out a Self–Earth Care Plan to help them think through ways that they can provide themselves and the earth support and care.

Each of our Self–Earth Care Plans will look different. Some of us may need to start with smaller, more manageable steps (although I am sure we would all like to save the world and all creatures and things on it). Making a plan for yourself must be something that makes you feel good and is achievable. If taking a walk in nature a few days a week is what you can manage in your schedule right now, that is terrific. If you volunteer with environmental groups or with organizations that work to protect and preserve natural spaces, that is terrific too. As counselors, we know the importance of self-care, setting boundaries, and having realistic expectations—and not just for our clients but for us too. As you move forward in your development as an ecotherapist, you will expand and explore different options that work for you best.

DEEPER ECOTHERAPY

As we now know, ecopsychology is the study of the connection between humans and nature, and ecotherapy is the methodology used to reconnect that relationship and heal clients integrating the natural world. Linda Buzzell, an expert in ecotherapy, coauthor of *Ecotherapy: Healing with Nature in Mind* (Buzzell & Chalquist, 2009), and founder of the International Association for Ecotherapy, uses the terms *Level 1* and *Level 2 ecotherapies* (Buzzell, 2016). Buzzell states that another name for Level 1 ecotherapy is human-centered nature therapy, which, simply stated, is going into nature to use it for its healing powers. There is plenty of evidence that as little as 5 minutes in nature improves one's mood and well-being (Frumkin et al., 2017; Louv, 2012), and so Level 1 ecotherapy is a good beginning into the field. Many of the therapists I have talked to at conferences or at presentations are intuitively doing Level 1 ecotherapy. They share with me stories about how it just felt right to stand up and take their client out of the office on a walk or bring the child client into a backyard for session. Buzzell (2016) argues, however, that Level 1 ecotherapy misses a critical point—that is, the effect on both the planet and human beings caused by the rapid destruction and loss of nature.

Buzzell (2016) calls Level 2 ecotherapy the "Circle of Reciprocal Healing" (p. 71). Buzzell states that "there can be no true human health on a sick planet" (p. 71). This level digs deeper from the anthropocentric view of human existence to a larger view that healing ourselves involves healing our planet. This also enables us to have a deeper understanding of the entire global, cultural, and political context of the natural world. Becoming a Level 2 ecotherapist does not mean that you must join a local activist group or hug trees (unless, of course, that's what you want to do) but instead lets you and then ultimately your clients think more deeply about our connection to nature. For some clients, understanding that some of their anxiety is caused by their deep worry about the earth is in itself a step in the right direction and, oddly, a relief for many who finally can understand and express that emotion. Others start to understand how they have always felt a deep connection to animals. I remember a client being able to articulate why birthdays and holidays were so stressful for her (beyond the family drama, of course). She started to understand that the packaging and over-consumerism of the holidays brought her a deep sense of worry about the waste and the cost of the environment to produce toys and goods that might soon be discarded and eventually placed into dumpsters and landfills.

Level 2 ecotherapists think about how to integrate these ideas into conversations with their clients. In addition, Level 2 ecotherapists are deliberate about their interactions with nature. If they use gardening or horticulture therapy as their ecotherapy method, they are careful to include plants that are indigenous to the location and are helpful to local wildlife. A Level 2 ecotherapist might take time to listen and even thank nature for the connection. Buzzell (2016) also describes Level 2 animal-assisted therapy as allowing the animal space and freedom to interact with human clients or as working with abused animals to help the animal's healing and, as a result, the client's own. Level 2 ecotherapy can look very different depending on the therapist and his or her preferred modality. As Buzzell notes, becoming a Level 2 ecotherapist may take time. As a therapist venturing into ecotherapy, you may need time to read and discover more about the different types of ecotherapies and then begin to integrate these thoughts and approaches into your own life. Next, when you feel ready, you can start to work with your clients through an ecotherapy lens. I know this was my own journey. The more I read and the longer I practiced, the better understanding I had about myself, my own connection to nature, and the ways that connection translated into my ecotherapy practice.

ECOPSYCHOLOGICAL THEORY

As discussed previously, ecopsychology is broadly known as the "what is" and ecotherapy as the "how to" in our therapeutic connection to nature. Kahn and Hasbach (2012) succinctly summarize the major tenets of ecopsychology:

1. Unconscious processes exist, including those of identification and repression, not only in relations with other people but to the earth itself.
2. Direct sensorial experience with the phenomenon of nature constitutes a foundational source of knowledge, joy, and a full realization of human potential.
3. As proposed by the theory of Gaia and deep ecology, human life is interdependent with other human life and with the nonhuman world.
4. Interaction with nature helps lead to optimum mental health and psychological development, often through developing inner peace, compassion, and trust and by providing a medium for engaging in selfless service. (pp. 119–120)

Hasbach (2012), a therapist who has been practicing ecotherapy for over two decades, expands on this initial foundation to include three more concepts:

5. Interaction with nature benefits people physically and psychologically.
6. We are biological beings with an evolutionary history and many patterns of thought and action that formed through coevolving with nature in our evolutionary history are with us still.
7. To flourish, we need to connect more deeply to wilderness. (pp. 120–124).

The wilderness is an important part of Hasbach's extended theory. Both Hasbach and her colleague Kahn (2012) write extensively on the concept of *rewilding of the human species*. They extend the concept of biophilia (human beings' propensity to connect with nature) and build on the evolution of human beings from their roots as creatures surviving in the wild. Our interactions with the wild can bring strong emotions. Certainly, those of us who have experienced living in the deep wilderness for longer periods of time know how transformative that experience can be. For many, the wilderness can cause deep fears. The darkness and creatures in the dark tease our nervous systems; spiders and snakes can cause panic attacks and shrieks of fear; the dirt and bacteria and illness (such as tick-borne illnesses) that are a part of nature also produce fear. Kahn and Hasbach

(2012) say we fear nature too much, especially in Western societies that crave order and control. The wild represents that which is untamed and unpredictable. We, as a modern species, have turned that fear of the unknown into anxiety. Kahn and Hasbach argue that we have lost touch with our wild sides and yet, at a deep level, actually crave these interactions. These feelings can be experienced in a single moment: locking eyes with a deer; seeing a heard of horses running through a field; witnessing a whale breaching high out of the ocean; having a butterfly land on your finger; experiencing the night sky without any light pollution; or, a recent phenomenon in the United States, watching the full solar eclipse. And yet so often we miss these moments or do not make opportunities to experience them. Kahn (2012) calls this *environmental generational amnesia*. Next we discuss how you fit in.

ECOTHERAPY AND COUNSELING

Counseling, while aligned with other helping professions, is guided more by holistic and humanistic philosophies and sees clients through a developmental lens (King, 2012). The discipline of counseling is well suited for the tenets of ecotherapy. Counselors view the world with open eyes, taking in rich perspectives from different cultural orientations and worldviews. Counselors use less of a medical model and more of a holistic model, celebrating the strengths and differences we all bring. Counselors are trained to be empathetic, kind, caring, respectful, and open-minded. Counselors assess clients by understanding their whole experience not just on a micro level but through a bigger picture, understanding that multiple influences, such as family, society, racism, systemic injustice, cultural beliefs, and religious orientations impact a client's mental well-being. Using a chosen theoretical lens, counselors work collaboratively with their clients to design treatment plans with goals and objectives to help clients deal with whatever issues bring them to therapy. Counselors value and celebrate all lives and work with their clients on helping them achieve their best selves.

Ecotherapy is lesser known in the counseling discipline and is taught in very few counseling programs. When surveyed, only 26% of counselors acknowledged learning anything in their graduate programs about the influence on the natural world on mental health (Wolsko & Hoyt, 2012). Even those with an understanding of the positive benefits of nature did not incorporate it in their practice because of a lack of understanding about how to do so. Barriers included a general lack of knowledge on how to include nature into practice as well as perceived limitations such as time and office location. With empirical evidence growing that supports the benefits of nature on physical and mental health, and with the wide-reaching impact that counselors have on the well-being of so many, the marriage of these two disciplines is well suited.

Reese and Myers (2012) highlighted the need to expand on counseling wellness to include "ecowellness." They define this as "a sense of appreciation, respect for, and awe of nature that results in feelings of connectedness with the natural environment and the enhancement of holistic wellness" (p. 400). They argue that this is a missing component in wellness models that counselors use to assess clients. Included in their understanding of ecowellness is access to nature, acknowledging that not all access to nature is equal and that such access is largely influenced by race and class. Another construct of ecowellness is an individual's environmental identity, or how access to nature impacts his or her own environmental identity. Individuals are more likely to have a stronger and healthier environmental identity if they had safe and positive access to nature as a child. Finally, Reese and Myers identify *transcendence* as another key factor in ecowellness. Transcendence is the ability to reach beyond oneself and connect to deeper levels of understanding or relationships. Reese and Myers address spirituality as well as community connections as important factors in this dimension. The researchers' conceptualization of ecowellness resulted in the development and validation of the Reese EcoWellness Inventory (Reese, Myers, Lewis, & Willse, 2015), designed to study the concepts of ecowellness.

Reese (2016) is a leading force in merging nature into the counseling discipline, acknowledging the missing aspect the natural world in our conceptualization of clients' well-being. He identified seven underlying factors as an important framework for counselors, especially those working in traditional settings, to assess a client's connection to nature and begin to introduce nature into their work with clients (Reese, 2016). These factors include having a strong working knowledge of ecowellness (or ecotherapy), above and beyond informed consent; honoring a client's nature worldview; protecting confidentiality; being clear with clients about the clinical intent of nature-based therapy and client advocacy; and having access to safe places in nature (Reese, 2016, p. 349). These key concepts are critical in setting up an ecotherapy practice, but first we must focus on you: How will you become an ecotherapist?

First, we focus on you. We explore your interest in the subject and ask you to begin to reflect on your relationship with nature—the ways that nature nurtures you and you nurture nature. You will begin to expand on your understanding about the reciprocity of nature. You will reflect on your thoughts and feelings associated with the condition of the planet and ways that these thoughts and feelings affect your mental health. You will explore your intent to become an ecotherapist. Then we discuss ways you can begin your practice, including ethical considerations in alignment with the American Counseling Association's Code of Ethics (2014) as well as practical and safety concerns.

In the following chapters, we also explore ways that you can integrate ecotherapy into your practice with children and/or adults, as well as in group or school settings. We discuss ecotherapy with the military population, a growing and effective modality for veterans and their families. We also explore the topic of *ecospirituality*, or the many ways that ecotherapy and spirituality (religious and nonreligious) are connected. We outline the different modalities of ecotherapy, including animal-assisted therapy, equine therapy, forest bathing, hiking therapy, horticulture therapy, and biophilic design, or ways that we can green our work and living spaces, including our indoor offices. Also included in this text are stories from counselors and counselors-in-training on their experience with ecotherapy. These vignettes demonstrate the concepts discussed in actual application. Each chapter integrates practical ways that counselors can infuse ecotherapy into their practice.

REFERENCES

American Counseling Association. (2014). *American Counseling Association Code of Ethics, 2014*. Retrieved from http://www.counseling.org/resources/aca-code-of-ethics.pdf

Bosson, J. K., Vandello, J. A., Michniewicz, K. S., & Lenes, J. G. (2012). American men's and women's beliefs about gender discrimination: For men, it's not quite a zero sum. *Masculinidades y cambio social*, 1(3), 210–239.

Buzzell, L. (2016). The many ecotherapies. In M. Jordan & J. Hinds (Eds.), *Ecotherapy: Theory, research & practice* (pp. 70–82). New York, NY: Macmillan.

Buzzell, L., & Chalquist, C. (Eds.). (2009). *Ecotherapy: Healing with nature in mind*. San Francisco, CA: Sierra Club Books.

Clinebell, H. (1996). *Ecotherapy: Healing ourselves, healing the earth*. Minneapolis, MN: Augsburg Fortress Press.

Conn, S. (1995). When the earth hurts, who responds? In T. Roszak, M. E. Gomes, & A. D. Kanner (Eds.), *Ecopsychology: Restoring the earth, healing the mind* (pp. 156–171). San Francisco, CA: Sierra Club Books.

Frumkin, H., Bratman, G. N., Breslow, S. J., Cochran, B., Kahn, P. H., Jr., Lawler, J. J., . . . Wood, S. A. (2017). Nature contact and human health: A research agenda. *Environmental Health Perspectives*, 125(7).

Hillman, J. (1995). A psyche the size of the earth: A psychological foreword. In T. Roszak, M. E. Gomes, & A. D. Kanner (Eds.), *Ecopsychology: Restoring the earth, healing the mind*, (pp. xvii–xxiii). San Francisco, CA: Sierra Club Books.

Jordan, M., & Hinds, J. (2016). *Ecotherapy: Theory, research & practice.* New York, NY: Macmillan.

Kahn, P. H., & Hasbach, P. H. (Eds.). (2012). *Ecopsychology: Science, totems, and the technological species.* Cambridge, MA: MIT Press.

King, J. (2012, December 14). *Defining counselor professional identity: What makes us unique among the mental health professions?* Chi Sigma Iota Webinars. Retrieved from http://www.csi-net.org/?webinars

Louv, R. (2005). *Last child in the woods: Saving our children from nature-deficit disorder.* Chapel Hill, NC: Algonquin Books of Chapel Hill.

Louv, R. (2012). *The nature principle: Reconnecting with life in a virtual age.* Chapel Hill, NC: Algonquin Books of Chapel Hill.

Reese, R. F. (2016). Ecowellness and guiding principles for the ethical integration of nature into counseling. *International Journal for the Advancement of Counselling, 38,* 345–357.

Reese, R. F., & Myers, J. E. (2012). EcoWellness: The missing factor in holistic wellness models. *Journal of Counseling and Development, 90,* 400–406.

Reese, R. F., Myers, J. E., Lewis, T. F., & Willse, J. T. (2015). Construction and initial validation of the Reese EcoWellness Inventory. *International Journal of the Advancement of Counselling, 37,* 124–142.

Roszak, T. (1995). Where psyche meets gaia. In T. Roszak, M. E. Gomes, & A. D. Kanner (Eds.), *Ecopsychology: Restoring the earth, healing the mind* (pp. 1–17). Berkeley: University of California Press.

Roszak, T. (2001). *The voice of the earth.* Grand Rapids, MI: Phanes Press.

Sabini, M. (2002). *The earth has a soul: CG Jung on nature, technology & modern life.* Berkeley, CA: North Atlantic Books.

Warren, K. J. (Eds.). (1997). *Ecofeminism: Women, culture, nature.* Bloomington: Indiana University Press.

Wolsko, C., & Hoyt, K. (2012). Employing the restorative capacity of nature: Pathways to practicing ecotherapy among mental health professionals. *Ecopsychology, 4,* 10–24.

Worell, J., & Remer P. (2003). *Feminist perspectives in therapy: Empowering diverse women.* Hoboken, NJ: Wiley.

PART II

Counseling and Nature

Interventions for Counselors in Everyday Practice

PART II

CHAPTER 3

ঔ

Nature and Play

Ecotherapy With Children

MEGAN E. DELANEY

MADDIE, AGE 7: When I am outside I feel strong and brave . . . happy and energetic.

GABRIELLA, AGE 9: Being outside, I feel like I'm free. I feel energetic and excited, like I'm going to have fun. There are no limits to the fun!

BEN, AGE 11: I live in a city. I love the summer because I get to go to camp in the woods. At camp I run and play outside with my friends. We swim and go hiking and this summer I tried rock climbing. That was awesome! Being at camp is the best part of the year.

Ask an older adult about their memories of childhood and many will describe running amok with neighborhood friends until either the sun went down or Mom yelled to come in for dinner. Without smart phones, cable TV, the Internet, PlayStations, YouTube, iPads—you name it—kids had fewer inside distractions. Many older adults remember parents shooing kids out of the house, warning them not to come back until it got dark. Of course, not everyone had access to safe neighborhoods, backyards, and parks to play in, and so a friend's stoop or a local basketball hoop would suffice. Many ponder the migration of the child from spending hours outside to the structured, indoor lives many children now live. Is it because of the ease and availability of electronic distractions and endless television shows? Or maybe because so many have affordable access to the Internet now. How much does the news portrayal of the dangers of children playing outside—they could get hurt, kidnapped, assaulted—influence this trend? Are kids are being overschedule so much that they don't have free time? Do kids have safe access to natural places? Regardless, this growing disconnection between children and the outdoors correlates with the increasing childhood ailments including anxiety, depression, attention deficit disorder, diabetes and obesity (Torio, Encinosa, Berdahl, McCormick, & Simpson, 2015).Nature and Play

In their earliest of experiences, children freely explore their surrounding environments (Arranz, Oliva, De Miguel, Olabarrieta, & Richards, 2010). With the curiosity that childhood brings, children explore the natural world on their hands and knees or while running in the woods or by a stream or lake or with any natural environment they can access (Lee, 2012). At the same time, these children are developing a sense of self, mostly molded in a social context by their parents, teachers, culture, religion, and racial and ethnic qualities (Arranz et al., 2010; Ginsburg, 2007). While these children are forming social relationships, some argue that they are also establishing a relationship with the natural world (Barrows, 1995; Louv, 2005; Lovejoy & Ray, 2001).

A child's natural curiosity, love of play, and tendency to explore make the outdoors an optimal classroom and playground. The natural world is filled with living examples, opportunities for creativity and exploration, teachable moments, and endless occasions for play (Sweatman & Warner, 2009). From the earliest of ages, babies, toddlers, and young children use exploratory play to interact with the world. In exploratory play, children manipulate what they find in order to learn more about the properties, textures, feelings, and uses of the objects they discover (Frost, Wortham, & Reifel, 2008; Ginsburg, 2007). Most children begin to parallel-play, or to play alongside another child or adult but not necessarily interact or involve the other with their play. As children develop, their play becomes more complex and involves others. The act of play helps a child develop executive functioning skills such as self-regulation, cognitive ability, and memory as well as social skills (Elkind, 2007; Ginsburg, 2007).

With each stage of development, the natural world can provide a boost to a child's budding knowledge and abilities. Infants need sensory inputs such as smell, sounds, touch, and taste as well as colors and textures. Toddlers are more active in exploring their environment while developing their independence and mastering large motor skills (Frost et al., 2008). Activities that allow for creativity and imagination as well as allow for active play work best for this age group. Young children need activities that support fine-motor skills while stimulating cognitive development and social skills. Depending on the developmental needs of the child, activities can include building, digging, running, climbing, as well as dramatic and pretend play (Elkind, 2007). Older children are ready to explore the deeper connections between themselves and the natural world and can benefit from the freedom, independence, and sometimes escape the natural world can provide (Barrows, 1995).

Despite the benefits and healing effects of the outdoors (Hartig, Mang, & Evans, 1991), there is dramatic decline in how much time children and their families are spending outside (Center for Behavioral Health Statistics and Quality, 2015). Children have increasingly busy schedules and often easy access to computers, smartphones, electronic games, and other technology (Juster, Hiromi, & Stafford, 2004; Louv, 2012). Reports from the American Academy of Pediatrics (AAP; 2016) indicate that children spend up to 7 hours a day on electronic devices despite the AAP's recommendations against it. The AAP suggests that children under the age of 2 should not interact with TVs or screens and that children and teens should have limited access, only 1 or 2 hours a day of high-quality programming or content. Some research suggests that the trend of spending childhood mostly indoors has contributed to the growing rates of childhood obesity, deficiencies in vitamin D, and other physical and mental issues in the younger generation (Rideout, Vandewater, & Wartella, 2003). Additional research suggests that hands-on contact with nature increases self-esteem and overall well-being (Berger & Lahad, 2013; Maller, Henderson-Wilson, & Townsend, 2009) and proximity to a natural environment near a child's home is found to decrease a child's level of stress and increase his or her perception of self-worth (Wells & Evans, 2003). Recently doctors are prescribing outdoor time as a way to tackle rising rates of obesity, heart disease, and other chronic conditions (see https://www.parkrx.org/).

Researchers believe there is a correlation in the increase of mental illness and the decrease of time spent outdoors (Burdette & Whitaker, 2005; Craig, Logan, & Prescott, 2016; Louv, 2005). Journalist Richard Louv (2005, 2012) extensively researched the lost connection with nature and coined the term *nature deficit disorder*. Louv insists this term is not intended as a medical diagnosis but more as a way of thinking about the disconnect children and adults have with the natural world. "Nature-deficit disorder describes the human costs of alienation from nature, among them: diminished use of the senses, attention difficulties and higher rates of physical and emotional illness" (Louv, 2005, p. 36). Experience with and access to natural spaces are important considerations in helping children and families reconnect to the natural world. A survey conducted by the Nature Conservancy (2011) asked children what inhibits them from going outside. While some children noted "it was uncomfortable to be outdoors due to things like bugs and heat," a large percentage of children said "they did not have transportation to natural areas," and "there were not natural areas near their homes" (p. 2). Results also indicated that those children with access to and positive experiences outdoors are twice as likely to want to go back, using the words "peaceful," "free," "calm," "happy," "adventurous," "alive," "curious," and "amazed" in describing their feelings of being outdoors (Nature Conservancy, 2011, p. 7).

Figure 3.1 Giving a tree a good hug is good for the spirit!

The purpose of this chapter is to suggest that mental health professionals can help their clients and families reconnect with the natural world by incorporating nature into therapy practice. This chapter provides some specific interventions and ideas on how counselors can integrate the natural world in their work with children. The important piece is play. How you, the therapist, bring nature into your work with children can go beyond the handful of ideas presented in this chapter. In fact, often children, once in nature, instinctually start exploring and playing on their own. Children are hardwired for exploring their environments (Louv, 2005). Following their lead often brings wonderful surprises and therapeutic breakthroughs.

ECOTHERAPY AND PLAY

Being "nurtured by nature" . . . means flinging wide our inner windows of grateful awareness of these gifts of life and deepening our intimate interaction with the natural world in ways that are both healing and enlivening. (Clinebell, 1996, p. 8)

Ecotherapists who work with children often include a play-based approach to therapy. Play therapy is widely used to treat children because it is often the most developmentally appropriate way to work through a child's emotional and mental health issues (Elkind, 2007). Most children under the age of 11 are unable to understand or verbally communicate abstract thoughts and feelings. Through the use of toys, dolls, or play materials, children act out or symbolically express their feelings and emotions, which allows the therapist to interpret and help the child work through his or her issues (Bratton, Ray, Rhine, & Jones, 2005). Interactive play helps children build relationships, such as with the therapist. Ecotherapists use play to help children develop a relationship with the natural world. Using nature in play-based therapeutic activities has the potential to build upon relationship skills, create new and enriching experiences to explore the natural world, as well as utilize nature for its healing properties.

ECOTHERAPY TECHNIQUES FOR CHILDREN

While counselors may differ in their theoretical approach, they all incorporate play in their work with children. Most play therapy occurs in a counselor's office; however, the aim of this chapter is to introduce how play therapy can be infused with the natural world. The following are several examples of ways that counselors can integrate ecotherapy into their practice.

Take the Office Outdoors

Most therapists conduct sessions in a private office space that allows for privacy and comfort. While most adults will sit on a chair or couch during therapy, children, especially younger children, often have a hard time sitting still for a traditional therapy appointment. Therapists who work with young clients have an office that includes games, dolls, dollhouses, puppets, and other interactive objects. The concept of taking the office outdoors depends on the therapist's comfort level, access to outdoor space, insurance limitations, and parent/guardian approval, yet it is a simple way to integrate nature, thus utilizing its power in everyday practice (Santostefano, 2004). If possible, a fenced or enclosed space free from distractions is ideal. Other considerations include safety issues such as the proximity to busy streets or other potential dangers, especially if you are working with a client who likes to run.

Optimally the therapy space would be safe and private with room for the child to explore. Just being outdoors allows for feeling open and free and for spontaneous and unstructured play, which in our overprescribed lifestyle is not something children are always able to experience (Hanscom & Louv, 2016; Louv, 2005). To start, take your planned activities outside and follow your own instincts as well as the child's lead. Sit under a tree and play a game, allow the child to build a house for her dolls in a special corner, bring the sand play outside, allow the child to use natural materials in his play, or build an outdoor shelter together. If you have the time and space, plant a small garden with your clients. The children can take time each session to water and nurture the plants and vegetables, watching them grow over time. Gardens that include lavender, sage, or other fragrant plants also provide a sensory experience and a deeper connection to the natural world (Chen, Ho, & Tu, 2013). With older children, taking a walk in a park or on the beach can reduce feelings of pressure and allow for conversations that feel more natural and spontaneous (Hegarty, 2010). Some children might prefer to play a sport together such as shooting hoops or playing catch.

Sensory Play

Sensory play is an important developmental activity for all children and helps to stimulate cognitive, linguistic, social, and emotional skills (Miller, Fuller, & Roetenberg, 2014; Smith, Mruzek, & Mozingo, 2015). Children with hyperactivity or sensory processing disorders or who may be on the autism spectrum are often prescribed specific sensory interventions to

Figure 3.2 Being outside with a young client gives them freedom to play and explore.

adapt responses to environmental and social input (Smith et al., 2015). Sensory play involves stimulating the senses: taste, touch, smell, sight, and sound. Sensory interventions can help children adapt their reactions to stimulus that might be overwhelming, as well as help those children who are underreactive to stimuli. The natural world is a wonderful place to engage a child's senses. Just exploring the surroundings, a child can feel, smell, see, and hear endless inputs. The therapist is able to adapt the therapeutic intention depending on the needs of the child. Some examples of sensory play are outlined next.

Grounding exercise: A therapist can help guide a child to listen, relax, and breathe to the sounds of birds, the breeze, or the babble of a brook or stream. Using the earth and trees as metaphors, a therapist can help a child with grounding exercises. The therapist guides the child through the visualization of standing tall and envisioning roots growing into the earth from the bottom of the child's feet. The child can extend his or her arms like branches and gently sway with the breeze. The therapist could ask the child how she feels (if developmentally appropriate) as the tree and suggest that she repeat this exercise at home or in a park or playground if she feels overwhelmed or out of control.

Sand play: Sand play offers an excellent opportunity for tactile play. Sand play is an especially powerful therapeutic tool for children who may not be able to verbalize their feelings. Using the sand tray, a child can portray feelings or circumstances that might otherwise be difficult to articulate. A therapist who does sand play with children can move sand play to an outdoor sand table and incorporate the typical toys and figures or guide the child to use items found outdoors. This typically nonverbal therapeutic technique allows children to create their scenario or scene in the sand while also benefitting from the power of being outdoors.

Tents or tunnel: A child feeling overwhelmed or stimulated often benefits from the small, safe place of a tent, a cozy corner, or a tunnel. Together, the therapist and child can create a space in an outdoor place that is covered and protected. If natural materials are present, the child could create and build a shelter, an exercise that can help to boost self-esteem and confidence. The therapist can help children think about creating their own safe place or cozy corner at home or in their yard to use to calm down or to be alone.

Heavy work: Heavy work is often used with children who have high arousal and energy levels. The concept of heavy work activities is to help a child's body receive the inputs it needs to regulate energy. This is especially true of children with underreactive neurological systems—those children who twirl, jump, run, and spin. Often these children are trying to stimulate their vestibular system, the area in the inner ear that registers movement (Miller, Fuller, & Roetenberg, 2014). The therapist can create heavy work in the outdoor space such as having a child roll a large log, push a rock or stone, shovel snow or rake leaves, jump rope, stack wood, or move large objects within the natural space. The combined interventions of heavy work and the natural world doubles the impact of the therapeutic activity.

Art Therapy in Nature

Art therapy is an alternative form of therapy that helps to facilitate change through the interaction of art materials, the client, and the therapist

(Dalley & Case, 2014). Using art materials and creative activities, the child channels his or her feelings into pictures, sculptures, masks, or other activities while the therapist interprets and interacts with the child through the art piece (Dalley & Case, 2014). Integrating nature and using natural items can be a powerful combination. The following are just two examples of art therapy incorporating nature; however, many art therapy interventions can easily be adapted to be done in nature, incorporate natural items, or use nature as a metaphor during the activity and client–therapist interaction.

Masks: Making masks with clients is a popular intervention for therapists incorporating art into their practice. Masks help therapists get a better understanding of how clients view themselves. A therapist can also explain the connection between the outside of the mask and the inside of the mask, in other words, how others might see you but how you feel inside. Masks can also be made to express a child's thoughts about his or her present and future self as a way of looking into the future and building confidence. Masks can also be a safe play to "hide" in order to express feelings that someone might not otherwise be able to outwardly express (Dunn-Snow & Joy-Smellie, 2000).

Materials needed: Paper masks found at an arts and crafts store and tape and glue.

Description: The counselor talks with the child about making the mask and explains the activity to the child depending on the purpose of the mask (how I see myself or how others see me or what I look like when I am sad, angry, happy, etc.). The counselor talks to the child about finding materials out in the natural world to use to decorate the mask (leaves, acorns, twigs, flowers, etc.). The child then uses the materials he or she collects to create the mask.

Masks are a powerful therapeutic tool and help clients to portray their inner thoughts and feelings (Dunn-Snow & Joy-Smellie, 2000). They can be an especially effective tool with children who might not have the developmental capability to verbalize how they feel. Combining this process with the natural benefits of being and exploring outdoors and discovering the materials from nature that the child will use for the mask is another way that nature can enhance the therapeutic process.

Totem Pole: In this exercise, the child uses a totem pole to create a story about him- or herself. The counselor can talk with the child about the history of totem poles and how Native American people built them to represent a story, a tribe, or a custom. The totem pole might also include an animal that is special and important to the child.

Materials needed: Paper, markers or paint glue, recycled coffee tins or recycled paper towel or toilet paper rolls, and natural things the child finds in the outdoors.

Description: The counselor sits with the child at the same level and talks about different animals that are in the natural world. The counselor asks about which animal the child likes most (or, if the child is older, what animal he or she relates to). Some questions the counselor can ask include:

- Have you felt connected with a particular animal but maybe don't even know why?
- What animals do you look for when you are out in nature? What animals do you like to see most when you go to the zoo?
- Is there an animal that always appears in your life, drawings, or dreams?

When a child picks an animal, the counselor can probe further to find out the connection that the child has with the animal. For example, if the child picks a horse as the favorite animal, the child might say "they are fast, strong, and free" and the counselor could expand upon that and, depending on the developmental level of the child, talk about ambition, drive, and power. The counselor can also explore with the child—is the horse wild or tame? What does that mean to the child? Think about three descriptive words that represent the animal and the child's connection. Together the counselor and child can think about what they would want to put on the totem pole. Depending on the age and developmental level of the child, the totem pole could have one or several stages. Using the horse example, the child who picked "fast," "strong," and "free" can create each section of the pole to represent those descriptive qualities. Encourage children to explore the natural space around them to find pieces of nature that they can include on their totem pole.

After the child completes the totem pole, the counselor and child can hold a ceremony to bless the totem pole and invite family and/or friends. In traditional Native American ceremonies, the host would give each attendant a gift, knowing that this act of giving will be reciprocal in the future. The "raising" of the totem pole can be followed by a party or celebration.

Nature as Homework

Counselors often give clients homework as a way to reinforce or further explore topics and ideas covered during the therapy session. One simple technique is to prescribe time in nature for both clients and their families. Helping a client and their families brainstorm ideas is a good first step. Make sure there are safe and accessible outdoor places near their home; if that is unknown, do some research on the parks and playgrounds nearby.

Give the client a realistic goal, such as 15 minutes a day for a walk outdoors or a total of 3 hours per week spending time together outdoors. Let a client know about local resources such as hiking clubs (which often have websites with local trails) and parks and recreation departments with outdoor activities. Encourage clients and their parents to utilize their own back or front yards, if available, to explore or play a game. Ask clients to journal their time spent outdoors and their mood and thoughts. (Parents might need to help and/or provide their own observations of the child's behavior.)

In collaboration with the National Wildlife Federation, the Natural Learning Initiative at North Carolina State University created a wonderful resource *Nature Play at Home: A Guide for Boosting Your Children's Healthy Development and Creativity* (Wilson, 2018). The guidebook (available as a free download at https://naturalearning.org/nature-play-home-released) is a user-friendly resource for families who need ideas and creative ways to get outdoors. The colorful and straightforward resource includes a large list of nature-based activities including water play, earth and mud play, backyard habitats, sand play, and even solutions for small spaces. Activities are labeled with an effort scale from minimal effort to substantial planning. The guidebook is also a great resource for counselors and therapists, who can use activities provided in sessions with their clients and/or work with clients on picking an activity they can do at home.

THE CASE OF JEFFREY

The following case is one that has long stayed with me. At the time that we met, Jeffrey was a 5-year-old boy who lived in a small suburban town in the Northeast. Jeffrey was about to enter kindergarten, and his family brought him to therapy due to Jeffrey's recent decline in speech, difficult behavior (mostly at preschool and camp), and limited social interaction with family and peers. Jeffrey had a diagnosis of pervasive developmental disorder—not otherwise specified, and he received early intervention services through his school district. At the time, he was placed in a self-contained preschool classroom for children with special needs and received 2 hours per week of occupational therapy and speech therapy.

Previous school evaluations described Jeffrey as "noncompliant," "difficult," and "unable to follow direction." School reports also characterized his behavior as "socially odd," including laughing and making faces while in school, which they construed as being "defiant." Jeffrey was reported to have experienced delayed speech, with his mother stating that he began talking at 3.5 years while early speech patterns included babbling and

Figure 3.3 Ecotherapy is good for kids in any season.

repetition, often known as "echolalia." At the time of our work together, Jeffrey was reported to understand most of what was said to him, but his mother and his teachers often stated that he did not acknowledge or answer questions. The parents had Jeffrey evaluated by a private speech therapist and the results indicated low expressive language and receptive language. The Child Study Team scored his language in the 5th percentile, but his mother reported that she believed this score did not reflect his intellect or abilities. Mom reported that Jeffrey has been able to read since the age of 3.

The short-term goal of my approach was to make a connection with Jeffrey, as rapport is key to any kind of long-term goals. Long-term goals included increasing verbal output and social skills. In this, I integrated a

DIR-Floortime approach, used by some therapists working with children on the autism spectrum or with other special needs. DIR stands for *developmental, individual-differences, and relationship-based*, which takes into consideration the unique qualities of each child, and, using that child as the lead, follows his or her natural curiosity and emotions while simultaneously promoting improvements in social, cognitive, and behavior ability (Pajareya & Nopmaneejumruslers, 2011). Initially, play therapy with Jeffery was conducted in a typical office setting. Jeffrey often picked up toys of interest and played independently. My attempts to interact with Jeffrey during play were largely ignored, and Jeffrey became aggravated and occasionally angry when interrupted. After several weeks, I still was struggling to find ways to engage with Jeffrey.

With approval from Jeffrey's parents, I moved our sessions outside into the enclosed area behind my office. I met with Jeffrey in this outdoor setting, bringing different toys, dolls, and games outside. During these meetings, I saw a dramatic change in Jeffrey's affect and mood. Jeffrey joyfully would run the perimeter of the yard, picking up objects as he saw them. Shortly after going outside, Jeffrey began to bring the objects to me. I mirrored his behavior, scavenging the yard for interesting items to share with Jeffrey. This was the first time that Jeffrey made eye contact with me. Over time, Jeffrey began to interact and communicate more. His eye contact increased, and his affect and communication skills slowly improved. A few weeks into our outdoor sessions, I put a sandbox outside and brought out the corresponding toys. This became Jeffrey's favorite place to play. He created elaborate scenes with the toys and other natural objects he found around the yard. The scenarios played out in the sand were very telling to me. Most scenes involved dinosaurs and a school bus where often the dinosaur did not want to get on the bus and would hide in a corner of the sandbox under a pile of leaves or sticks with most of the other cars and dolls on the opposite end. Through this play, I was able to begin to understand the inside of this little boy's mind. When I would state something like "that dinosaur is all by himself; I wonder if he might feel lonely and sad," Jeffrey would turn his head and look intently at me. Over time, Jeffrey and I developed a stronger bond as evident by increased eye contact, play that was more elaborate, improved verbal communication, and better proximity of physical space during play. Jeffrey's mood and affect began to improve in and outside of therapy.

Over time, Jeffrey made progress in therapy, at home, and at school. His verbal and nonverbal communication skills improved, specifically in eye contact and response rate to verbal questions and queues. His mom has also noticed the improvements, and with my encouragement, now makes time each day to be sure Jeffrey has time to play outside. She also tries to take Jeffrey for longer outdoor trips on weekends. In addition, I began to collaborate with Jeffrey's school counselor, teachers, and occupational and speech therapists to provide a more integrative and collaborative routine of care.

Jeffrey was a difficult case. Long after I stopped working with him, I heard from his mom that he had regressed. Of course, children on the autism spectrum need intensive, ongoing interventions and can experience cyclical gains and losses (Seligman & Reichenberg, 2007). Hearing about your client's struggles is one of the most difficult aspect of this work. Still, we keep faith that our time together with our clients provides resiliency and long-term positive effects. Talking to Jeffrey's mom again, I reminded her how much fun we had playing outside. She mentioned that they had not been doing outdoor play as much and would make time to reconnect. Of course, that will not solve all of Jeffrey's ongoing issues, but it might provide some respite and bonding time for both mother and son.

With the current trend in increased use of electronic devices and screen time and decreased time in outdoor play, it is no wonder that children are struggling with attention, focus, concentration, as well as increased stress and anxiety (Torio et al., 2015). Over the years of working with children, I have witnessed directly the difference in our relationship as soon as we are outside. The children are more relaxed, smile more, are quicker to engage in activities, and genuinely look forward to coming to therapy. The natural world provides open-ended possibilities for play and exploration. Combining the imagination of the therapist and child as well as the abundance of inspiration and resources provided in nature, the natural world is a powerful tool and ally.

REFERENCES

American Academy of Pediatrics. (2016). *Media and children.* Retrieved from https://www.aap.org/en-us/advocacy-and-policy/aap-health-initiatives/Pages/Media-and-Children.aspx

Arranz, E. B., Oliva, A., De Miguel, M., Olabarrieta, F., & Richards, M. (2010). Quality of family context and cognitive development: A cross sectional and longitudinal study. *Journal of Family Studies, 16*(2), 130–142.

Barrows, A. (1995). The ecopsychology of child development. In T. Roszak, M. E. Gomes, & A. D. Kanner (Eds.), *Ecopsychology: Restoring the earth, healing the mind* (pp. 101–110). Berkeley: University of California Press.

Berger, R., & Lahad, M. (2013). *The healing forest in post-crisis work with children: A nature therapy and expressive arts program for groups.* Philadelphia, PA: Jessica Kingsley.

Bratton, S. C., Ray, D., Rhine, T., & Jones, L. (2005). The efficacy of play therapy with children: A meta-analytic review of treatment outcomes. *Professional Psychology: Research and Practice, 36*(4), 376–390.

Burdette, H., & Whitaker, R. (2005). Resurrecting free play in young children: Looking beyond fitness and fatness to attention, affiliation, and affect. *Pediatrics & Adolescent Medicine, 159*(1), 46–50.

Center for Behavioral Health Statistics and Quality. (2015). Behavioral health trends in the United States: Results from the 2014 National Survey on Drug Use and Health (HHS Publication No. SMA 15-4927, NSDUH Series H-50). Retrieved from http://www.samhsa.gov/ data/

Chen, H. M, Ho, C. I., & Tu, H. M. (2013). Understanding biophilia leisure as facilitating well-being and the environment: An examination of participants' attitudes toward horticultural activity. *Leisure Sciences, 35*, 301–319.

Clinebell, H. (1996). *Ecotherapy: Healing ourselves, healing the earth*. Minneapolis, MN: Augsburg Fortress Press.

Craig, J. M., Logan, A. C., & Prescott, S. L. (2016). Natural environments, nature relatedness and the ecological theater: Connecting satellites and sequencing to shinrin-yoku. *Journal of Physiological Anthropology, 35*(1). doi:10.1186/s40101-016-0083-9

Dalley, T., & Case, C. (2014). *The handbook of art therapy*. New York, NY: Routledge.

Dunn-Snow, P., & Joy-Smellie, S. (2000). Teaching art therapy techniques: Maskmaking, a case in point. *Art Therapy, 17*(2), 125–131. doi.org/10.1080/07421656.2000.10129512

Elkind, D. (2007). *The power of play: How spontaneous, imaginative, activities lead to happier, healthier children*. Cambridge, MA: Da Capo Press.

Frost, J. L., Wortham, S., & Reifel, S. (2008). Characteristics of social play. In J. L Frost, S. Wortham, & R. Reifel (Eds.), *Play and child development* (pp. 1–3). Upper Saddle River, NJ: Pearson/Merrill Prentice Hall.

Ginsburg, K. R. (2007). The importance of play in promoting healthy child development and maintaining strong parent-child bonds. *Pediatrics, 119*, 182–191.

Hanscom, A. J., & Louv, R. (2016). *Balanced and barefoot: How unrestricted outdoor play makes for strong, confident, and capable children*. Oakland, CA: New Harbor.

Hartig, T., Mang, M., & Evans, G. W. (1991). Restorative effects of natural environmental experiences. *Environment and Behavior, 23*(1), 3–26.

Hegarty, J. R. (2010). Out of the consulting room and into the woods? Experiences of nature-connectedness and self-healing. *European Journal of Ecopsychology, 1*(1), 64–84.

Juster, F. T., Hiromi, O., & Stafford, F. P. (2004). *Changing times of American youth: 1981–2003*. Ann Arbor: Institute for Social Research, University of Michigan.

Lee, P. C. (2012). The human child's nature orientation. *Child Development Perspectives, 6*(2), 193–198.

Louv, R. (2005). *Last child in the woods: Saving our children from nature-deficit disorder*. Chapel Hill, NC: Algonquin Books of Chapel Hill.

Louv, R. (2012). *The nature principle: Reconnecting with life in a virtual age*. Chapel Hill, NC: Algonquin Books of Chapel Hill.

Lovejoy, F. H., & Ray, J. J. (2001). Attitude toward the environment as a special case of attitude toward all living things. *The Journal of Social Psychology, 123*, 285–286.

Maller, C., Henderson-Wilson, C., & Townsend, M. (2009). Rediscovering nature in everyday settings: Or how to create healthy environments and healthy people. *EcoHealth, 6*(4), 553–556.

Miller, L. J., Fuller, D. A., & Roetenberg, J. (2014). *Sensational kids, revised edition: Hope and help for children with sensory processing disorder (SPD)*. New York, NY: Penguin.

Nature Conservancy. (2011). Connecting America's youth to nature. Retrieved from Nature.org.

Pajareya, K., & Nopmaneejumruslers, K. (2011). A pilot randomized controlled trial of DIR/Floortime™ parent training intervention for pre-school children with autistic spectrum disorders. *Autism, 15*(5), 563–577.

Rideout, V. J., Vandewater, E. A., & Wartella, E. A., (2003). *Zero to six: Electronic media in the lives of infants, toddlers and preschoolers*. Retrieved from https://www.kff.org

Torio, C. M., Encinosa, W., Berdahl, T., McCormick, M. C., & Simpson, L. A. (2015). Annual report on health care for children and youth in the United States: national estimates of cost, utilization and expenditures for children with mental health conditions. *Academic pediatrics, 15*(1), 19–35.

Santostefano, S. (2004). *Child therapy in the great outdoors: A relational view*. Hillsdale, NJ: Analytic Press.

Seligman, L., & Reichenberg, L. W. (2007). *Selecting effective treatments: A comprehensive, systematic guide to treating mental disorders*. Hoboken, NJ: John Wiley & Sons.

Smith, T., Mruzek, D. W., & Mozingo, D. (2015). Sensory integration therapy. In R. M. Fox & J. A. Mulick (Eds.), *Controversial therapies for autism and intellectual disabilities: Fad, fashion, and science in professional practice* (pp. 104–106). Philadelphia, PA: Jessica Kingsley.

Sweatman, M., & Warner, A. (2009). Integrating nature experiences into early childhood education. *Canadian Children, 34*(2), 4–9.

Wells, N. M., & Evans, G. W. (2003). Nearby nature: A buffer of life stress among rural children. *Environment & Behavior, 35*(3), 311–330.

Wilson, R. (2018). *Nature and young children: Encouraging creative play and learning in natural environments* (3rd ed.). New York, NY: Routledge.

CHAPTER 3A

COUNSELING WITH NATURE: A REFLECTION

Daniel G. Zebrowski

Incorporating nature and other outdoor activities into therapy has been impactful for many of my clients in various levels of care. My first experience in this field was working with children and adolescents in group homes, partial care settings, and intensive outpatient programs while in graduate school. Since earning two master's degrees, I have specialized in working with clients in the foster care and treatment home settings, intensive in-home counseling for clients living with a parent or guardian, as well as clients in my private practice. My approach, which often combines existential interventions in the outdoors with cognitive behavioral therapy, humanism, and positive psychology, has enabled many of my clients to overcome barriers to growth.

Whether holding sessions fishing, in a county park, or on a beach, boardwalk, or hiking trail, nature seems to aid in many aspects of growth for clients of all ages and with a wide range of challenges. It teaches and promotes clarity and calm. Despite the tension in clients' homes or within themselves, they often seem to communicate and process with more clarity when in nature. Many clients who find technology a welcome distraction willingly put it aside when allowed to enjoy certain outdoor settings that they normally do not experience. From my understanding, nature's assistance with clarity and calm seems the most evident in clients with anxiety, mood disorders, and/or sensory issues. Distractions or triggers from their usual environment are often replaced with serenity and peace in these settings. Also, clients who have a difficult time in an office setting for energy or mood reasons will often engage more effectively when moving outdoors.

However, as a disclaimer, this may not be true for certain beaches at the Jersey Shore in the summer, so choose wisely!

Other aspects of growth aided by nature include the ability to heal, recharge, and to be resilient. These abilities are demonstrated by our foliage, landscape, beaches, and animals. Without directly illuminating this, many clients seem to pick up on ways nature bounces back from periods of distress. When these clients are surrounded by natural examples of growth, they often indicate through discussion, affect, and behavior that the same is attainable for them. This has been a theme for many of my clients who live along the shore line that was destroyed by Super Storm Sandy in 2012. Many of these beaches and communities are still recovering as of this writing.

Certain activities, interventions, and concepts seem easier for clients to embrace when in nature. While yoga enthusiasts, Buddhists, and certain martial arts practitioners have been harnessing the mindfulness and meditative power of nature for centuries, it is a relatively new approach for clinically trained therapists. Relaxation techniques such as progressive muscle relaxation, deep breathing techniques, and visualizations are much more effective in a peaceful park than the living room of a busy house. Flow activities such as hiking, sea glass hunting, bird watching, and leaf collecting seem to allow for genuine conversation with young people who can normally be guarded in other situations. Serene settings that allow for reflection are also some of the best stages for grief and loss interventions.

A specific grief and loss activity I have used that has helped provide closure for several children, with nature's assistance, is as follows. They are encouraged to draw or write about thoughts and emotions surrounding their loss, their vision for the future, and/or how the loved one will continue to help them or "live on in their actions." The children are then asked to choose a way to send their message. Some of the choices have included sending the message with a biodegradable balloon lantern; putting it in a bottle, which is thrown in the ocean, lake, or river; and burning it, with assistance (only suitable for certain clients). The client chooses the location that is sometimes a meaningful one or simply a peaceful one. Settings have included beaches, scenic overlooks, county parks, and cemeteries. Assessment for appropriateness of this activity is needed for each client. No matter the location, the environment seems to sooth clients both before and after sending their message. One client watched his lantern rise above the clouds and expressed how he now felt his father knew how he really felt and that he would always remember this experience. Another cried for the first time following a loss as he threw his message into a local inlet that he used to fish in with his uncle.

Another activity that has been aided by nature is an anxiety awareness visualization. We discuss how anxiety typically comes in waves and then passes, allowing children to realize symptoms are temporary and can be managed. This discussion has been followed up with trips to the beach to watch waves, discuss how they pass and how they have different patterns and sizes, and how surfers manage them. This is then related back to triggers of anxiety and effective coping skills for various levels of symptoms. This has been particularly useful for children who have experienced panic attacks and have felt they cannot control them.

An activity that is meant to help build on the concepts of resilience and adaptability can take place on a beach or a hiking trail. The young client is asked to find several examples of natural things that have overcome challenges, obstacles, or distress. Some children have chosen flowers or plants that have grown in unlikely places such as cracks in a pavement or in a wooden fence. Others have chosen trees that have been knocked sideways only to continue growing upright or plants that are clearly stretching for sunlight. One of the more memorable sessions included a boy who was diagnosed with posttraumatic stress disorder and a rare brain disorder called Chiari malformation. While walking on the beach he found a sea gull bouncing around on one leg. We watched and discussed how the gull was still functioning despite his struggle. This led to the boy seeking out other examples of adaptability on his own, which he would bring to future sessions.

Fishing with clients who enjoy it or are open to it teaches and promotes many traits. As most who fish know, it requires patience, focus, adaptability, and problem-solving and at the same time can be very relaxing. The various situations that can arise while fishing in a lake, river, or ocean allow for illumination of these traits and ways to utilize positive reinforcement when the client applies them. A tangled line, a snagged hook, boredom, or a catch can all be opportunities to instill or reinforce positive traits or skills in between other discussions. The various peaceful settings allow for reflection and calm while clients learn a skill and add to identity formation as well as self-worth. I have been very fortunate to be in a position to help others with the help of nature. My hope in writing this is that you can also encourage your clients, students, or children to step outside their comfort zones of isolation, distraction, or whatever they are struggling with and find new comfort in the natural settings that are most likely very close to their homes.

CHAPTER 4

Ecotherapy With Adults

Reclaiming Relationships and Reconnecting to the Natural World

MEGAN E. DELANEY

Joseph came to see me at the insistence of his wife. New to therapy, Joseph was skeptical and hesitant. He thought that people who see therapists were "crazy" or just "unable to do what they are supposed to do" in everyday life. Joseph was a married father of two children who were still in school and living at home. While he and his wife lived comfortably in a suburban town, his daily life was stressful. He had a rhythm to his life, but lately he had become sullen, bored, and sad. After a typical 12-hour day of combined working and commuting, Joseph did not have much energy left for anything else. His wife, who also commuted and worked, had picked up the majority of the other work around the house. Their relationship had suffered over the years as the grind of daily life left them with little time and less energy to do much else. The stress of making ends meet weighed heavy and never seemed to get easier. Yet with the house, the kids, and the future—paying college tuition, saving for retirement, and helping with his aging parents—Joseph knew there was little to do but get up and continue with his routine.Joseph and I spent some sessions getting to know each other. He was reluctant to talk too much and seemed uncomfortable in his skin. My indoor office is small, on a busy street, and, for privacy, the blinds are kept mostly closed. We met on the couch at first because the weather was cold and rainy those first few weeks. I was worried, after the first few meetings, that he would not return. However, he did, like clockwork, which made sense in his scheduled and predictable life. Above all things, Joseph was reliable and consistent. After the third session, I spoke to Joseph about meeting in a local park to walk and talk rather than meet inside. He agreed, and, going forward, we met at the park. The transformation for me was obvious, even though I did not know Joseph that well yet. His face softened; he looked more alert and alive. He walked with a brisk pace but would stop and notice things, especially birds. We would be walking and then he would stop and get quiet. He would listen to the bird songs, wondering how he could figure out what species was making that call. We really started to work. While we walked, Joseph told me about his job, his work climate, and his coworkers. He struggled with getting older at work and watching the younger employees come in and take over projects and responsibilities. He thought that they were different than he was at their age. He said they did not respect the older generation, were impulsive, and thought they "knew it all." He was alarmed that everyone was on cell phones and computers during meetings: "How is anyone listening to anything being said?" He felt as if, despite his years of experience and his considerable working knowledge, he was becoming invisible. I asked him about his office space: What was it like inside? He groaned. It was corporate and utilitarian. He used to have an office with a window looking out on a courtyard. Now, he said, unless you were in the most upper management, you had a workspace: a cubicle configuration in a large open space that was noisy and utilitarian. We talked about how he felt when he was at work. It was not surprising to me that he felt suffocated and, despite being surrounded by others, very isolated and alone. The windows were in the perimeter offices, and so there was barely any natural light. The office lacked any color or natural elements and was basically a sea of people, computers, files, and papers. While he used to like his work, Joseph now felt like he could not keep up. Deadlines were tight, and the pressure was always on to work fast and under budget. He told me how he used to love certain aspects of his job. He was able to be creative, think critically, make decisions, and be in control. When a project was completed, he felt satisfied. He told me he did not have any of those emotional reactions anymore. He now dreaded getting up every day, and it was becoming harder to get out of bed. There were many things at play for Joseph. He was a middle-aged man in the thick of raising children and at the height of his career. Both of these tasks bring enormous amounts of pressure. Typical of many men, his identity and sense of worth largely surrounded his career. He lived with constant anxiety about becoming a failure, losing his job, and not being able to provide for his family. He did not have other activities in his life that brought him satisfaction, and his network of friends rotated around the social life created by his wife. He found that he had little time to fit in exercise. While he used to take lunch breaks, he did not anymore, eating at his desk the food he bought from the downstairs deli. He had gained weight over the years and lacked energy. He knew his relationship with his wife was suffering, yet he did not know where to begin. So we began with the birds. I brought a local bird book for our area to one of our meetings. I know a few bird songs, so we began with the robins, sparrows, and cardinals. We brought a journal and wrote down what birds we saw on our walks. Over the next several weeks, Joseph walked, talked, and sometimes silently listened for birds and recorded in his journal what we saw that day. In between sightings, we talked about Joseph's childhood, his expectations for his future, and his depressed mood and lack of energy.

The State of Adulthood

Although global life expectancy has more than doubled since the 1900s, good health still depends on whether one lives in a wealthy or poor country (Centers for Disease Control and Prevention [CDC], 2017b). Even in wealthier countries such as the United States, sedentary lifestyles are taking a toll, despite the advances of modern medicine. Heart disease and cancer remain the most common causes of death in the United States, while respiratory disease, obesity, diabetes, hypertension, stroke, and suicide are other leading causes (CDC, 2017a). Another major cause of death is suicide. Since 2000, almost all causes of death in the United States have seen decreases, yet suicide is on the rise (CDC, 2018). In 2015, mental health expenditures totaled over $186 million, including inpatient, outpatient, and residential care; retail prescription drugs; and insurance administration. This was an increase of 67% since 2004 and over 400% since 1986 (National Center for Health Statistics, 2016). Outpatient services and prescription drugs account for the same percentage of expenditures. Yet many Americans do not receive adequate mental health care. According to the National Alliance on Mental Health (NAMI, 2019). One in five Americans experience a mental health condition, and 1 in 10 live with chronic mental health issues, yet nearly 60% of adults with a mental illness did not receive mental health services in the previous year. Americans suffering from mental health conditions who are American Indian, Alaskan Native, Asian, Black, and/or Hispanic American are even less likely than White Americans to pursue mental health care (NAMI, 2019).

Barriers to quality healthcare continue to plague multicultural communities. These barriers include access to care; quality of care received; stigmas, especially with mental health; and systemic racism (NAMI, 2019). Yet it is widely known that mental health and substance use disorders are chronic, costing individuals and society a substantial amount. Often these costs are barriers to treatment, if treatment is even available. Without treatment, mental health problems compound into issues such as chronic unemployment, poverty, and even death (NAMI, 2019). Mental health professionals see clients every day who are distressed. Counselors strive to provide excellent care while juggling a caseload of clients, managing billing and insurance companies, potentially marketing their private practice, and keeping up with continuing education credits and licensing credits as well as current research and treatment options. A counselor's own self-care is just as important, although it is often sidelined for the needs of others.

If you have adult clients, you know that this work is challenging. Each adult comes in with his or her own baggage, years of collecting experiences, pain, broken and damaged relationships, and patterns of thoughts and behaviors. If we think beyond the individual, we know systemically that many of our clients also have internalized messages of anxiety, fear, alienation, and marginalization that consciously or subconsciously affect their state of mind and their self-esteem. As therapists, we begin to peel back the layers to see what is at the core of our clients' understanding and beliefs. As an ecotherapist working with adults, I build each new client's experience with the natural world into my intake questionnaires and our initial conversations. Like other ecotherapists, I ask clients questions about early experiences with nature, childhood memories, or special places frequented on their own or with family. I ask new clients if they enjoy nature now and, if so, in what capacity. I also explore their experiences with gardening, pets, or other animals. I ask about their fears about nature. What do they worry about when they think of nature? Do they worry about ticks, bugs, poison ivy, wild animals? Or do they have bigger worries, such as fears of floods, hurricanes, thunderstorms, or other natural occurrences? As an ecotherapist, I gauge their relationship with nature and, at the same time, the extent of their understanding and care of the natural world. It gives me some insight on their level of connection, empathy, and concern about things other than themselves. It also gives me a place to start.

Ecotherapy is not for all adults. In my experience, I have had only one client unwilling to take counseling outdoors. Her anxiety ran deep—all the way down to a fear of turtles. However, that was an interesting place to start a conversation. We sat in my office and talked about her fears, which stemmed from an overprotective father who died young, leaving her feeling overwhelmed with the uncertainty and unpredictability of life. These conversations led to discussions of fear, control, anxiety, and relationships. Ironically, she hated being indoors. She felt cramped in her office, could never sit still very long, hated exercising unless it was outdoors, and loved being at the beach. During our time together, we used nature as a metaphor for many instances in her life. For example, a tree near her office being swallowed by an overgrown vine reminded her of the suffocation she felt from her overbearing father. Over time, her understanding of her issues improved, as did her relationship with the natural world. For homework, she spent time in nature using specific strategies to reduce anxiety while outside (deep breathing and five-senses awareness). She eventually became involved with her town parks department, helping to clear trails and maintain the community garden. One day she came to see me beaming with pride and excitement. She had actually held a turtle on a school outing with her son! Before you start your work, be sure to talk explicitly to your clients about their understanding, experiences, feelings, and hesitations about the natural world.

COMBINING THEORIES

Many of you reading this book are already be using a theoretical base to conceptualize and create treatment plans for your clients. While some may disagree, I think that ecotherapy is capable of merging with many other theoretical orientations. I utilize relational–cultural theory (RCT) in my framework for the conceptualization of my adult clients. RCT was developed in tandem with the feminist movement in the 1970s and propelled by Jean Baker Miller's (1976) pioneering book *Toward a New Psychology of Women*. RCT was built upon the premise that, throughout the lifespan, human beings grow through and toward connections with others (Jordan, 2010). RCT theorists state that we need connections with others to flourish, even to stay alive, and that isolation is a major contributor to suffering of people at both the personal and the cultural level. RCT provides a model for doing therapy that emphasizes movement out of isolation into mutually beneficial relationships and challenges other theories that suggest that independence is the highest achievement in development (Jordan, 2010).

Relationships are the center of RCT, as therapists work on establishing a mutually compassionate relationship with their clients. RCT therapy helps *repair empathic failures* and *alters relational expectations* that may have formed in early influential relationships (Jordan, 2010). This takes deep and vulnerable work with the therapist and client. Clients see, know, and feel (or empathize with) the therapist, therefore beginning to repair the damage caused by past relationships and possible isolation. The client and therapist move toward a *growth-fostering relationship* and connection with each other. The ideal is clients learn skills of authenticity, mutual empathy, and empowerment and translate those skills back into their own relationships. The therapist also helps the client understand that conflict is inevitable and *good conflict* may even be important. Miller (1976) suggested that people experience the most change and growth when they encounter conflict and have the skills and confidence to work through these differences.

Miller suggested that the "Five Good Things" that occur in growth-fostering relationships include

1. Sense of zest or energy
2. Increased sense of worth
3. Clarity: Increased knowledge of oneself and the other person in the relationship
4. Productivity: Ability and motivation to take action both in the relationship and outside of it
5. Desire for more connection: In reaction to satisfaction of relational experience. (as cited in Jordan & Dooley, 2001, p. 3)

Growth and change occur when clients can experience this type of relationship within their own lives. Culture is also very important for RCT therapists, especially the ways the larger culture and context of power and control affect the nature and extent of healthy relationships. Therefore, a core tenet of RCT is social justice and giving a voice to marginalized people. RCT is based on a change in attitude and understanding rather than a set of techniques. Therapists help the client work through relational images, understand and acknowledge the power of the social context, and build relational resilience (Jordan, 2010).

In my perspective, RCT integrates well with ecotherapy on several levels. The core of RCT is the understanding and development of relationships. Ecotherapists build or repair relationships with the natural world. The natural world is a wonderful place for people to start the healing process for broken or reclaimed relationships. The natural world is gracious, giving, and forgiving. It unconditionally accepts and nurtures. We can explore relationships in several ways. We can start by asking our clients to describe their relationship with nature from their early childhood memories. From these stories, we can get a sense of our client's childhood and early memories. Often that leads into conversation about family and early relationships with parents and siblings. More often than not, families are at the root of our relationship patterns (Esposito & Hattem, 2017). In my experience, clients either foster a love of nature through family engagement (camping trips, hikes, barbecues in the park with extended family) or use nature as a respite from family ("I escaped into the woods near my house rather than be home with my angry father," or "The beach was the only place I could find peace from the tension in my house"). Some have fears of nature: "My mom was afraid that I would be snatched up by a bad man, so I wasn't allowed to play in the park by my house. I still feel scared when I walk in parks or in the woods." These narratives are important parts of our clients' life story. They can also be wonderful connections to lost memories as a tool for healing. For example, the overanxious mother who would not let her daughter out of the house to play eventually fostered the daughter's own anxiety. After working with a therapist, this client was able to see the pattern of her lost relationship with nature. As a child, she would sit at the window, longing to be outside with other kids, and yet she felt guilt and fear as an adult when walking through a park. Reconnecting her relationship with nature helped her ease some of her anxious feelings and let go of the anxiety she was storing for her mother.

Relational cultural therapists consider the influence of culture in the conceptualization of clients. Our clients' cultural backgrounds might bring different relationships with nature. One friend described her happiest memories of barbecues in the park with her family:

> We lived in the city and had little access to nature, but when the weather got warm, every Sunday, we all took the subway together and met our extended family at the park. Being with the whole family, aunts, uncles, cousins, is important to my family. So is cooking, dancing, and singing. But none of us had a large place to gather or access to a backyard. So the park was our special place. We listened to music from my *abuela*'s country and ate my *tía*'s special mole. I spent the whole day running around the playground and exploring the trees and the lake with my cousins. I looked forward to it all week long.

It is important to talk to your clients about their cultural and ethnic background and the impact on their identity and beliefs. It is also important to understand how that culture and/or ethnicity may be marginalized and/or impacted by the dominant culture (Jordan, 2010). Digging deeper, we look at how cultural identity and issues of suppression may be embedded in clients' conscious or unconscious understanding of themselves in the context of multiple layers of society. As ecotherapists, we also want to explore our clients' culture and ethnicity and their relationship with the natural world in order to honor their experiences. What this looks like can vary by individual and his or her cultural practices.

Another key principle in RCT is social justice. Counselors are charged with being advocates at the micro and macro levels with diverse clients, in multiple settings across the discipline (Ratts, Toporek, & Lewis, 2010). This can involve connecting our clients with critical resources as well as advocating on behalf of marginalized populations and those with little to no voice. Marginalized populations that need advocacy may include those with physical or cognitive disabilities, young children, the elderly, and those with mental health conditions. Many of these clients rely on others for their own safety and well-being and can easily fall victim to neglect, abuse, and exploitation (Varghese, 2015). Ecotherapists argue that nature, including plants and animals, fits within the category of the voiceless. Advocacy for the natural world is an equally important cause. We also teach our clients how to be advocates themselves. As we know, advocacy can boost self-efficacy and self-worth (Kiselica & Robinson, 2001). It can also help clients who feel lost or without a purpose feel like they are making a small effort somewhere in their corner of the world. For those with social anxiety, it is a way to connect to others with like-minded ideas while doing something helpful. As ecotherapists, we meet the clients at their level and help them connect to causes that resonate with them. This can range from something as simple as picking up trash in their local parks to volunteering with a local animal shelter or an environmental organization.

As described earlier, it is possible to integrate ecotherapy with other theoretical concepts as long as the core tenets of ecotherapy, in particular the reciprocity of our relationships with nature, are set. As you hone your skills as an ecotherapist, this will become clearer with time and practice. There are many ways to add activities, homework, and techniques into your ecotherapy practice with adults. I encourage you to think about ways your preferred theory may be enhanced with ecotherapy. Your creativity and your own personal connection can be good starting points. Try it, solicit feedback from your clients, and modify as needed. In the meantime, the following are just a handful of ideas that work for me when working with adult clients.

USING METAPHORS

A metaphor is a figure of speech used to describe a behavior or an item that is not literally applicable. Metaphors are used in all different areas of life to help us learn information (in relation to other ideas) as well as organize and understand different situations. Because metaphor helps us learn and understand new information as well as process information in new ways, it is a great tool for counselors. Metaphors can be client driven or counselor driven. Client-driven metaphors can be very enlightening for clients, helping them understand their issue in a different way. Sometimes the metaphor takes away from clients' direct pain or emotion but allows them to project their thoughts in an abstract way. Counselor-driven metaphors are more intentional. We use metaphors specifically to enhance or support our therapeutic intervention in order to help our clients make a different connection or understand a concept in a new way (Wagener, 2017).

When I work with my clients, we start here, using memories, metaphors, and examples as well as relationship language (mutuality, empathy, unconditional support, the ability to forgive, calmness, and patience). Nature metaphors are abundant and easily translatable. I might ask a client to lean against a tree and describe the feeling of being supported and secure. Clients describe how they feel, knowing that despite how much weight they might put on the tree, the tree will hold them steady. We can then talk about the people in their lives who provide that kind of support (or don't). We might talk about the grass or clover beneath us that, despite the traffic and the consistent trample, can still spring up again. We can look at tree limbs that, despite the density of the forest around them, still find a way to reach for the sun. We can look at fallen pieces of the forest that are regenerating new life. These metaphors can be powerful examples of our own capabilities.

Nature also provides an abundance of metaphors about relationships. One of the most obvious relationships is flowering plants and bees. The bee and flower have a have a relationship based on mutualism in which both species benefit. Bees provide flowers with reproductive abilities by spreading pollen from the flower. Flowers give bees pollen and nectar that the bees take back to their colonies. Bees and ants are also wonderful metaphors for cooperation and reciprocity. One of my students told me a story about a breakthrough she had with an adolescent client. This client was fighting with her mother, often around the task of doing chores in the house. My student and the client were out for a walk and talk, admiring the bees. The client talked about how busy the bees were, and my student used it a chance for a nature metaphor. My student asked the client what the bees do. "Well, they do all this work to help the colony and the queen bee"—and then the client got it: "Ahhh, kind of like my mom and me." On a recent walk with an overworked and anxious client we came across a woolly bear caterpillar on the ground. I'm sure he was sprinting in caterpillar terms, but to us, he was moving slowly and deliberately down the path. Without being prompted, my client said, "I could take a lesson from this caterpillar and slow down a little." We laughed, but the woolly bear caterpillar demonstrated the exact lesson she was trying to hear.

PLANTING A PATCH

Taking a piece of land and making it into a small patch of something beautiful or edible (or beautiful and edible) is a wonderful exercise to prescribe to a client. Horticultural therapy connects an individual to the earth at a physical level and provides direct sensory input. In my neck of the woods, we can easily grow vegetables and plants, as long as we protect them from deer. However, if clients have never gardened before or believes they just "kill plants," I often have them start with something small. For the real beginner, I make suggestions of hardy plants that require little maintenance. Together we might make a succulent garden with supplies I bring to session. Working together is a great way to be busy and let the conversation flow. Clients leave the session with their plants and direct instructions on how to care for them. We write the instructions down on an index card, so they can keep it right next to the plant as a reminder.

For the more adventurous, we might think together about designing an herb window box. We can draw the design together, make the list of supplies, and assign the construction as a homework assignment. Clients can pinch a few herbs from the box to add to meals they might be cooking. When late spring or summer comes around, I might encourage a client to design and plant a container pot. With a container pot, you do not need your own lawn—just a place to put the pot in the sun. Container pots can be planted with anything the client wishes to add. I love basil, tomato plants, and peppers. It is fun to watch the plants grow and become edible. Depending on the client, some instruction from you might be necessary (how and when to water and prune, how much sun, etc.). Flowers are also wonderful, but be sure to do some homework together. How high do the flowers grow? How long do they flower (once or throughout the summer)? What kind of pruning do they need? How much water? What type of sun and for how long? Taking the time to research and create the pot will help its longevity and output. Of course, this type of metaphor can also be translated into the research and care clients' relationships might need. Each relationship needs a little research, understanding, and care. If a client is frustrated with a child who acts out each time he or she has to go somewhere new, creating chaos for the whole family, we might have to take the time to understand the needs of this particular child. Transitions are particularly hard because they create anxiety in this sensitive child. These children might need a little more "watering" and "care." In other words, we research together how best to create a regular routine so that a sensitive child anticipates and then handles change. An unexpected change is just like moving a plant from one space to another abruptly. They drop leaves and droop. We have to be sensitive to sudden changes and take care to create the environment it needs to thrive.

If a client loves to garden or wants to learn more, you can suggest volunteering at a local community garden or cultivating his or her own spot in the garden. Community gardens are a communal piece of land, either private or public, where people can cultivate a small piece of the land for their own. These gardens are wonderful opportunities for people to connect socially while basking in all that nature has to offer. In the gardens, clients can grow vegetables, herbs, and flowers. This potentially offers a healthier lifestyle by adding to an individual's consumption of healthy fruits and vegetables. It can also beautify a piece of earth, especially in city neighborhoods. Community gardens also support a cleaner environment by adding oxygen to the air and reducing rain runoff, and they are often places where people compost for fertilizer. Community gardens can provide educational opportunities for schools or scout groups and are correlated with stronger communities (Macias, 2008).

JOINING A HIKING GROUP

Another relatively simple step for clients is to help them find and join a local hiking group. Many communities have local parks and recreation organizations that offer opportunities to get into the parks. In my county, the parks department has a variety of different hiking opportunities. Some hikes are led by naturalists, which is a wonderful way to learn more about the local environment. Other opportunities include hiking clubs that meet at different locations each week for a hike. It is important to do some research about the group to make sure it is accessible to your client and fits within your client's physical capabilities. Check your local town, county, or even state park websites for information local to you. There are also national organizations that organize outdoor opportunities. One example of such an organization is Hike It Baby (https://hikeitbaby.com/). With the tagline "Parenting is an adventure. Bring it outside," Hike It Baby includes volunteers who act as hike hosts or branch ambassadors. These folks create safe, accessible, inclusive opportunities to have families with young children get outside, meet each other, and get some fresh air and exercise. REI (Recreational Equipment, Inc.) Co-Op is a retail organization that sells merchandise related to the outdoors, but the website (www.rei.com) also has information about classes and events, often free, at its locations as well as outside opportunities searchable by zip code. Hiking groups offer a multitude of benefits for our clients. Saying we are going to do something does

Figure 4.1 A flower garden is one way for an adult client to reconnect with nature.

not always produce results (I am going to go to the gym three times this week!), but having a group waiting for you provides more accountability. Hiking groups provide a double dose of good health: exposure to nature and interaction with other people.

GOING ON A FAMILY PICNIC

A simple homework assignment that I often talk to clients about is setting up time to be in nature with family. Often I see clients in the grind of their daily lives. Family time can be hard to navigate, with busy schedules

Figure 4.2 Walking or hiking groups are wonderful opportunities for adults to connect to others while basking in the benefits of the natural world.

and the pull of multiple commitments. Yet we know how important taking time to be with family is to healthy relationships. I find that families can be stuck in their houses, a common place for congregating. Sometimes, however, this can be a place of stagnation (dishes to do, laundry to be folded, homework piling up, TVs blaring, electronics buzzing). A way to get out of the house and together in nature is to go on a family picnic. I encourage families to do this collaboratively and commit to a time and place. I also encourage the picnic to be an electronics-free zone. This can be hard for kids (and parents!) but is critically important to allow for engaging with each other at a deeper level. I encourage the most skeptical families to start small: I tell them not to attempt a picnic after a 5-mile hike, but instead pick a local place and pack a blanket and lunch. Family picnics can be translated into family trips to the beach, family hikes, or family paddling excursions, or they can stay with the picnic. The main thing is getting outside, unplugged from the demands of our busy lives, and plugged into nature and each other.

TAKING MINI-BREAKS AND MINI-SOLOS

I help every client think about how to incorporate nature into his or her everyday life. Often I hear folks tell me how good they feel when they get to spend time in nature, yet they do not know how to fit it in their schedule. The good news is that the research says as little as 5 minutes in nature can make us feel better (Williams, 2017). Thus I talk to clients about taking nature breaks. For office-bound clients, that can mean leaving the building for a quick walk around the block or eating their lunch in the local park or under a tree. I encourage kids to run in the grass barefoot, especially if they feel angry or frustrated. A mini-break can be just what someone needs to get a little boost of energy. For other clients, especially those who have truly embraced their understanding and need for nature, I prescribe mini-solos. A mini-solo is time that a client spends alone, in quiet contemplation, while in a natural setting. Like any meditation or mindfulness practice, this kind of exercise takes time and a certain level of commitment. Yet so many of us do not have the dedicated time to allow ourselves to just be. This time can be dedicated to contemplation, rest, reflection, and a chance to test vulnerability and trust in ourselves. All of the bodily senses become acutely active during a solo—we see, hear, smell, and feel our surroundings more clearly. Clients have memories of the birds and animals they observed and can describe in great detail what the location looked like. Often they feel accomplished and proud of their ability to test their own limits and emerge from solo time rested and refreshed, with clarity on an issue or a solution to a problem.

GREENING YOUR PLACE IN SPACE

Another concept that I introduce to clients is biophilic design. Biophilic design is a way of connecting people to nature within their own homes, work spaces, and communities (Kellert, Heerwagen, & Mador, 2011). Biophilic design is another way for people to establish their connection to the natural

Figure 4.3 Taking a moment to sit on a bench can help you relax and recharge.

world by designing their living, working, and community spaces with nature in mind—what designers call "built environments." Research on biophilic design has shown positive results in productivity, overall mood, and reduction of stress (Ryan, Browning, Clancy, Andrews, & Kallianpurkar, 2014). Biophilic design on a large scale incorporates architects, engineers, and interior designers, but for our purposes we keep it simple. While I would love to re-create all of my indoor spaces to be like being outdoors, I know I can only control my own environment.

I talk with my clients about what we can control. This is usually their homes and their spaces at work (within reason). Then we discuss the aspects of nature that appeal to them most. This might be green plants, flowers, bright colors, or subtle hues. It could also be sounds or smells. We discuss their living and working spaces; corporate offices in particular can be sterile. We can make tweaks in our lives to make our indoor spaces greener. This might be as simple as turning our desk to have a view out the window; bringing pictures of nature into our spaces; adding plant life (fake plants work fine too, if your client is convinced they don't have a green thumb); or adding specific nature colors like blues, greens, or yellows. Other ideas can be adding a noise machine that may include sounds of nature; lighting a candle (if allowed) that has scents of their favorite places;

or, for rooms without windows, adding a picture of a nature scene or adding natural lighting and turning off the fluorescent overheads. These little improvements can help our clients feel better throughout the day.

Circling Back

Joseph and I worked together for several months in order to understand and reflect on his own story. Over that time, he became quite the bird lover and joined a local Audubon association, where he made new friends and connections. The greatest lesson of our time together, he told me, was that his work identity did not have to define him. He still had to work, for now, to support his family, but he was more relaxed at work and less reactive to stressors he could not control. He took mini-breaks during the day to get a touch of nature and to reenergize. He added elements of nature to his home and his work space: pictures of his family doing a fun activity outdoors, plants on his desk, and a small lamp that emits a gentle glow. Even his coworkers commented on how they felt less stress just being in his space at the office. Overall, he was more relaxed and, as a byproduct, more productive at work. He had more energy for himself, his spouse, and his children. Of course, not all of his issues were resolved; he was still in a job he didn't love. But he felt rejuvenated and more capable of tackling new issues as they arose. He also shifted his focus, rebalancing his understanding of what was important to him, including things he could control and things he could not. We agreed that some of his newfound understanding was the result of the therapeutic process, but Joseph reflected that his reconnection with nature was a catalyst for change.

Not all clients are capable of change, and we, as therapists, cannot change our clients. But we can act as supportive guides who occasionally offer an alternative path. As ecotherapists, we offer a double dose of wellness, time in nature, and the healing work of counseling. The idealist in me hopes the more adults we return to nature, the more likely they will bring along their loved ones and children too, forming a rippling effect that benefits not only the human species but also the world around us.

REFERENCES

Centers for Disease Control and Prevention. (2017a). *Leading causes of death.* Retrieved from https://www.cdc.gov/nchs/fastats/leading-causes-of-death.htm.

Centers for Disease Control and Prevention. (2017b). *Life expectancy*. Retrieved from https://www.cdc.gov/nchs/fastats/life-expectancy.htm.

Centers for Disease Control and Prevention. (2018, June 7). *Suicide rates rising across the U.S.* Retrieved from https://www.cdc.gov/media/releases/2018/p0607-suicide-prevention.html

Esposito, J., & Hattem, A. (2017). *Introduction to family counseling: A case study approach*. Washington, DC: SAGE.

Jordan, J. V. (2010). *Relational-cultural therapy*. Washington, DC: American Psychological Association.

Jordan, J., & Dooley, C. (2001). *Relational practice in action: A group manual*. Wellesley, MA: Stone Center.

Kellert, S. R., Heerwagen, J., & Mador, M. (2011). *Biophilic design: The theory, science and practice of bringing buildings to life*. Hoboken, NJ: Wiley.

Kiselica, M. S., & Robinson, M. (2001). Bringing advocacy counseling to life: The history, issues, and human dramas of social justice work in counseling. *Journal of Counseling and Development, 79*, 387–397. doi:10.1002/j.1556-6676.2001.tb01985.x

Macias, T. (2008). Working toward a just, equitable, and local food system: The social impact of community-based agriculture. *Social Science Quarterly, 89*, 1086–1101. doi:10.1111/j.1540-6237.2008.00566.x

Miller, J. B. (1976). *Toward a new psychology of women*. Boston, MA: Beacon Press.

National Alliance of Mental Health. (2019). *Mental health conditions*. Retrieved from https://www.nami.org/Learn-More/Mental-Health-Conditions

National Center for Health Statistics. (2016). *Health, United States. With chartbook on long-term trends in health*. Hyattsville, MD: Author.

Ratts, M. J., Toporek, M. J., & Lewis, J. A. (2010). *ACA advocacy competencies: A social justice framework for counselors*. Alexandria, VA: American Counseling Association.

Ryan, C. O., Browning, W. D., Clancy, J. O., Andrews, S. L., & Kallianpurkar, N. B. (2014). Biophilic design patterns: Emerging nature-based parameters for health and well-being in the built environment. *International Journal of Architectural Research, 8*(2), 62–76. doi:10.26687/archnet-ijar.v8i2.436

Varghese, P. (2015). Advocacy in mental health: Offering a voice to the voiceless. *Indian Journal of Social Psychiatry, 31*(1), 4–8. doi:10.4103/0971-9962.161987

Wagener, A. E. (2017). Metaphor in professional counseling. *The Professional Counselor, 7*, 144–154. doi:10.15241/aew.7.2.144

Williams, F. (2017). *The nature fix: Why nature makes us happier, healthier and more creative*. New York, NY: W. W. Norton.

CHAPTER 4A

NATURE'S EXPRESSWAY

Rashmi Kamath Talpady

For someone who spent more than half of three decades of her life reading under a tree, the knowledge that outdoors is therapeutic sure came as a surprise. Perhaps, it has to do with the fact that I grew up by the ocean and my childhood house was surrounded by an expanse of woods and greens. Both the sea and our wild-grown, albeit well-kept, garden was an awe-inspiring sight to most who visited us, something that did not fail to amuse my sister and me. Fortunate as I was, like many others, I was short-sighted and did not comprehend the opulence and unlimited access I had to the natural world. Sensitivity to nature and the need to preserve natural resources has been very much inherent to me. Nonetheless, it is only recently that I have gained a clearer perspective on Mother Nature and my relationship with her.

The natural world is undoubtedly a salubrious force by virtue of all that it does to the human mind and body; however, it is only in the recent past that it has been considered for utilization as a structured therapy. It has been my observation that as far as rudimentary concepts of ecotherapy are concerned, they are, although not ambiguous, abstract and open for creative interpretations. In recent times, the Japanese culture of *shinrin yoku*, widely acknowledged as forest bathing, has been gaining momentum. The idea behind forest bathing is to mindfully experience wilderness through the sense organs (shinrin-yoku.org). As someone with intentions to work alongside nature as a cotherapist, the concept of employing it to achieve sensory tranquility on a primal level conforms to what I think forms the foundation to therapeutically embodying the spirit of the ecological system. This vignette discusses a way that I would choose to integrate the ecosystem into my future practice—zeroing in on a specific sense organ, or a combination of two or more, in a way that caters to clients and their subjective sense of remediation and emotional prosperity.

OLFACTION

A strong sense of smell is perhaps the sharpest tool of survival for all the species who scavenge in search of food. As an evolved species, we humans seldom rely on our sense of smell for survival. In fact, I believe, conscious utilization of the olfactory sense is very limited. According to the ancient Ayurvedic science, the nasal route is considered as the gateway to the brain and is a prime site for drug (herbal!) administration (Charaka Samhita, 400–200 BCE). As a new mother holding my newborn at the hospital, I wondered how long it would be before my baby began to recognize me. Guess what? Her nose knew how to detect me faster than it takes a gadget to catch an available wi-fi. In Indian homes, it is habitual to burn sandalwood- and flower-flavored incense in the morning (to begin the day afresh) and at dusk (to calm the mind before dinner) as a part of everyday prayer ritual. It is this keen sense of smell that absorbs the fragrance emitted by trees and flowers that does a reverse stimulation of amygdala's flight-or-fight response (Williams, 2018, p. 28). Is it any wonder that even a 10-minute walk by the park is enough to temporarily ground a troubled mind? In my opinion, this parasympathetic simulation is the most potent tool at our disposal as ecotherapists. Imagine walking into a room and smelling that strong waft of freshly brewed coffee—yes, that! Extrapolating into the counseling lingo, it is helping clients identify their proverbial caffeine in nature and guiding them in making it a regular part of their life.

AUDITION

I am one of those who finds it hard to focus when exposed to an array of noises to the point that I experience total brain freeze—there is no way I can drive on a busy highway with open windows. Contrarily, I usually have a playlist of jazz instrumentals or nature sounds running on a loop to let my creativity flow. In my brain, the former is a noise and the latter a symphony. What that means is, even if we do not realize it, the brain is continuously processing sounds; the ones that we perceive as "noise" stimulate stress (Williams, 2018, p. 88) and the harmonious ones trigger the release of dopamine in the mesolimbic pathway thus allowing for emotional regulation (Williams, 2018, p. 99). My sister recently went on a solo trip to an island far from the main city and was surprised that she woke up earlier than her usual time and was feeling happier as opposed to feeling grumpy at being woken. The difference, she said, was the chirping birds outside her window that did the job and not the usual hustle bustle of moving vehicles. Figuring out the "noise" that is adding to the client's stressors and significant addition of nature sounds that the client positively responds to would be one of my primary considerations for selection of therapy activity.

It is ritualistic in Indian temples to ring copper bells before sitting down to meditate. As a child, I was taught that the vibrations of the bell are close to the AUM sounds, which the Hindus believe is the first and only sound of the universe. It grounds the ringer to the present moment by inching him or her closer to the sound that connects the cosmos. Now I am not suggesting we install bells all around the house (but that would be so cool!). I am instead suggesting that, in addition to differentiating sounds that the clients identify as stressful from those that they relax into, we explore modulations that help in anchoring the restless mind to the present.

VISION

A month after my miscarriage last summer, my husband and I made an impromptu plan to drive through the Shenandoah National Park scenic highway. It was close to sunset, and the winding road had an orangish glow to it, with irregular blotches of darkness and streaming evening sunlight due to the thick canopy of trees above. That drive was as beautiful as it was sad; however, I found myself just living it instead of being the usual swirling mess I was those days. Of course, the drive ended, and I went back to pitying myself. However, it did shift something in me, and I'd like to think that it was a grounding experience. Did nature make me forget my pain? No. If anything, I was hurting even more. But it was the first time I allowed myself to experience the pain without trying to control it. I was not surprised, to say the least, when I learned of the fact that rumination in the natural setting is markedly different from a reflection that is done otherwise (William, 2017, p. 181). I do not mean to suggest that this would be the case with everyone, but being there, watching all the colors of the wilderness in its highest glory, just drained me of all my pretenses. It felt much easier to just give in and grieve. As I mentioned, I went back to my usual ways, but with a renewed sense of what I needed to heal. It is my firm belief that rumination is both a significant part of living as well as successful psychotherapy, and I want that kind of deep introspection for people who trust me with their time and money. For clients who need that gentle push, a silent walk in a setting that they resonate with would probably be my primary go-to.

SOMATOSENSATION

I have never been into gardening or owned a garden. My idea of being a gardener is limited to buying succulents, for I somehow manage to kill the plants that I bring home. My grandmother, on the other hand, was an avid gardener, and she was always short of words in expressing how happy it made her—I never saw her more comfortable than when she was knee-deep in a hole and covered in dirt. And it's not just her, I have heard different versions of similar joy from many people who find it incredibly calming to work with plants. Despite having no personal experience of my own in this arena, I can't help but wonder how therapeutic a session it would be for a client who does not feel ready to talk but is willing to work with his or her hands. There is a nurturing element associated with sowing that is empowering. Besides, while the activity has a prominent element of here-and-now, it is also opportune regarding allowing the mind to do its quiet reflections. Nonetheless, the option does not have to be limited to gardening alone. As far as the sense of touch is concerned, for me, nothing holds a candle to the feeling of immersing myself into a waterbody. But I would not be astonished if my clients' idea of healing touch is much more adventurous than taking a dip in the ocean. A significant part of my job is to explore that which clicks and bring it into session in a manner that is safe and within my zone of professional competence.

GUSTATION

Of all the senses, taste is perhaps the most challenging of all. In my opinion, the best possible way of incorporating flavor therapeutically is encouraging the client to adopt a healthy diet. In a psychotherapy setting, food habits are hardly ever a topic of discussion, perhaps because there is no known association of food with the mood. If that is true, why do we crave to eat when confronted with overwhelming feelings? I grew up in a culture that laid strong emphasis on utilizing a combination of seasonal fruits and freshly cooked meat and vegetables in addition to eating according to an individual's body type; not only that, it also expounded upon the association between good food and a healthy mind (Charaka Samhitha, 400–200

BCE). The key, I believe, is to break the norm and open talk regarding clients' food habits and identify those they perceive as soothing. If we must eat to feel better, let's do it right!

Every client is unique, and it is fitting that the therapeutic aspect of nature is very much subjective as well. While some seek the thrill of adventure in the surge of pure adrenaline, others—like me—enjoy the wind in their hair with feet planted firmly on the ground. The expanse of imagination and creativity that could be tapped into in combining ecosystems with conventional therapy is most undoubtedly unparalleled. However, in my opinion, it boils down to two things—recognizing obstacles that impede emotional healing/growth and utilizing what nature has to offer.

Remember that therapy activities should be planned as per the client's will and comfort. Likewise, it is imperative that counselors work within the boundary of their competence, familiarize themselves before bringing in the client, and stick to the ethical guideless to ensure a positive experience for the client. Furthermore, I assume that counselors only need to find a way to connect clients to an aspect of nature that suits them best; the rest is taken care of by the chemistry that sizzles between the client and Mother Nature. The truth is she is there, evergreen, arms open always. And I can say this, because, despite growing up in an era that preceded the influx of technology, letting the warm waves crash over my bare feet seemed like the best possible way to end a day spent reading on the sand.

REFERENCES

Shinrin yoku. (n.d.). Shinrin-yoku forest medicine. Retrieved from http://www.shinrin-yoku.org/shinrin-yoku.html

Williams, F. (2018). *The nature fix: Why nature makes us happier, healthier, and more creative*. New York, NY: W. W. Norton.

CHAPTER 5

Group Work in the Natural World

SARAH I. SPRINGER, EMMI MCCAULEY, AND MALLORY SHEKLIAN

INTRODUCTION

Symptoms associated with depression and anxiety continue to be prevalent in our society across the lifespan. Isolation is a common reality for many who struggle with these symptoms, and images of lying on the couch in the therapist's office uncovering childhood memories may not seem like an inviting option. A variety of treatment modalities are needed to address these and related (e.g., bipolar disorder, attention deficit hyperactivity disorder) symptomatology, and therapists must be equipped with the knowledge and skills to initiate these interventions.

Unfortunately, stigmas continue to exist surrounding mental health counseling in mainstream society. While having a therapist may seem trendy is some communities, the idea of speaking about issues to a complete stranger is foreign and daunting for many people. Mental health counselors recognize this reality and continue to seek out opportunities to increase client attendance and overall treatment adherence. While individual talk therapy can be beneficial for a host of client challenges, growing bodies of research include counselors expanding the design and boundaries of counseling to include more creative outlets within the structure of different counseling modalities. Creative interventions within the realm of art, drama, and music therapy are more commonly found among a variety of age groups, as they help to encourage client growth by bridging traditional images of talk therapy with other forms of self-expression. Emerging in the therapeutic literature are also orientations and intervention that help to connect the natural world with clients' physical, emotional, and spiritual identities.

Consider your experiences growing up in nature. Whether you have firsthand knowledge of outdoor learning or have experienced nature vicariously through TV and movies, take a moment to return to your childhood by remembering or picturing in your mind the following examples: How did it feel to breathe fresh air on a scout-sponsored nature trail or when you experienced the wind hitting your hair as you kicked around a soccer ball with teammates? What about enjoying moments by a campfire with friends or picking weeds from your garden with a family member? Whether or not you've experienced any or all of these situations personally, imagine, in this moment, what your body might feel like to share these experiences with others on a cloudless 75° day. Counselors who integrate nature into their practices have the opportunity to unite people through similar shared experiences and promote valuable therapeutic outcomes within the context of group counseling.

NATURE-BASED INTERVENTIONS IN GROUP SETTINGS

Outdoor learning has long since been recognized for the educational value it can bring to groups of students in K-12 settings (Gresalfi Barnes, &Cross, 2012; Benfield, Rainbold, Bell, & Donovan, 2013). Nature's connection to improved cognition and focus (Chawla, 2015; Li & Sullivan, 2016; Louv, 2008) as well as enthusiasm for the learning process (Blair, 2010) encourage educational leaders to provide continued opportunities for children to benefit from and give back to the earth. Making meaning of experiences together in a group setting, however, also depends on the facilitator leading the group. Whether through an outdoor classroom in K-12 where children are learning to plant and maintain their flower beds, a ropes course utilized within the context of a course as a bonding experience for undergraduate students, or even an orientation to graduate counseling students learning the power of vulnerability (Schimmel, Daniels, Wassif, & Jacobs; 2016), educators are teaching students to nurture their relationships with nature while simultaneously gaining academic and social benefits from using nature as a teaching tool. Nature's ability to nurture our psychological, behavioral, and emotional selves in the context of group settings has also been recognized for its therapeutic value by school counselors in the educational setting. Examples of this include Flom,

Johnson, Hubbard, and Reidt (2011) discussion around the integration of nature into large group developmental guidance lessons and Glass and Shoffner's (2001) six-week adventure-based small group outline for children in the school setting. Counselor educators Duffy, Springer, Delaney and Luke (2019) even integrated ecotherapy interventions into their respective human development graduate courses in order to didactically teach skills, provide experiential learning, and promote self-awareness through targeted process questions.

Eliciting therapeutic benefit from nature-based activities in a group setting, however, is more than just taking a group out in nature and asking them to talk about how they feel in the present moment. There is an interplay between nature's impact on the individual and the shared experiences of recognizing the relationship group members collectively have with each other within the context of the natural world. Adventure-based counseling represents a recognized application of group work and nature-based counseling across the lifespan; its utility regarding mental health outcomes specifically is less discussed. What we do understand from group work literature is that in order to provide group-based intervention with meaningful therapeutic outcomes, group facilitators must have the knowledge, skills, and awareness of group dynamics to be effective leaders (Gladding,

Figure 5.1 Ecotherapy group work.

2015). The next section briefly discusses group counseling as a therapeutic modality and highlights core tenets leaders must understand to effectively provide group interventions with fidelity.

GROUP COUNSELING IN A NUTSHELL

Group work is an important and efficacious treatment modality comprised of two or more clients who identify themselves as collectively belonging to a setting in which there are mutually defined outcomes (Gladding, 2015). The Association for Specialists in Group Work (ASGW, 2000), a division of the American Counseling Association, suggests that "the goals of the group may include the accomplishment of tasks related to work, education, personal development, personal and interpersonal problem solving, or remediation of mental and emotional disorders" (pp. 2–3). Using nature as both a metaphor and a counseling setting, group leaders can address these goals by providing an extended therapeutic environment that helps clients work on these areas of personal development in a more open setting.

Group counseling as an intervention is designed and organized by a trained leader who "facilitate[s] interactions among the members, help[s] them learn from one another, assist[s] them in establishing personal goals, and encourage[s] them to translate their insights into concrete plans" (Corey, 2008, p. 5). Throughout this process, the facilitator identifies opportunities to help members develop insight or intrapersonal knowledge, connect with other members interpersonally, and identify commonalities through shared experiences with other members of the group. This is accomplished through interventions at the individual or personal level (e.g., sharing an experience with the group of finding a plant in nature that reminds them of their childhood), subsystem or interpersonal level (e.g., discussing what it felt like to trust another person during an activity on a ropes course), and whole-group level (e.g., discovering common fears of being in the water during a paddle board intervention). As an example, a group leader might help individual members to process their anxiety about trusting people by encouraging others to share their reactions to watching a member take a risk to engage in a ropes activity. Members give and receive feedback and thus provide support to the struggling member (subsystem). The facilitator may then support this member by helping him or her process any insight (intrapersonal) gained from this feedback. The facilitator may identify and share an observation that many members of the group seem to have experienced similar challenges and begin to process with the group what it feels like to know that others may have similar struggles (group as a system). These interventions contribute to the unique nature of the group counseling experience and differentiates this treatment modality from individual counseling. Facilitators may use "process questions" to intervene at these various levels. Sample questions that address these levels of intervention within the case example are provided at the end of the chapter.

Tenets of Group Counseling

As suggested by the ASGW (2000), there are four categories of groups: task/work, psychoeducation, counseling, and psychotherapy. Psychoeducation groups used for prevention or early intervention for at-risk populations are often centered on particular content areas. These groups are generally short term and include instructional strategies to support members with everyday challenges (e.g., stress management). Psychoeducation groups tend to be some of the most prevalent in practice and are often created within the context of adventure-based counseling.

Regardless of the theoretical orientation, to achieve the potential for positive therapeutic outcomes, trained group leaders must understand group dynamics; these are often realized across various stages of the group process and inspired by what Yalom and Leszcz (2005) call as the 11 therapeutic factors. These factors intimately involved in the change process are briefly described next and contextualized within a description of Tuckman and Jensen's (1976) five-stage group work model.

Therapeutic Factors

Yalom and Leszcz (2005) identified 11 interconnected processes occurring through the life of a group that offer therapeutic value to clients. The distinction between these may not always be readily apparent or even necessary to differentiate, but according to Yalom and Leszcz the following identified therapeutic factors collectively reflect the complexity of human experiences and offer ways in which to understand the intrapersonal and interpersonal benefits of group work.

> **Instillation of hope:** A belief that things will improve
> **Universality:** We are all in this together
> **Imparting information:** Here's what's working for me

Altruism: Helping for the greater good
Corrective recapitulation of the primary family group: You remind me of my critical mother: Working through and resolving conflicts with familial relationships within the context of the group
Development of socialization techniques: Practicing social skill development with members of the group
Imitative behavior: Vicarious learning
Interpersonal learning: Meaningful feedback exchanges that promote relational insight
Cohesiveness: I can be vulnerable here: A sense of closeness among the group
Catharsis: Expression of emotion
Existential factors: Addressing meaning, mortality, and the inevitability of human isolation

Counselors use a variety of process questions to draw out these factors. Examples are provided throughout the intervention section of this chapter and within the case example. We look at where group leaders might see opportunities to initiate process questions that elicit the therapeutic factors across group stages next.

Group Stages

Group members interact with one another in various ways depending on their levels of safety and comfort and the norms established and agreed upon by both leaders and group members. Consider how different it might feel to share a personal challenge like fear of swimming on your first day in a group with "strangers" versus sharing your anxiety about watching a family member almost drown in the ocean after you have gotten to know and trust these people over the last six weeks. Safety and trust are the cornerstone of group counseling. Understanding the power behind the bidirectional relationship between group members' safety and group dynamics can be understood by examining each of Tuckman's (1976) five stages of group. According to Tuckman, *forming, storming, norming, performing,* and *adjourning* represent the life and movement of the group as members work toward both independent (e.g., social anxiety) and collective group (e.g., experience others authentically) goals. As individual members make progress toward these goals, the group in its entirety experiences dynamics uniquely found in each stage; if recognized and addressed meaningfully, leaders can use content (e.g., gardening activity) with accompanying process questions (e.g., "How did sharing a wish for members as you pulled weeds from the garden assist with both managing your anxiety giving feedback to others *and* simultaneously nurture the natural world, which provided space for this group?") to help group members make meaning of their experiences with each other in the natural world. Initiating these types of process questions extends group content by promoting intrapersonal awareness and eliciting altruism and self-expression ("I can nurture nature while nature nurtures me").

The *forming* stage of group is the initial period where members get to know each other and look for acceptance by seeking approval and establishing personal and group goals (Gladding, 2015). A leader may look for and draw out therapeutic factors such as group cohesiveness, imparting information, and universality. During the second and third stages of group, *storming* and *norming*, members go through periods of angst as they may vie for control, form subgroups with members perceived to be similar to them, and begin to establish norms that help the group progress toward cultivating a safe, trusting, and nurturing environment. Additional therapeutic factors such as socializing techniques, interpersonal learning, and imitative behavior may be seen and drawn out during these stages. The working or *performing* stage is where the most productive work is done in the group. Therapeutic factors like the recapitulation of the family experience, catharsis, and instillation of hope may be experienced and highlighted through this stage. Finally, the *adjourning* stage is where members experience the ending of the group and the various emotions that often accompany termination. Existential factors and altruism may be two additional therapeutic factors observed at this stage. While these stages are not necessarily linear (group members may return to various stages as things change between members and within the overall group dynamics), and the 11 identified therapeutic factors may be present across many stages, effective group counselors plan content and process questions with an eye toward the life of the group and an ear for drawing out the therapeutic factors that represent the cornerstone of group dynamics.

The following case example offers a rationale and realistic picture of the design and implementation of an ecotherapy psychoeducation group for college-age students. Given that the transition to college is a vulnerable time and adolescents are susceptible to a variety of stressors, we chose to offer an outline of this ecotherapy group as a way to show how this population can discover stress management techniques by learning to develop or rekindle their relationship with the natural world.

CASE EXAMPLE: MINDFULNESS-BASED ECOTHERAPY GROUP FOR COLLEGE STUDENTS

College students often use maladaptive coping strategies to manage stress and the emergence of their independence (Bland, Melton, Welle, & Bigham, 2012). These habits may result in negative consequences, and there is a growing need to support students with more adaptive coping strategies. Emerging research suggests that the college-aged population may benefit from exposure to nature-based techniques to help reduce stress and promote healthier decision-making (Bowen & Neill, 2013; Roberts, Stroud, Hoag, & Massey, 2017). The following provides clinicians with steps for organizing the group as well as a week-by-week description of each eight-week ecotherapy group session.

Promoting the Group and Screening

As the facilitator of an ecotherapy group, it is necessary to ensure that prospective members are deemed appropriate to attend an outdoor, physical setting. For this particular group, clearance from a doctor is required to participate. Flyers concerning the intentions and parameters of the sessions are posted in various places around the college campus, as well as contact information for the facilitator. The flyer includes the requirements of the group, such as the ability to complete a highly physical task such as a ropes course and the ability to hike a moderate distance. Prospective members must be aware of the physical activities required before reaching out to the group facilitator. An equine therapy activity is involved; therefore, the flyer mentions that the group may not be suitable for those with severe allergies to animal dander. The flyer also mentions that transportation to and from group activities is not provided. All genders are welcome to join.

Prospective students are encouraged to reach out to the facilitator with their interest via email, and, from there, facilitators disseminate an initial screening questionnaire. Some questions on the questionnaire include: How do you currently cope with stress? What is your current relationship with nature? What is your favorite memory in an outdoor setting? Can you remember a time where you had a difficult or negative experience in nature? What is something you expect to get out of this group? What are your concerns about being a member of this group? Prospective participants must also be screened for any mental health concerns. An inventory such as the Beck Depression Inventory is administered as a second-level screening process to ensure that any severe mental health issues are flagged and addressed using other primary interventions before participating in a secondary treatment.

Informed Consent

The consent form discusses the goals and objectives for the group and reiterates the potential risks. Confidentiality and its limits must be addressed, such as the fact that there is a possibility members will be seen in a public setting by others outside of the group, the physical risks involved, and so on. This consent form also contains a detailed description of the meeting times and places where each session is held, as well as where the group will meet in the event that the weather is not conducive to outdoor activities. In these cases, a conference room is reserved in the university's student center. The informed consent also provides the address of the location of the first meeting. Members meet in the parking lot of the designated location and from there walk down to their final meeting location together.

Week One: Introduction

The first session takes place at a local park with hiking trails. The trail is aligned on either side by trees with the intent that group members can hear the sounds of nature such as birds chirping and the leaves rustling in the wind. Facilitators suggest that members utilize their walk to destress and become more fully present. Members reach a picnic table that overlooks the bay as well as a small pier, where they can hear waves lapping the shore from boats driving by in the distance. Facilitators can choose to use other venues that afford participants opportunities to hear a variety of sounds in the natural world.

The facilitators introduce themselves again, discuss the tenets of both mindfulness and ecotherapy, and relate them back to the purpose of the group. Members are asked to introduce themselves and participate in an icebreaker exercise to learn each other's names. Various icebreakers can be catered to encompass a nature-related theme, such as "What is the best memory you have in nature?" or something as simple as "What comes to mind when you think of the word 'nature?'" Facilitators might use one of the questions formally used on the screening questionnaire to expand on members' previous responses.

Since the members are at the forming stage and just getting to know each other, group leaders encourage them to share common stressors they are experiencing while enrolled in college. One of the goals of the group leader here is to promote the therapeutic factor of cohesion through social connectedness. Do group members share similar anxieties when anticipating tests? Are they having a difficult time balancing school on top of their personal lives? Are they involved in any organizations on campus that are causing them stress? The facilitator leads this discussion and points out commonalities between members to link them together, promoting hope and universality within the group dynamic. Some process questions include: X, how does it feel to know that Y shares those same fears of performing poorly in class? Z, how does it feel to know you are not alone in experiencing anxiety while supporting yourself financially on top of completing school work?

The group facilitator should help members to connect, feel safe, and establish independent as well as mutually defined group goals. Ask members why they chose to participate in the group. What do they hope to get out of this experience? Facilitators maintain the focus on the here and now. Some group goals and rules that can be established between members are confidentiality, safety, participation, punctuality, absences, courtesy, and any other topics the group may wish to address. There is also a participation contract that members sign that addresses the roles each member will fulfill. These include but are not limited to confidentiality, attendance and participation, group informed consent, courtesy, and the facilitator's name and contact information.

Week Two: Practicing Mindfulness

Members meet in the same location as week one, keeping the structure constant since the group is still in its forming stage. Stability is important in the first few sessions of a group, as too much change too quickly can delay members from feeling comfortable enough to build a solid relationship with one other.

Given that the topic for the week is mindfulness, group members are encouraged to participate in a walking meditation as they follow the trail down to the water. Some members of the group may have been practicing mindfulness while walking down the path before the first session without even realizing they were doing so. The purpose of this time is to highlight the intentionality with which participants will listen to the nature around them (e.g., bird chirping, leaves rustling). Participants may also be encouraged to consider the absence of familiar hustle and bustle. Some group members may notice that they have been occupied elsewhere in their thoughts, such as thinking about something stressful they were dealing with in their lives or perhaps battling nerves about what the group process would look like. A walking meditation encourages these members to remain present, focusing on and preparing to be more grounded throughout the session. A simple walking meditation may entail encouraging participants to feel their feet hitting the ground with each step, noticing where the earth connects with the soles of their feet, or perhaps simply listening to and recognizing the sounds of nature around them.

During the second week of a new group meeting, members are typically still hesitant and shy, therefore an icebreaker is utilized again at the beginning of the session. Members are asked to first repeat their names and then state what it is they noticed most on their brief walk to the water. This is a simple yet effective way to build up to the mindfulness activity for the week and may be seamlessly incorporated into the main activity. An important goal is to continue to foster trust through openness and shared experiences. The following describes a simple mindfulness activity in detail.

Encourage the group to take three deep breaths. Ask members to feel the places the sun is hitting their skin, to think about what that feels like; encourage members to feel the air moving across their skin and the earth supporting their bodies on the ground. Encourage the group to connect with their breath, focusing on each inhale and each exhale, thinking about how the air they are breathing is shared with the trees around them. This is an opportunity to slowly introduce a second goal of ecotherapy, which includes incorporating the symbiotic relationship between people and their ecosystem. More specifically, this may include how the air we inhale is provided by the nature around us, and how the air we exhale helps to sustain that ecosystem in return.

Keep in mind that grounding and meditation exercises may be very challenging for some. It can be overwhelming to focus in on thoughts and feelings in the body so closely, especially for those under high levels of stress or who have experienced trauma. This is an example of when it is important as a group leader to be able to read the energy of the group and determine how long each part of the meditation should last. Members should be talked through the exercises accordingly, being reminded that it is normal for thoughts to wander or to feel some discomfort. Facilitators can gently urge group members to bring their thoughts back to the breath and the simplicity of the meditation.

The session ends with a gratitude exercise. Ask members to recognize how special it is to be a part of such a diverse ecosystem, to be able to decide whether they want to accept its gifts and nurture it in return. Afterwards, the facilitators lead a discussion processing the activity. Members are encouraged to openly discuss what they were feeling and thinking throughout the exercise. Process questions may include asking about times during the activity that members found it to be easier or harder to stay present or what it was like to maintain a here-and-now focus in the presence of other group members. The entirety of this activity is an opportunity to encourage universality among the group if one or more members divulge that they had difficulty practicing the meditation. This may also encourage the beginnings of group cohesion, or members starting to feel a sense of connection among each other.

Week Three: Letting Go

The group again meets at the picnic table by the water, where the session begins with a recap of the previous week. Members are encouraged to freely discuss their thoughts and feelings surrounding the exercise and how they felt before versus how they felt after. By this point, group members should be beginning to feel more comfortable, and individual personalities start to show through.

The topic of week three's session is "Letting Go of the Past and the Future," which help members become aware of what is keeping them from remaining in the present moment. This activity sheds light on whether members of the group are focusing their awareness more on the past, or the future, or perhaps both. To begin, all members are seated around the picnic table. The facilitators distribute a pen and piece of paper to each member and ask that they write down a list of things that cause them stress. After the list is created, the facilitator asks that members then write down a "P" for the things on the list that happened in the past and an "F" for what they might be stressing about for the future (Hall, 2016). The point of this exercise is for members to realize that, for most of them, very few things that cause them stress are happening in the present moment. This leads to the topic for the group's process discussion. An example of a process question can include, "How many of the stressors you are dealing with now are rooted in the present moment?" "Are most of the things you are stressed about (i.e., upcoming midterms or graduation) things that are happening right now, or are they going to take place in the future?" "What is it like to hear other people talk about similar future stressors?" This activity can bring an instillation of hope between members. Members are able to see firsthand if their thoughts about the past and the future are preventing them from living in the present.

Leaders may intervene at the intrapersonal level to help members share more of their own experiences ("When was a time where you felt you had trouble moving on from something that happened in the past?"), and they may also help to bridge members at the subgroup level by asking a question such as, "Can anyone else in the group relate?" or "Has anyone in the group experienced something similar that they would like to share?" The leader may also make a group-level process comment like "It sounds like we experience stress at various times of our days and that being outdoors provides opportunities to inhale a little bit more deeply and refocus our minds to the present moment" to help build community and cultivate safety.

It is important to point out that these activities will bring a group closer together, but as people become closer there is also more opportunity for conflicting experiences and opinions. Members could begin to disagree or recognize various points of view, indicative of the storming stage, and the group leader should be aware of this to navigate through it effectively.

Following the processing activity, the facilitators then discuss within the group different ways that members can use nature as a resource to help them remain present. For example, when they are somewhere surrounded by nature, they can take some time to do a mindfulness exercise (Cordes, 2014): take a deep breath, name five things that can be seen, four things that can be heard, three things that can be touched, two things that can be smelled, and one thing that can be tasted. This exercise can be done anywhere and can be a useful tool for remaining present and grounded. The group leader can kick off the exercise by providing an example of what it looks like. Through these activities, interpersonal communication fosters relational connectedness and members begin to also note the bidirectional relationship with nature (i.e., how we can nurture nature and how nature can nurture us in return).

The group is concluded with a homework assignment: to be mindful of what is continuing to cause you stress throughout your week, write it down, and bring it to the following session.

Week Four: Acceptance

Since this is the fourth time the group is meeting, the facilitator should address that they are now at the halfway mark. Be sure to check in with the members about how they are currently feeling and see where their thought processes are. Next, have members walk down toward the bay and out onto the pier to go over the homework activity. The group leader has a large bowl filled with water, and, one by one, members share what they wrote

Figure 5.2 Ecotherapy group taking time to watch the ocean.

down on their list of stressful thoughts they were experiencing throughout the week.

Sharing common stressors brings the therapeutic factor of universality to the group, allowing members to realize they are not alone in experiencing commonalities in many aspects of their lives. Some examples of these common stressors may be relationship issues, a big test they have been anxiously studying for, or the lack of time management between academics and personal life. The group leader then has members come up individually and place the paper in the water-filled bowl, watching their stress list disappear.

After the activity ends, the facilitator asks what it was like to watch what they wrote down slowly disappear in the water. Some process questions about this activity may include: "Do you remember what you were stressed out about five years ago?" "The things you wrote on the paper—will they still matter five years from now, or even next year?" "What can you learn from this?" "What can you do to be in control of your thoughts and not let them have power over you?"

The facilitator then breaks the group up to walk through the park and each member picks something up in nature that he or she connects with on a personal level. Some examples of this can be a feather hidden in the leaves, a crooked stick, a multicolored leaf, or a flower. On their walk, members are also asked to pick up a large rock. The group then meets back at the picnic table and shares with the group why they chose that object. Did they have a difficult time choosing an object? What do the other members think about why they chose that? This brings about group cohesiveness through sharing their thoughts about how they view themselves versus how other group members view them. Some process questions include: "What does it feel like to share something so personal with the group?" "Was there a fear that you would be judged for choosing the object you chose, or for why you chose it?" "Do you feel accepted?" "What does it mean to be accepted by someone?" "How can nature help you accept yourself?"

To conclude the topic of acceptance, members meet at the picnic table with their rock and pick one word or sentence to paint on it. This helps them start their day with a positive self-affirmation with the goal of obtaining self-acceptance. The facilitators can have a list of examples for members to choose from, or members can create their own. Some examples include "hope," "faith," "grateful," "blessed," "strength," "heal," "beautiful," "I got this," and "Take a deep breath." They can place this rock somewhere in their dorm room or home where they will see it daily as a reminder for self-compassion and unconditional self-acceptance. This rock also symbolizes what they have learned thus far about themselves in their group ecotherapy sessions.

Week Five: Living in the Present

The fifth group session is centered on "living in the now"; therefore an activity that requires constant attention is appropriate. In this example, a ropes course is used. This activity requires group members to not only be fully present but also to work as a team to accomplish a task. This part of the group is a reminder of why it is so important to ensure that group members are physically capable, given that the ropes course is a highly physical activity. Group safety must be discussed prior to the activity, including a lesson on how to properly use the belays and harnesses. The facilitators first ask the group to discuss fears or doubts they may have or challenges they faced throughout the week.

Ropes courses are ideal for team and self-esteem building and serve many purposes at this stage of the group. Utilizing a ropes course can foster problem-solving skills, trust, coping skills, communication, a positive outlook, and self-efficacy—all skills that can be translated into everyday life (Sweetser, 2018). By week five, members may be entering the storming phase, in which relationships are getting stronger, and members may begin to disagree and challenge one other. An activity such as the ropes course may push people into the storming mode at an accelerated rate, given that group members naturally differ in their styles of accomplishing a task. In an activity such as the ropes course, group members are forced to work together to accomplish a common goal. In this regard, it is important for the group leader to be able to assist group members in safely and successfully navigating this stage.

Some of the activities that take place in the ropes course are the trust fall, the catwalk, the dangle duo, and the leap of faith. The trust fall happens first as a warm-up activity on the ground. Member 1 stands directly in front of Member 2, with his or her back to Member 2. Member 1 closes his or her eyes and falls backwards, and Member 2 catches him or her. This exercise is a perfect way to foster trust among members and also teach them how to let go of control. The catwalk is a solo activity in which a log is suspended between two trees and the individual must cross over and ascend down. The "leap of faith" is also an individual activity where members climb to a platform and then must leap and hit a buoy suspended in the air in front of them. The individual free-falls in the air before the harness catches him or her and lowers him or her down to the ground. The ropes course then progresses to a partner exercise, where two people climb a ladder together and utilize one another's strength to climb upwards (Sweetser, 2018).

Many of the group members may exhibit fear throughout this exercise, and while it can be a time for storming to occur, it can also be a wonderful opportunity for group cohesion and instillation of hope among members. Members will naturally encourage one another and push one another to confront their fears. Upon completion of the course, there is a debriefing and processing session among the facilitators and members. Some processing questions include: "What did you find to be the most positive aspect of completing the ropes course?" "What were some of the more challenging aspects?" "How do you feel now, having completed the course?" "What was it like to work together as a team and rely on a partner to complete the activities?" The facilitators should be able to teach members how to apply skills they may have learned on the ropes course to their everyday lives.

Week Six: Animal-Assisted Healing

During week six, the group is introduced to animal-assisted therapy. Developing a bond with an animal provides innumerable benefits to the human psyche, including more developed self-worth, trust, and self-regulation. Horses in particular are especially fitting in conjunction with mental health due to their size, power, and sensitivity to human emotions and body language (EAGALA, 2018). In the case of group ecotherapy, members have the chance to not only interact with the horses but also with each other. Members have the opportunity to think differently than they are used to, utilizing problem-solving skills and learning different ways to relate to one another and the animal. Group members who may find themselves disconnecting under the stressors of college life may find themselves coming back into the present to focus on the large and powerful animal beside or beneath them.

The group meets at a local equine therapy facility, where members are given a brief tour of the barn and some background on the nature of horses. The session begins with a check-in on anything the members may feel like sharing before beginning the group, including feelings toward the activity. However, during the exercise itself, much of the beauty of equine therapy comes from the fact that talking is not necessary, making it an ideal modality for members who may be less inclined to share.

The members are brought into the outdoor paddock with the horses and encouraged to be mindful of how they are feeling. The horses may walk up to the members, exploring the new addition to their environment. It is important to take note of members' body language—some may seem timid or afraid, and others may seem comfortable. The facilitators asks the group what they notice about the horses and how members of the herd interact with one another. Group members learn how to groom and tack up the horses, and then they proceed into the arena where they first lead the horses on foot. Members get to know the animals little by little, gaining a feel for what it is like to walk beside such a powerful yet gentle animal. Members are continuously reminded throughout the session to be mindful and remain present.

Following this exercise, it is time for members of the group to mount their horses. Some individuals may feel timid or afraid and should be encouraged to express these feelings to the group. This is a great opportunity for members to have a shared experience, as others may be experiencing similar emotions. It is especially important at this time for the group to remain grounded in the present moment, as not doing so can be dangerous when mounted on the horse. Members should be encouraged to feel the weight of their bodies sitting in the saddle and the movements of the horses' shoulder blades moving back and forth beneath them, carrying them. Different exercises may be incorporated into the session, including team-building and mindfulness exercises, at the discretion of the equine therapist (EAGALA, 2018).

At the end of the lesson, members lead their horses back to the barn, where they untack and groom them before putting them back out into the pasture. Encourage the group to express gratitude to their horses for allowing them the experience to connect with them. Members then join together outside and discuss their shared experience. Group members are encouraged to discuss how they felt during the experience and what they may have noticed happening in their bodies, physically and emotionally. Some process questions include: "What did it feel like to be in the presence of such a large animal, trusting it to carry your weight?" "Did you feel a connection with your horse?" "Did you find your thoughts wandering during the experience?" "If so, what brought you back to the present?" The group is encouraged to express anything else they wish to share at this time. Facilitators thank the group for being open to new experiences and sharing their thoughts.

Week Seven: Horticultural Therapy

Week seven takes place at a greenhouse. Members are seated around a table where various tropical plants are arranged. The horticulture therapist describes the care and characteristics of each plant, and then members are asked to choose one they feel they connect with most. The facilitator asks members if they would be willing to share why they chose the plant they did, after which each member is given a clay pot to decorate throughout the session. At the end of the group session, members re-pot their plants into their new containers.

Gardening may help members gain a sense of self-confidence and purpose, which may be especially applicable to the college-aged population. College is a time of branching out and gaining independence, and fostering the growth of a plant can provide members with a sense of self-satisfaction as a result of watching a living entity thrive under their care. Linden and Grut (2002) aptly describe therapeutic gardening as an opportunity to use metaphors to deepen members' connections with nature. Seeds and plants often go dormant in the winter, giving the impression that they will not come back to life. On the contrary, plants that appear dead in the winter will re-emerge and thrive in the springtime. College-aged individuals in particular may be able to relate to the feeling of wanting to "go dormant," perhaps especially after a grueling round of final exams. Group members may also be able to relate to the feeling of being "uprooted," possibly as a result of moving away from home to attend college or due to other circumstances. Members of the group can use these metaphors from nature in their own lives during times they may be feeling

Figure 5.3 Equine assisted group therapy.

like there is no hope, remembering that all living things have ups and down and nothing is permanent; after being uprooted or neglected, even the most tired plant can once again flourish with the proper care. This is an opportunity to incorporate some process questions into the group, having members revisit a time when they may have felt like there was no hope and ways they can practice self-care in the future during those times.

It is important to call attention to the fact that this session is the second to last time the group will be meeting. Group members may have mixed feelings about this: some may be fearful, some sad, some relieved, and some may feel a mixture of these emotions. The group leader should take time to help the group navigate these potentially confusing and conflicting emotions.

Week Eight: Wrap-Up/Take Away

For the final week, the group meets again at the same location as week one (the picnic tables at the park), bringing the group full circle. Since this is the final session, the facilitator has the members review and summarize the group experience. Some debriefing questions may include: "What were the benefits of being a member in this group?" "What have you learned about yourself? others?" "Would you recommend this group to a friend?" "Are there any sessions that you wish could have been longer/shorter?" "What can be improved?" "How can you take what you have learned and apply it to the stress of being a college student?" "Do you view nature differently now versus before the group experience?" These questions should be based on the individual goals set by each member at the onset of the group.

Have members recall and share special moments that stick out to them from the past eight weeks. The group facilitator should point out individual growth and changes within each member, and members are encouraged to provide positive feedback to the others in the group. Providing feedback is imperative when closing out a group and can be a useful tool for members to continue to make meaningful changes (Gladding, 2015). To conclude the group, farewells are addressed. The facilitator can revisit the previous sessions and remind the members that they will always have the tools they learned throughout the group, as well as the positive self-affirmation/self-acceptance stones and plants as a reminder of the time they spent with the group.

Figure 5.4 Getting the group grounded with feet in the sand.

SUMMARY

The purpose of this chapter was to discuss the practice of group counseling and highlight group leadership skills and group dynamics that may impact clients participating in an ecotherapy group setting. This chapter describes the theoretical underpinnings of group counseling and suggests ways in which group leaders can manage group dynamics through the use of targeted group process questions. Specific examples of ecotherapy group interventions are provided and group leadership considerations in a variety of settings are suggested to help leaders draw out various therapeutic factors that impact group dynamics at different stages of the group's process.

REFERENCES

Association for Specialists in Group Work (ASGW). (2000). Association for Specialists in Group Work: Professional Training Standards for the Training of Group Workers. Retrieved from http://www.asgw.org/pdf/training_standards.pdf.

Benfield, J. A., Rainbolt, G. N., Bell, P. A., & Donovan, G. H. (2015). Classrooms with nature views: Evidence of differing student perceptions and behaviors. *Environment and Behavior, 47*(2), 140–157. https://doi.org/10.1177/0013916513499583.

Bland, H. W., Melton, B. F., Welle, P., & Bigham, L. (2012). Stress tolerance: New challenges for millennial college students. *College Student Journal, 46*(2), 362–375.

Blair, D. (2010). The child in the garden: An evaluative review of the benefits of school gardening. *Journal of Environmental Education, 40*(2), 15–38.

Bowen, D. J., & Neill, J. T. (2013). A meta-analysis of adventure therapy outcomes and moderators. *The Open Psychology Journal, 6*, 28–53. doi:10.2174/1874350120130802001

Cordes, S. (2014). Easy grounding exercises to calm the nervous system. Retrieved from http://www.drcordes.com/blog/2014/11/24/easy-grounding-exercises-to-calm-the-nervous-system.

Corey, G. (2008). *Theory and Practice of Group Counseling* (7th Ed). Belmont, CA: Thomson Brooks/Cole.

Chawla, L. (2015). Benefits of nature contact for children. *Journal of Planning Literature, 30*(4), 433–452. https://doi.org/10.1177/0885412215595441.

Duffy, J., Springer, S. I., Delaney, M., & Luke, M. (2019). Eco-Education: Integrating nature into the counselor education classroom. *Journal of Creativity in Mental Health*, 1–14. doi:10.1080/15401383.2019.1640152.

Equine Assisted Growth and Learning Association (EAGALA). (2018.). Retrieved from https://www.eagala.org/model.

Flom, B., Johnson, C., Hubbard, J., & Reidt, D. (2011). The natural school counselor: Using nature to promote mental health in schools. *Journal of*

Creativity in mental health, 6(2), 118–131. https://doi.org/10.1080/15401383.2011.579869.

Gladding, S. T. (2015). *Groups: A counseling specialty* (7th ed.). Upper Saddle River, NJ: Pearson.

Glass, J. S., & Shoffner, M. F. (2001). Adventure-based counseling in schools. *Professional School Counseling, 5*(1), 42.

Gresalfi, M. S., Barnes, J., & Cross, D. (2012). When does an opportunity become an opportunity? Unpacking classroom practice through the lens of ecological psychology. *Educational Studies in Mathematics, 80*(1-2), 249–267.

Hall, C. (2016). *Mindfulness-based ecotherapy: Facilitator manual.* n.p.

Li, D., & Sullivan, W. C. (2016). Impact of views to school landscapes on recovery from stress and mental fatigue. *Landscape and Urban Planning, 148,* 149–158. https://doi.org/10.1016/j.landurbplan.2015.12.015.

Linden, S., & Grut, J. (2002). *The healing fields: Working with psychotherapy and nature to rebuild shattered lives.* London, England: Frances Lincoln.

Louv, R. (2008). *Last child in the woods: Saving our children from nature-deficit disorder.* Chapel Hill, NC: Algonquin Books of Chapel Hill.

Promises Behavioral Health. (2019). Ropes course therapy. Retrieved from https://www.elementsbehavioralhealth.com/therapies/ropes-course-therapy/

Roberts, S. D., Stroud, D., Hoag, M. J., & Massey, K. E. (2017). Outdoor behavioral healthcare: A longitudinal assessment of young adult outcomes. *Journal of Counseling & Development, 95*(1), 45–55. doi:10.1002/jcad.12116

Sweester. (2018). High ropes course. Retrieved from https://www.sweetser.org/training-institute/focus-through-adventure-challenge-ropes-course/.

Schimmel, C. J., Daniels, J. A., Wassif, J., & Jacobs, E. (2016). Learning the ropes: A creative orientation approach for counseling students. *Journal of Creativity in Mental Health, 11*(1), 27–38. https://doi.org/10.1080/15401383.2015.1095663.

Tuckman, B. W., & Jensen, M. A. (1977). Stages in small group development revisited. *Group and Organisation Studies, 2*(4), 419–427. https://doi.org/10.1177/105960117700200404.

Yalom, I. D., & Leszcz, M. (2005). *The theory and practice of group psychotherapy* (5th ed.). New York, NY: Basic Books.

CHAPTER 5A

SKIPPING STONES

Bethany Sheridan

Growing up on the Jersey shore afforded me many beach days throughout my childhood, which fostered a deep sense of connection to nature, especially to the water. Being the child of two athletes, I was always involved in sports and outdoor activities, such as soccer, camping, and Girl Scouts. This love of being outdoors was shared by my friends and neighbors; we could always be found playing kickball or riding our bikes during the day and looking for frogs at night. When I think of my childhood, I think of playing with chalk, going to the beach, riding bikes, and just generally being outdoors. Fortunately, my parents encouraged and fostered a relationship with nature that has continued to evolve and be present in my adult life.

Throughout college, I studied holistic health and worked outdoors in summer camps and as a lifeguard. I was hungry to learn more about the healing potential of the natural world. However, after losing my father to suicide during my first year of college, I decided to focus on psychology and the helping professions. I went to see many counselors myself, often in sterile rooms inside stuffy buildings. I was uncomfortable sitting in windowless rooms yet looking at posters of flowers and water on the walls; I wanted to run, to scream, to move. My first experience with ecotherapy was as a client; after seeing many therapists, I finally found one I connected with, and he conducted our sessions while walking next to a lake. The healing power of nature transformed from something I was studying to something incredibly deep and meaningful that I was experiencing.

As I moved on in my education, I ultimately decided I want to pursue a career as a counselor. I enrolled in a mental health counseling master's program and continued to learn how natural elements can be incorporated into counseling sessions. I was fortunate enough to study with many great professors who took classes outside at times and discussed the physical, emotional, and spiritual impacts of being in nature. With a head full of my own positive personal experiences, knowledge I had gained from school, and the hope of helping others, I was thrilled to accept my first counseling job at a rehabilitation facility for clients with drug and alcohol disorders. However, I quickly realized that the practical realities of counseling in a large agency were quite different than the ideal conditions I had envisioned in my mind.

For the clients in treatment, they attended four groups per day, an hour long each, met with their individual counselor at least once or twice per week, and had additional morning and evening groups at the residence, on top of the counseling homework they were expected to do in their free time. All of the groups and sessions were conducted inside, in very sterile and plain offices because there were not enough offices for each counselor to have his or her own. Therefore, we were unable to decorate our offices as they were constantly changing locations. During one particularly rowdy group session, I asked the clients why no one was interested in the group and what I could do to make the session better. Without hesitation, a client looked at me and said, "How about you let us move around? You know how long we've been sitting in these metal chairs under these fluorescent lights? Nobody around here gives a damn! We ain't seen the sun in days!" While I could see many issues with the structure of the program and the limits of what I could do, it was the first time it had explicitly been brought to my attention that these clients were stuck indoors almost exclusively during their time there. My heart ached for them as this realization dawned on me, and I knew I had to do something.

I went to my supervisor and the other counselors and was given permission to conduct a group outside. Fortunately, the facility was located about five minutes walking time from a large lakefront area, where we agreed to go. Of course, clients were given the option to stay inside and the limits of confidentiality were discussed, as we were going to a public place, but everyone wanted to go. As a brand-new counselor, leading large groups was intimidating enough, but taking a group outside was terrifying. I was nervous that I would lose control of the group, that someone would try to run off, or that I would fail my clients in some way.

During my first outdoor group, I asked the clients what they wanted to get out of group and out of treatment. Nearly everyone was in agreement that they "just wanted to get outside" and had difficulty expressing what they wanted in the long term. We spent our first group walking near the edge of the lake and talking about what treatment had been like for them. Memories of my own experiences walking by a lake came back to me, and while I was still unsure of myself, I was reminded to trust the process. Clients spoke about feeling like objects, like the way they were being treated was impersonal, as if they were just a number or another faceless drug addict. I hung back, letting the clients do most of the talking to process their feelings and experiences. This information was important for me to reflect on: how had I let them down and what could I do to be better? I needed to listen.

As group progressed, I started incorporating guided meditations. Being in the natural world, we didn't have to imagine that we were being warmed by the sun or that we could see a beautiful lake; I used what was in front of me. More and more, I began to incorporate what Mother Nature had already provided me with. I stopped telling clients to close their eyes during meditation and instead we started to focus on the beauty around us. We began to walk more, to move more, and slowly my background in yoga made its way to counseling after a client requested to do a physical activity. During group one day, she said, "It's really nice that you took us out here, but all we do all day is sit in group after group; can't we do like yoga or something?"

This simple request prompted me to re-evaluate what I could do to meet their needs. I could absolutely incorporate yoga and more movement into sessions. The first time I led a yoga session, there was a lot of nervous laughter in the air. Most of the male clients were making jokes to ease their own discomfort, others stood around nervously, and a few quietly waited for instruction. I could feel the awkward discomfort and clients' uncertainty in the first few minutes after we began. I pressed on, and the laughter began to fade, the awkward tension started to disappear, and soon we were in sync as a cohesive group. As we settled into our meditation at the end of the yoga session, it felt as if a physical weight had been lifted. For the first time since I had started working there, I couldn't feel anxiety, anger, or restlessness from the group. They were finally able to be at ease, if only for a short time out of their day.

As we began to establish ourselves as a group, clients started showing new members how they were expected to behave in the group. When I first started the group, I felt like I was all by myself trying to establish group norms and boundaries. However, as time progressed clients began to take ownership of the group, which shaped how the group functioned. Due to the nature of inpatient treatment, the turnover rate for clients is anywhere from 2 to 4 weeks, so we did not have a typical therapeutic group timeframe to work in. However, because we met daily, we were able to establish a group identity. I remember during one session a new client was giving me a hard time; he was cursing at me, refusing to participate, and trying to get the other clients riled up. Before I could even respond to him, another client said, "That's not how we talk to Bethany and that's not how we do group here. If you don't want to come you can just stay inside." The other group members supported this sentiment, and I realized we had truly started something special, something the clients wanted to protect.

As I became more comfortable with the group, we were able to start trying new things. Many of the clients came to treatment feeling angry, ashamed, guilty, and completely stigmatized by society. I wanted to address these feelings, so I decided to make use of the many rocks and stones around us. I asked the clients to gather rocks, one for each of the difficult feelings they were experiencing. They were to get a rock that physically represented the emotions they were carrying around. Clients were pretty resistant to this idea at first, and I was nervous they would use the rocks inappropriately. Many of the clients voiced their feelings about this activity by saying that it was stupid, it wasn't going to help, and that rocks couldn't possibly represent how they felt, but they did it anyway. After they had all collected their rocks, we talked about what feelings they were representing. Clients were given the space to process some of the reasons they picked up a rock and quickly found they shared a lot of the same feelings. It was clear that an activity clients were unsure of at first had started to take them to a deep place where they could process difficult feelings.

A common theme was guilt. Every single client in group that day spoke about the guilt they felt from the destruction and heartache that their addictions had caused. They had lost their homes, their children, their parents, their loved ones; they had damaged their own health and happiness; they let down their gods and spirits—they all had a story about the guilt that was ravaging them. While we were processing, I asked them to hold the rock they had picked to represent this guilt and imagine they were putting all of that guilt into the rock as they spoke. One client said the rock got heavier and heavier as it took on this burden for him. At the end of our session, I asked the clients to let go of this guilt—to acknowledge it, to feel it, and to let it go. They looked at me like I was completely psychotic. I was met with cries of "We can't just let it go!" and "It's not that simple!" or "But I'll always feel this way." I asked them to try. At this point, we had built up enough trust and they agreed to try. They threw those rocks as hard and far as they could into the lake. A few clients let out a yell as they watched the rocks sink below the water. A few clients cried as they started to let go of what had been holding them down. I don't know that anyone's guilt was completely absolved that day, but something had opened up in them. There was a complete shift in the air, and I was a part of something more powerful than I can put into words.

Many months had passed since that day, and I was getting ready to move across the country and leave my job behind when a former client came in to see me. It is such an honor to have a client come back because so often I can never know how a client's journey progressed after he or she leaves treatment. It was the client who had given me a hard time. This was a client who nearly got kicked out of treatment for bad behavior and, frankly, one for whom much of the staff had little hope of truly recovering. He had come to thank me for my group and to apologize for his behavior. He was employed, living in a sober community, and was right in front of me asking for forgiveness for the things he had said. He told me that going outside for that group was the highlight of his day and that I helped him more than I could know. I know that this was not the work of just me; we were both part of something bigger than us—we experienced a deep and meaningful connection not only to other people but to the natural world. There have been many days I questioned my career choice, my counseling choices, and whether or not what I was doing was truly helpful. I often go back to this moment to remind myself how far a person can come when given the chance. Although I was incredibly saddened to be leaving something that had become so beautiful and powerful, I knew that a tradition was started that would continue to help many others, and with that, I continue upon on my own journey.

CHAPTER 6

cVo

Incorporating Nature in Schools

JASON T. DUFFY AND MIRANDA BRUMBER

INTRODUCTION

Come forth into the light of things, let Nature be your teacher.
—William Wordsworth

With the increased focus in most public schools on standardized tests and district rankings emanating from places like *U.S. News and World Report*, many K-12 students in the United States find themselves increasingly learning the skills and content they need in order to excel in these measures (William, 2010). Concurrent with this standardized test-based focus in our public schools, we have seen a simultaneous uptick in the number of children and adolescents struggling with emotion-based mental health issues (Merikangas et al., 2010). Ironically, the United States, considered by most measures to be the wealthiest (monetarily) nation on earth (Desjardins, 2018), falls well below the student-based achievement scores of many other industrialized countries (Funk & Rainie, 2018). There are numerous variables responsible for this trend; however, one that has been hypothesized anecdotally and supported by a growing body of research is the ever-increasing divorce between our nation's youth and the natural world, a place imbued with the ability to assist as a pedagogical tool as well as to stem the tide of many mental health issues (Juster et al., 2004; Louv, 2015).

This chapter highlights the growing mental health issues facing many of the United States' students, exploring the link between mental health and learning and development, and provides examples of how school-based mental health personnel (i.e., school counselors, social workers, and school psychologists) can incorporate the natural world into their work in order to promote holistic wellness in their students and, additionally, support the learning taking place in the classroom. Finally, the chapter ends with a case study that illustrates the use of the natural world with an "at-risk" student in a public high school in Upstate New York.

STUDENT MENTAL HEALTH AND LEARNING

Americans are inundated with messages about success—in school, in a profession, in parenting, in relationships—without appreciating that successful performance rests on a foundation of mental health.

—U.S. Department of Health and Human Services (1999)

There is a growing body of research that indicates that mental health issues such as depression and anxiety negatively impact both behavior and academic achievement in school settings (Flom, Johnson, Hubbard, & Reidt, 2011; McLeod, Uemura, & Rohrman, 2012). These findings are concerning because recent literature indicates that 13% to 14% of students meet the criteria for a significant mental health disorder each school year in the United States. By some estimates, the percentage is much higher; however, even the lower estimate of 13% is problematic when considering it means that 13 out of 100 students are dealing with a significant mental health disorder. With the average high school containing just around 500 students (Public School Review, n.d.), this means that about 70 students are dealing with a significant mental health problem. Many teachers and school counselors can speak energetically about the impact a single student struggling with mental health issues can have on the school environment as well as how much of the school's resources must, at times, be allocated to such students rather than toward the primary purpose of education.

Students that meet the criteria for mental health disorders tend to struggle more with attendance, grades, testing, appropriate behavior, and social interaction involving both peers and adults (Love, 2004). According to Boston University's Center for Psychiatric Rehabilitation (n.d.), the reason for the decrease in school performance correlates to the impact mental health disorders have on student variables such as sustaining concentration, screening out problematic environmental stimuli, maintaining physical and psychological stamina, handling pressure, navigating multitasking, responding to transitions, and handling critical feedback.

There is some recognition of these mental health and school-based success correlations. For example, mental health diagnoses are often the impetus for students 504 Plans and Individualized Education Plans. The Vocational Rehabilitation Act of 1973 allows for mental health diagnoses to be the rationale for providing school-based interventions for students, ranging from extended time on tests to a more restrictive intervention such as placement in a specialized 6-1-1 setting (1 teacher, 1 teacher assistant, and 6 students). Although such allowances are important for students struggling with mental health disorders in the school setting, the question remains: Are there other interventions that school staff and faculty can employ to help students struggling with mental health issues feel better and actualize their full potential?

USING NATURE TO TREAT MENTAL HEALTH DISORDERS IN SCHOOLS

I felt my lungs inflate with the onrush of scenery—air, mountains, trees, people. I thought, "This is what it is to be happy."

—Sylvia Plath

As previous chapters have illustrated, nature is a source of remedy and balm for many mental health related issues. Research has indicated that symptoms related to depression, anxiety, anger, and overall emotional dysregulation issues among other mental health issues can be lessened when people are exposed to the natural world directly (e.g., a walk in a wooded area, tending a garden inside or outside, listening to the sounds of the natural world) or, at times, through other means, such as pictures, sounds, mental imagery, and so on (Flom et al., 2011; Louv, 2008; Pope et al., 2015). For example, a 2015 study conducted by Stanford University researchers found that a brief walk in the woods can decrease depressive symptoms and give participants more conscious awareness of their emotions and more control over them (Bratman, Hamilton, Hahn, Daily, & Gross, 2015). Another study indicated that small amounts of exposure to green space (forest, grassy areas, etc.) can improve self-esteem through the enhancement of mood (Barton & Pretty, 2010). The authors of this study end their paper by calling for public housing and landscape planners to find ways to integrate natural spaces into their designs.

Such benefits of the natural world extend to many aspects of health for children and adolescents. For example, a growing body of research indicates that children's social, psychological, academic, and physical health is positively impacted when they have daily contact with nature (Flom et al., 2011). For example, a Dutch study (Maas et al., 2009) examining the official health records of over 300,000 participants found that the overall wellness of participants was higher for those who lived closer to green spaces (woods, natural waterways, fields), especially for children. Much of this research indicates that even a minimum amount of exposure to nature positively impacts various facets of functioning that directly impact the capacity to learn, such as cognitive ability, emotional stability, and focus (McCurdy et al., 2010). One such study conducted with third graders found that student off-task behavior decreased by 54% after spending even a small amount of time outdoors in natural spaces (e.g., grassy areas outside the building, small fields) just prior to an indoor school-based lesson (Kuo et al., 2018). These types of nature-based activities have also been studied with tweens (between child and teen) and teens in school settings with the same results: Students exposed to outdoor activities (free time in natural settings, outdoor lessons) demonstrate fewer attentional issues, retain more information for a longer amount of time, experience less stress, and are more motivated to learn (Dettweiler, Becker, Auestad, Simon, & Kirsch, 2017; Dettweiler, Lauterbach, Becker, & Simon, 2017; Dettweiler, Ünlü, Lauterbach, Becker, & Gschrey, 2015). The benefits of nature in schools in relation to wellness are legion; however, too often the exposure to nature in schools is either extremely small or nonexistent.

Figure 6.1 Taking the classroom outside.

Why are we neglecting this wonderous elixir that can help our students' mental health and learning? The answer is complex, but some of it appears to relate to the misguided perception that we do not have enough time and/or that we do not have access to natural environments in many school settings. The next section provides various activities that can be integrated into school environments, including some that can be utilized regardless of the context of the school.

INTEGRATING THE THERAPEUTIC BENEFITS OF NATURE IN SCHOOLS

Go for a Walk

For much of a school day, students are surrounded by walls and the artificial light of the typical classroom setting. School counselors taking opportunities with students to go outside or into areas of the school that provide a view of the natural world—even through a window—can promote well-being. Research emanating from various sources has indicated that even small amounts of exposure to natural light through a window may decrease symptoms associated with depression and increase energy levels in individuals (Holt, 2015; Louv, 2008). Additionally, students who are able to view natural settings (trees, grass, natural water sources, etc.) through classroom windows have reported decreased stress and have even scored better on standardized tests, according to research conducted at the University of Illinois at Urbana-Champaign (Li & Sullivan, 2016). Therefore, although walking in a natural area (wooded area, field, grassy spot, etc.) with a student for a period of time would be wonderful in terms of promoting wellness, it is possible to reap some of the rewards of nature by simply exposing students safely (let's not cause sunburns!) to sunlight and natural settings through windows. Such time engaging with natural settings can be done during discussions about scheduling classes, doing a psychosocial assessment, mediating a disagreement between two students, or just as a supplemental support for a student struggling with depression, anxiety, panic attacks, or other mental health related issues. Research indicates that the student does not even need to know that the natural world is being used as an intervention for positive outcomes to occur (Louv, 2008). There are numerous possibilities, and the creativity of the mental health professional is the only limitation.

One thing to consider is how to discuss using the natural world as a viable intervention for students with potentially skeptic administrators or those concerned about liability. Parents may also be worried about having students outside of the school walls, and you may want to consider whether a consent form is needed prior to embarking on outdoor activities. Being prepared to share some of the statistics and findings related to the efficacy of nature-based interventions is a good first step; being able to articulate specifically your plan for the outdoor activity is also key. This chapter, for example, may be helpful to provide to individuals who want to learn more about nature-based interventions as well as the research-based support for their efficacy. It is also important to make sure that safety is considered when taking students outside as there are numerous potential issues that can arise—traffic, wildlife, the elements (heat, sunburn, exposure to cold, etc.), a student running off, and so on. This brings up a second point: It is important to use nature-based activities that are developmentally appropriate for the student(s) you are working with. For example, a more structured activity outdoors may be needed for a second-grade student as she may struggle with just walking in a natural area without integrated activities and become easily bored and, therefore, behaviorally challenged. On the other hand, a junior in high school may be perfectly engaged with the natural world and positively affected simply by going on an unstructured walk with you for 15 minutes after a heated dispute with a teacher or fellow classmate.

Tend to a Garden

Since many schools are located in places where going outside to experience the benefits of nature is not an option, another approach is to bring nature into your office or work space (classroom, hallways, etc.). This approach may also be used when weather or time constraints are not conducive to time outside. Having a small potted garden in your office or various potted plants can promote the feeling of being in nature for students even while they are still sitting in an office or classroom setting. There is research indicating that having individuals with mental health issues tend to the needs of a plant (e.g., watering, trimming, adjusting for light needs, repotting, adding soil) or garden can promote improved mental health (Seixas, Williamson, Barker, & Vickerstaff, 2017). Additionally, just the presence of plants in an indoor setting can bring about improvement in overall psychological wellness (Bringslimark, Hartig, & Patil, 2009; Nieuwenhuis, Knight, Postmes, & Haslam, 2014).

Incredibly, some research has even indicated that briefly focusing attention on pictures of nature-based scenes such as forest, mountains, lakes,

Figure 6.2 The joy of children discovering nature can be as simple as holding a frog for the first time.

and fields can promote wellness by decreasing stress (Berg et al., 2015). Whether just using the plants or pictures in an ornamental fashion within an office or classroom or being intentional about integrating these things into activities with students, the benefits are potentially myriad. The bottom line is there are many ways to integrate nature into school and office settings in ways that promote student as well as employee well-being. Advocating for increased foliage or nature-based pictures and decorative material inside of school buildings is another approach that can parallel the way school counselors create their own office space. Have fun and be creative!

Mindfulness Meditation . . . With a Twist

Over the past decade, the rise in popularity of mindfulness and guided relaxation in schools in place of detention or other types of consequences has been well documented (Semple, Droutman, & Reid, 2016). Some schools have developed rooms where students can stop in throughout the day to take part in mindfulness and relaxation exercises to rejuvenate themselves or to deal with problematic emotions or thoughts. Within many of these settings, students are asked to visualize natural settings (mental imagery) and, among other things, to explore their senses, thoughts, and emotions within these mental imagery settings as a way to help bring them into the present moment rather than focusing on the past or future, places that often trigger depression and anxiety. Many times, these rejuvenating school settings are staffed by a school counselor or another mental health professional who has some basic knowledge and/or training related to mindfulness and guided relaxation.

These types of exercises can also be used in classroom settings by teachers or within the counseling office for individuals and groups. If possible, one might consider combining this technique with a "green" space. If leaving the school building is not a possibility, simply using a sound machine (or app) that produces sounds of nature (e.g., rain falling, thunder, a running creek) or cracking a window to let the sounds and smells of the outdoors into the classroom or office can be helpful and bring parts the natural world into the exercises.

Figure 6.3 Children feel grounded with the earth beneath their body.

Bringing Nature Indoors... Part 2

As mentioned before, simply having images of greenery around the office can improve well-being. The space in which you are working with students is nearly as important as the work you are doing with them. When options are limited for outside excursions, bring nature indoors! Sandplay has been a widely trusted therapy technique with children and is a variation on naturally occurring soil. Developing children need tactile input, and for many, this can provide a sense of calm (Momeni & Kahrizi, 2015). Aside from sand (or clay), you may also consider having a container of leaves, grass, rocks, or pebbles handy. These various natural objects can be used in a variety of ways. For example, children may use these items as nature-made "fidget" tools. You can also incorporate them metaphorically into counseling through the use of the sandtray or other creative means. You might also allow for free exploration of these nature-based items. Performing swap-outs of everyday items, for example, twigs in place of craft sticks, is an inexpensive and rewarding trick to incorporating products of nature in the counseling office. Albeit buckets of sand, water, leaves, or rocks found outside may be messy, these types of natural objects as primary or supplemental material in the counseling context are beneficial.

CONCLUSION

In this chapter, the benefits of nature related to student development and learning were discussed. As stated, a growing body of research has demonstrated the impact of mental health on learning and social engagement in the school environment. Various studies as well as anecdotal evidence indicate that exposing students to appropriate natural settings and nature-based activities can improve mental health issues such as depression and anxiety and bring about positive changes for students in the school environment. Additionally, various nature-based activities were discussed to aid the reader in integrating nature into their work in school settings.

CASE STUDY

JD was a sophomore at a high school in the northeastern United States. He had transferred to the school during seventh grade and had, since the beginning, experienced social issues, such as verbal and physical fights with peers, being disrespectful toward teachers, and consistently earning average to below average grades and test scores even though he had performed well on school-based aptitude tests. JD lived with his single mother and had limited interaction with his father; his dad lived in another state. His mother was an administrator in a local city school district and was at her "wit's end" related to the issues that her son consistently had at school as well as at home. Mom reported that she had trouble controlling him at home (getting him to do homework, talking about what had happened at school, cleaning up after himself, and being respectful), and he was quick to anger when "things don't go his way"; however, she said he had more problems at school. Many of the teachers in the high school knew JD by reputation and a few discussed how they had "tried to connect and help him" but had finally "given up" because they grew so frustrated with his "attitude" and "behavior" in the classroom and halls. His name was consistently brought up in the faculty lounge and not for good reasons! JD did play on the JV football team (the one extracurricular activity he did) and did reasonably well as one of its starting wide receivers; however, even the football coach—a very laid-back guy and the high school vice principal—had benched JD in the past and had reprimanded him during games and practices numerous times due to his "bad attitude."

My work with JD began during his sophomore year after he was transferred to me when his ninth-grade counselor retired. Upon meeting with JD a couple of times, he stated that he always felt extremely "anxious" when he was at school and felt like he always had to be "protecting himself" because people always "mess with me." JD did not view the school as a safe place, and he was regularly in what he called a "ready to beat ass" mindset as he sat in class, ate in the cafeteria, and walked the halls. It also became clear that JD's issues were emanating from several places. First, JD struggled with his sense of identity. As a light-skinned African American (his mom was Caucasian and dad was African American), he felt like he didn't really fit in with the other "black kids" and believed he wasn't really a "white kid" either. Having moved to the district in seventh grade, he felt like he had started from a place of disadvantage socially and had never really been able to catch up, as many of the students in his classes had known each other since kindergarten or before. Additionally, JD had been diagnosed with attention deficit hyperactivity disorder in fifth grade by his pediatrician and was fairly consistent with his medication (20 milligrams methylphenidate XR). His dosage had remained the same for about a year, and he reported that it did help him with his focus and gave him a boost of energy.

I understood from JD's history with his past counselors, faculty, and administrators that I needed to approach our work together in a novel way. Luckily, I had recently read Richard Louv's *Last Child in the Woods: Saving*

Our Children from Nature Deficit Disorder and was full of ideas related to integrating nature into my work with students. I had always been good at connecting with what a few of my colleagues termed "the naughty students," but I felt that mixing up my usual approach with JD was going to be necessary in order to create a strong, trusting relationship as well as to work toward helping him find more success socially and academically in school.

I was hesitant to get him involved with any of my counseling groups (one of which intentionally utilized the outdoors as an intervention) because he had such problematic relationships with peers. During our first meeting, after asking if he would be open to doing so and getting permission from the building principal, I took JD outside to the wooded area behind the building, a place that has several paths. As we walked one of the paths that first day we discussed his experiences in the school district and what he was hoping to get out of our time together. He stated that he had "no idea" and that he "hated school" and wished he could just "drop out." He had been assigned to see me once a week for 20 to 30 minutes during his lunch by the assistant principal (his football coach) as a way to help him transition into and find success during his 10th-grade year. When we were done with our walk, I asked him how it felt to be outdoors, and he said that he liked being outside of the school walls and that he felt more relaxed. I asked him if he would like to meet outdoors—weather permitting—for our sessions, and he quickly said yes.

Over the next few meetings we simply walked the paths behind the school and talked about his overall life, his school experiences, football (he was a big NFL Eagles fan), and anything else that was on his mind; I didn't push anything in particular. JD always seemed to me to be in a better place emotionally and cognitively after our walks outside. Additionally, I always asked him how he was feeling prior to our walks using a 1 to 5 Likert scale (1 = totally chill to 5 = panic mode), and his level of stress and anxiety almost always decreased after our walks when I checked in again using the Likert scale.

I checked in several times and asked what it was about our time together that he believed assisted his emotional and mental state, and he consistently said that the combination of talking about things freely with me and being outside helped him feel better about his life. As time progressed, we had days when going outside was not an option. On those days, we used a sound machine in my office that created the sound of a rainforest, thunderstorm, rain, running creek, or ocean waves. JD said he liked the natural sounds and felt that although he found it annoying at first, especially since he would rather be outside, he ended up "getting into it" as time went by, and he enjoyed choosing what nature sound would be playing on the sound machine during our time together. We also had indoor days when we integrated guided imagery consisting of the imagining the paths (using all five senses) we walked when outside. On these days, we would usually start our time together by closing our eyes and taking turns guiding the other using words through a part of one of the paths. At first JD was hesitant to be the leader during these 2- to 3-minute activities; however, after I had modeled it a few times, he was willing to give it a try.

Of course, some of our discussions and work related to his sense of identity, mediating here-and-now issues with teachers, and problem-solving issues in his classes (getting behind on homework, etc.); however, we spent much of our time doing these in the natural setting behind the school, listening to the sounds of nature, and doing activities like guided imagery. Although JD still had issues with peers, struggles in the classroom academically, and a few run-ins with teachers, he demonstrated measurable improvement related to attendance, GPA, and the number of overall conflicts with others. Unfortunately, due to a change in JD's mom's work and living circumstances, JD had to leave during the summer between his sophomore and junior year to live with his dad in another state. We never got to say goodbye as he left school at the end of his sophomore year not knowing when he would be back.

It was four years later that I received a letter from JD. He had received his high school diploma and had opted to join the Marines. In the letter he stated that he only made it through high school because of the time we had spent together. He said that when he arrived at his new school and was assigned a counselor, they worked out a deal where he could go stand, walk, or sit in the senior garden when he became frustrated or just needed a break—as long as he didn't misuse this privilege. He explained to the counselor that being in this type of setting helped him "do better in school" and "not get in fights." JD said that he would never forget our walks together and many times thought of our time together when he was outside in a natural setting. He included a picture of him in his Marine uniform and, sure enough, he posed for the picture standing outside in front of some trees and other foliage—very fitting, even if he had not consciously done this for any reason in particular.

REFERENCES

Barton, J., & Pretty, J. (2010). What is the best dose of nature and green exercise for improving mental health? A multi-study analysis. *Environmental Science & Technology,*44(10), 3947–3955. doi:10.1021/es903183r.

Berg, M. V., Maas, J., Muller, R., Braun, A., Kaandorp, W., Lien, R. V., . . . Berg, A. V. (2015). Autonomic nervous system responses to viewing green and built settings: Differentiating between sympathetic and parasympathetic activity. *International Journal of Environmental Research and Public Health, 12*(12), 15860–15874. doi:10.3390/ijerph121215026.

Bratman, G. N., Hamilton, J. P., Hahn, K. S., Daily, G. C., & Gross, J. J. (2015). Nature experience reduces rumination and sub-genual prefrontal cortex activation. *Proceedings of the National Academy of Sciences of the United States of America, 112*(28), 8567–8572. doi:10.1073/pnas.1510459112.

Bringslimark, T., Hartig, T., & Patil, G. G. (2009). The psychological benefits of indoor plants: A critical review of the experimental literature. *Journal of Environmental Psychology, 29*, 422–433.

Campbell, S. B., & von Stauffenberg, C. (2007). Child characteristics and family processes that predict behavioral readiness for school. In A. Booth & A. C. Crouter (Eds.), *Disparities in school readiness: How families contribute to transitions into school* (pp. 225–258). Mahwah, NJ: Lawrence Erlbaum.

Center for Psychiatric Rehabilitation. (n.d.). How does mental illness interfere with school performance? Retrieved from https://cpr.bu.edu/resources/reasonable-accommodations/how-does-mental-illness-interfere-with-school-performance/

Desjardins, J. (2018, May 5). Ranked: The 10 wealthiest countries in the world. Retrieved from http://www.visualcapitalist.com/chart-the-10-wealthiest-countries-in-the-world/

Dettweiler, U., Becker, C., Auestad, B. H., Simon, P., & Kirsch, P. (2017). Stress in school: Some empirical hints on the circadian cortisol rhythm of children in outdoor and indoor classes. *International Journal of Environmental Resources in Public Health, 14*(5), 476–500. doi:10.3390/ijerph14050475

Dettweiler, D., Lauterbach, G., Becker, C., & Simon, P. (2017). A Bayesian mixed-methods analysis of basic psychological needs satisfaction through outdoor learning and its influence on motivational behavior in science class. *Frontiers in Psychology, 8*, 2235. doi:10.3389/fpsyg.2017.02235/full

Dettweiler, U., Ünlü, A., Lauterbach, G., Becker, C., & Gschrey, B. (2015). Investigating the motivational behavior of pupils during outdoor science teaching within self-determination theory. *Frontiers in Psychology, 6*. doi:10.3389/fpsyg.2015.00125

Flom, B., Johnson, C., Hubbard, J., & Reidt, D. (2011). The natural school counselor: Using nature to promote mental health in schools. *Journal of Creativity in Mental Health, 6*(2), 118–131. doi:10.1080/15401383.2011.57969

Holt, S. (2015). Cochrane corner commentary: Light therapy for non-seasonal depression. *Advances in Integrative Medicine, 2*(1), 66–67. doi:10.1016/j.aimed.2015.02.003.

Juster, F. T., Ono, H., & Stafford, F. P. (2004). *Changing times of American youth: 1981–2003*. Institute for Social Research, University of Michigan, Ann Arbor, Michigan, 1–15.

Funk, C., & Rainie, L. (2018, April 26). Public and scientists' views on science and society. Pew Research Center. Retrieved from http://www.pewinternet.org/2015/01/29/public-and-scientists-views-on-science-and-society/

Kuo, M., Browning, M. H., & Penner, M. L. (2018). Do Lessons in Nature Boost Subsequent Classroom Engagement? Refueling Students in Flight. *Frontiers in Psychololgy, 8*(2253). doi:10.3389/fpsyg.2017.02253

Li, D., & Sullivan, W. C. (2016). Impact of views to school landscapes on recovery from stress and mental fatigue. *Landscape and Urban Planning, 148*, 149–158. doi:10.1016/j.landurbplan.2015.12.015

McCurdy, L. E., Winterbottom, K. E., Mehta, S. S., & Roberts, J. R. (2010). Using nature and outdoor activity to improve children's health. *Current Problems in Pediatric and Adolescent Health Care, 40*(5), 102–117.

Louv, R. (2008). *Last child in the woods: Saving our children from nature-deficit disorder*. Chapel Hill, NC: Algonquin books.

Louv, R. (2015, September 12). Back to school, forward to nature:: Ten ways teachers can fortify their students with vitamin N. Retrieved from https://www.childrenandnature.org/2015/08/16/back-to-school-forward-to-nature-ten-ways-teachers-can-fortify-their-students-with-vitamin-n/

Love, R. J. (2004). The predictive relationship of self-efficacy, disruptive classroom behavior, self-reported grade point average and school attendance with working alliance among at-risk high school students. *Dissertation Abstracts International: Section B: The Sciences and Engineering*. ProQuest Information & Learning. Retrieved from https://login.ezproxy.oswego.edu/login?url=http://search.ebscohost.com/login.aspx?direct=true&db=psyh&AN=2004-99020-344&site=ehost-live&scope=site

Maas, J., Verheij, R. A., de Vries, S., Spreeuwenberg, P., Schellevis, F. G., & Groenewegen, P. P. (2009). Morbidity is related to a green living environment. *Journal of Epidemiology & Community Health, 63*(12), 967–973.

McLeod, J. D., Uemura, R., & Rohrman, S. (2012). Adolescent mental health, behavior problems, and academic achievement. *Journal of Health and Social Behavior, 53*(4), 482–497. doi:10.1177/0022146512462888

Momeni, K., & Somaye, K. (2015). The effectiveness of sand play therapy on the reduction of aggression in preschool children. *Quarterly Developmental Psychology: (Journal of Iranian Psychologists), 11*(42), 147–157.

Merikangas, K. R., He, J., Burstein, M., Swanson, S. A., Avenevoli, S., Cui, L., ... Swendsen, J. (2010). Lifetime prevalence of mental disorders in U.S. adolescents: Results from the National Comorbidity Survey Replication–Adolescent Supplement (NCS-A). *Journal of the American Academy of Child & Adolescent Psychiatry, 49*(10), 980–989. doi:10.1016/j.jaac.2010.05.017

Nieuwenhuis, M., Knight, C., Postmes, T., & Haslam, S. A. (2014). The relative benefits of green versus lean office space: Three field experiments. *Journal of Experimental Psychology: Applied, 20*(3), 199–214. doi:10.1037/xap0000024.

Public School Review. (n.d.). Average public school student size. Retrieved from https://www.publicschoolreview.com/average-school-size-stats/national-data.

Seixas, M. D., Williamson, D., Barker, G., & Vickerstaff, R. (2017). Horticultural therapy in a psychiatric in-patient setting. *BJPsych. International, 14*(4), 87–89. doi:10.1192/s2056474000002087.

Semple, R. J., Droutman, V., & Reid, B. A. (2017). Mindfulness goes to school: Things learned (so far) from research and real-world experiences. *Psychology in the Schools, 54*(1), 29–52. https://doi.org/10.1002/pits.21981.

Wiliam, D. (2010). Standardized testing and school accountability. *Educational Psychologist, 45*(2), 107–122. https://doi.org/10.1080/00461521003703060.

CHAPTER 6A

THE JOY OF EXPLORATION: ECOTHERAPY WITH MIDDLE SCHOOL CHILDREN

Cory Brosch

Living on a dead-end street flanked by cornfields in a small rural/suburban town in central New York, I spent my childhood outside regardless of the season. My father, a dentist who was an entomologist at heart, and my mother, a teacher with an artist's soul, infused respect and consideration for the natural world in every aspect of our lives. Our modest ranch home was situated on a three-quarter acre lot. We had a vegetable and herb garden, fruit trees, grape vines, chickens, a goat, rabbits, and a dog. Amid all of this, the best part of my childhood home was the adjacent vacant lot.

This small lot had trees to climb, a small creek that changed with the season, wildflowers to pick, and soft grassy areas in which to sit and think. While it was right next door to my house, I could feel a million miles away and on my own. In some parts among the cottonwood trees, I could not see my house. I built forts, threw rocks in the creek, caught frogs, and built dams. I could spend hours in that lot just observing nature. Some days would be for self-reflection and contemplation, feeling small in a big world. Other days, I would make new discoveries whether it was a new bird nest or that Joe Pye weeds have hollow stems. I felt free and developed a sense of self as well as a feeling of connection to other living things. As a child, I had no idea how important my own little realm would be to who I would become.

I began college as a biology major. While I loved each biology course, I felt a desire to pursue elementary education. With my education in elementary education as well as my experience in the classroom, I understood the importance of outdoor recess, hands-on learning, and a child's natural attraction to animals. I often took my students on walks and infused nature and the outdoors into lesson planning. When I had my own children, I wanted the same personal nature experience for them. I bought a house adjacent to a nature preserve owned by the school district. This preserve was also adjacent to the middle school. The trail from my yard connected to the trails of the preserve. My children began to have their own natural space to explore and experiment. I developed a new understanding and appreciation from my view of watching them interact with nature. When my children were outside, they were so happy. They got along better with each other. They seemed to be able to focus for hours on an activity. Best of all for any mother of young boys, they slept well at night.

Little did I know at the time that this house–nature preserve trail connection would parallel my career path and professional projects. I decided to return to college to get a second master's degree in counseling. During my graduate studies, I came across a small blurb about ecotherapy. This blurb was a beacon to me. I wanted to learn all I could about this type of counseling. At the time, there was little research, but what I did learn resonated in my soul. Ecotherapy was a culmination of all my studies in biology, education, and counseling. In biology classes, I learned that species are connected to their habitats and climates. Behaviors are related to survival. In the classroom, it was evident that students did not learn in a vacuum. Their family systems, personality, and the school environment all contribute to a student's success. As a clinical mental health counselor, I learned that a client's personal coping skills, family system, culture, and life's experience all factor into the process of change and growth. Ecotherapy stresses the importance of an individual's connection to the natural world and the state of the global environment to his or her mental health. Ecotherapy seemed to be where I was heading since childhood in that vacant lot.

MIDDLE SCHOOL ECOTHERAPY GROUPS

During my master's program for mental health counseling, I was fortunate to do an independent study in ecotherapy. As a project for the independent study, I went to the local middle school, which has its own nature preserve—a nature preserve I was familiar with because it was connected to my property. This middle school consists of only seventh and eighth graders. For the seventh graders, this is the first time in their school lives that they do not get a daily recess. At the time of my project, the seventh graders had an advisory period built into their schedule for career guidance, extra help, and other programs. Some students were fortunate enough to have advisory scheduled before or after lunch. The school counselors selected students with that type of schedule, which gave me almost an hour and half to work with the students. The school counselors referred students who were struggling with self-esteem and/or anxiety challenges that interfered with their school achievement. I ran two groups using ecotherapy interventions to help with self-esteem as well as anxiety symptoms. One group consisted of three students who struggled with mainly internalizing symptoms of stress and anxiety including feelings of sadness, being withdrawn, loneliness, and somatic complaints. The second group was comprised of three students whose anxiety manifested externally as behavioral difficulties, acting out, and aggressiveness. The groups were held two times per week for five weeks. My teaching background was helpful in planning and organizing sessions to utilize our time in the most efficient way. Sessions began with an introduction and check-in while students ate their lunches, followed by an ecotherapy activity that incorporated a specific topic and closed with a group discussion and conclusion or check-out.

ECOTHERAPY ACTIVITIES

On the first day of the group, the students were unsure of what to expect. I began with an introduction to the group, including psychoeducation about stress, anxiety, and depression; ecotherapy; and group expectations. After the talk, I took the group outside. As a teacher and a counselor, I strive to meet my students or clients where they are. I can't expect a student to read if they don't know letters and sounds. With ecotherapy, I also meet the clients where they are. I need to understand their comfort and connection to the natural world. I started with a simple color walk. Students were instructed to choose a color. As we walked around the school grounds, they were to take notice of as many objects as they could find of their chosen color. They were to call out the object and color as they noticed it. Students became competitive as we walked. We ended the walk by sitting at a picnic table discussing the experience. Students who were quiet and hesitant at the beginning of the session were talkative and cheerful for this closing discussion. The activity helped to bring awareness of the outside world and expand their observational skills. I was also able to gauge any discomfort for parts of nature, such as a fear of bees or a disgust of mud. I was also able to discover knowledge by how students labeled what they saw.

INCORPORATING MINDFULNESS

Throughout the next 5 weeks, most activities were held outdoors. During the second session, one student suggested they bring their lunch outside to have more time in the outdoors. Eating outside became a therapeutic part of the group. Many of the ecotherapy activities planned for the groups incorporated mindfulness. For example, during one session we laid in the grass looking up at the blue sky with white fluffy clouds. As we watched the clouds float by, coming and going from our view, I introduced mindfulness skills of being aware of our thoughts and feelings without having to act. Students remarked on the calmness they felt. I reinforced the relaxing qualities of watching clouds as well as the students' ability to generalize this activity by encouraging them to do this at home or anytime they were outside or near a window. A second mindfulness activity the group enjoyed was incorporating a breathing exercise with awareness of the outside world. As a group, we practiced deep breathing. On the inhalation, students were instructed to close their eyes. With a pause to hold the breath, they were instructed to open their eyes and be aware of the world around them. After the exhalation, they were to finish the statement, "I notice." Bringing attention to the present seems to be easier in nature. Students had a wide range of observations in this activity. Another breathing activity helped to differentiate internal observations and external observations. On the inhalation, students were instructed to take notice of what was going on the inside, such as thoughts, feelings, tension, pain, and so on. On the exhalation, they were instructed to take notice of sensations from their environment, such as birds singing, the sun on their faces, the feel of the ground on their feet, and the smell of the pine trees.

THE USE OF NATURE METAPHORS

Nature is often filled with survival and coping metaphors. During one session, we took a walk focusing on trees. We noticed trees that swayed in the wind, trees that grew out of fallen trees, and trees with broken limbs. We discussed lessons we could learn from trees about coping and surviving. Students became talkative and silly at times. By the end of the session, students were able to apply a lesson to their own lives. One student pointed out that when a wind comes, a tree just sways with the wind because it cannot move or go somewhere else. This opened a discussed on how to deal with problems at school or home when we can't just leave. We all practiced being a tree, sitting or standing in place, letting the wind blow or bugs fly around us.

ECOTHERAPY ACTIVITIES INDOORS

Because I could not control the weather, I had an activity on hand that could be held indoors. One rainy day with thunderstorms, it was clear to me and the students that we would not be venturing into the woods. They were clearly downtrodden and disappointed. While they ate lunch in the classroom, we were able to discuss what being outside has meant to them. I surprised them with seed-starting kits. Each student had a seed tray to fill with dirt, using his or her bare hands. Some students were hesitant to get dirty at first, but once they touched the dirt and held it in their hands, they relaxed. Students picked the seeds they would like to plant. It became apparent that, for some students, this was their first experience planting. Others discussed having gardens at home. As a group we discussed what their seeds needed to sprout. We furthered this to discuss what the students needed to sprout and grow. Some students gave concrete answers of food, water, and clothes. Others gave abstract answers of freedom, creativity, respect, and knowledge. During subsequent meetings after this activity, students were excited to discuss the progress of their seeds. During group discussion, I focused my reflections on their hope, awareness of self and others, and nurturing a resilient spirit.

ECOTHERAPY ACTIVITIES THAT FOSTER RESILIENCE

Planting seeds not only taught the students about what a plant needs to thrive but also prompted the students to consider what they need to thrive and become the best versions of themselves. Making connections from the planting activity to their own lives, I facilitated a discussion on not only what we need to thrive but also barriers to our growth, specifically negative self-talk. We took a walk to different flower beds on the school property. I pointed out the weeds. We discussed how weeds get in the way of the flowers. Students used words like "suffocate," "take away sunshine," "crowd," and "hog the nutrients." We took out the weeds in the flower bed to give the plants space to grow and bloom. I used the term "mental weeds" to discuss negative self-talk. Students shared some of their own mental weeds that get in the way of self-esteem. Students connected with the idea that good self-esteem is necessary to thrive, or "bloom."

THE JOY OF EXPLORATION

While all my sessions were planned and I had activities in mind, I quickly learned after a few sessions how green my students were to the outside world. The wonder for the natural world was palpable. Many of the students did not have a vacant lot like I did to explore and learn about the outdoors. In the nature preserve, there was a pond. It had a small deck that overlooked the water. We would use this space to eat and have group discussions. On one sunny day, turtles were sunning themselves on a log. The group was captivated. All they wanted to do was find turtles and frogs. I quickly adapted that day's activity to accommodate this curiosity. I was amazed at how quickly this group of self-conscious adolescents lost their concerns about peer opinions and what is cool. The joy of exploration emerged, and they were carefree. They were excited to share their discoveries with their groupmates. Complacency quickly turned to passion and exuberance. Later sessions' formats were adjusted to incorporate free time for ecoplay. This free time, even if only 10 minutes, was some of the most valued time by the group.

In summary, the two groups engaged in activities that increased their connection to nature and also incorporated meditation, mindfulness, exploration, teambuilding, and appreciation for other living things. Through experiencing nature together, a cohesiveness among the members of the groups emerged. Students who were not friends became close in the group. Group members began to be open about their own lives and struggles. Students reported feeling more relaxed and happier on group days. I found myself also feeling happier after spending a session in the woods with the group. Nurturing this connection to the natural world improved students' functioning in school as well as their overall well-being. Upon termination of the group, students reported fewer feelings of anxiety, stress, and worry. Natural environments can be restorative and healing and foster a deeper connection with self and others.

CHAPTER 7

Nature-Based Interventions for the Military/Veteran Population

NICOLE M. ARCURI SANDERS
AND KELLIE FORZIAT-PYTEL

INTRODUCTION

A variety of theories and techniques are applicable for counseling individuals who are part of the active military (i.e., active duty service member [known as "service member" throughout], guard, or reserve) and veteran population. A more recent approach to working with this population includes nature-based interventions. Nature-based interventions are applicable for service members or veterans, their spouses, and their child(ren), and they can be used in individual, couple, or family-based counseling services. As discussed in previous chapters, nature-based interventions bring about psychological healing through the relationship that individuals have with nature (Buzzell & Chalquist, 2009). Individuals in the military population face unique stressors directly linked to the components of military culture and the military lifestyle (Hall, 2016). The approach of using nature-based interventions with this population may not be a new concept to researchers and mental health providers, but there are limited published research studies on its use and effectiveness. In more recent years, some research has shed light on using nature-based interventions with veterans, but little information is available pertaining to counseling work with the service member, spouse, children, and family as a whole. In this chapter, several connections are discussed including (a) military culture as it relates to counseling and the use of nature-based approaches, (b) military specific mental health issues, (c) two interventions to highlight nature-based approaches, and (d) why research related to this topic and population may be scarce.

MILITARY CULTURE

We live in a world full of cultures that dictate how we function in everyday living. All of us have our own unique belief systems, values, traditions, and language that has developed overtime based on the context in which we live (Hays & Erford, 2014). The military culture mimics this idea; the military is founded on its own beliefs, values, traditions, language, and even laws (Exum, Coll, & Weiss, 2011; Gooddale, Abb, & Moyer, 2012). Service members' worldview and behavior is formed by this culture (Greenberg, Langston, & Gould, 2007). For most individuals, outside of this culture (i.e., "civilians"), it may be misunderstood. Important components of this culture include a shared sense of purpose surrounding a mission, the attitude of a warrior, a tight sense of community, intense training, frequent moving, and a hierarchy chain of command that dictates the service members every move (Hall, 2016).

The military emphasizes training and commitment of soldiers to the missions at stake. As a result, service members are disbursed all around the world in order to fulfill these missions; this is referred to as a *deployment* (Blaisure, Saathoff-Wells, Pereira, MacDermid Wadsworth, & Dombro, 2012). Deployments vary in terms of location, length, and purpose (Department of Defense [DoD], 2012). For example, one service member may deploy to Yuma, Arizona, in the United States (state-side deployment) for three months for an operational training mission whereas another service member may deploy to Izmir in Turkey for an overseas combat mission. Some deployments are combat related while others are not. Despite the type of deployment, psychologically, the service member experiences stress. Service members experiencing operational or combat-related deployments are exposed to prolonged separation and lack of communication from support systems, reduced quality of life, numerous high-stress situations, and exposure to environmental stressors (Psychological Health Center of Excellence [PHCoE], n.d.). For combat deployments, service members also may experience stressors related to personal injury, moral injury (i.e., responsible for death), and witnessing the death of others (Drescher et al., 2011; PHCoE, n.d.).

When training and a mission is involved, spouses and children also have a mission to support their service member from home. For example, the service member will be away from their home frequently based on where their mission takes him or her. The family has to adjust to this separation and remain in support of the service member as he or she is gone, even though there may be times where that service member is really needed at home (i.e., to help with the children at home) (Laser & Stephens, 2011; Lester & Flake, 2013; Pryce et al., 2012).

To be successful working with this culture, counselors must have a thorough understanding of the language (e.g., acronyms), a general understanding of military occupational specialties (i.e., jobs within the military), rank (which shows skill and status within), and military installation operations (e.g., chain of command, laws and regulations) (Blaisure et al., 2012). Culture impacts the service member and the family; all family members are impacted individually and as a family unit. This is outlined next.

Service Members/Veterans

Just like choosing any other job, the military service member chooses the military for a number of different reasons. Common reasons for joining may having prior family members who serve or served, benefits (e.g., healthcare and educational funds), identity, as a way of leaving a current life situation (Hall, 2016), travel opportunities, and patriotism (Exum, Coll, & Weiss, 2011). In respect to current life situation, the reasons to seek service can vary; for example, individuals may want to escape their local community, family dynamics, economic restrictiveness due to location, or a multitude of other conditions. However, those in this situation see this opportunity as a chance to change the path of their future. The service member may join by enlisting or commissioning; this difference is determined by level of skill and educational level entering the service (Pryce et al., 2012; Today'sMilitary.com, 2017).

After an individual enlists as a soldier/sailor/airman, or commissions as an officer in any of the branches of service, the military then has the ability to dictate that person's entire life and, by extension, the lives of his or her spouse and children. Service members must view the military and their assigned unit's mission as the top priority (Blaisure et al., 2012). Service members live with discipline and personal sacrifice, giving up their rights to important things such as privacy, a political voice, family time, and, in combat situations, their life (Blaisure et al., 2012). Cultures that exist among branches should be explored too, as this may impact the service member's values and mottos for life; additionally this will help paint a picture of the surrounding job/life mission (U.S. Department of Veterans Affairs, 2014).

Service members may be torn between what is best for the military and for their family (Blaisure et al., 2012; Hall, 2016). For example, the military family may not want to move from their current community given the support and resources they have, but the service member must move them anyway because of a transfer to another military installation. Given the military culture and lifestyle as just described, service members experience a variety of mental and physical health consequences, which are discussed in more detail later in the chapter (Blaisure et al., 2012; Exum et al., 2011; Pincus, House, Christenson, & Alder, 2001; Pryce et al., 2012).

Veterans, on the other hand, have completed their military service. They can be at various stages of the transition process back to the civilian life after many years of being part of a vastly different military culture and community. Given transition struggles or consequences of serving (e.g., trauma), they may find themselves in need of counseling services (Arcuri, Forziat, Erb, Schmouder, & Jensen, 2016).

Spouses

During the service member's active duty status, spouses have their own mission to take care of the home and the children, if applicable, during all occasions where the service member needs to be away. Spouses in the military struggle with maintaining meaningful employment (often due to moving and child care; Castaneda & Harrell, 2008), temporary single parenting, child care, and constant relocating as well as adapting to life when the service member is not there (Drummet, Coleman, & Cable, 2003; DeVoe & Ross, 2012; Faber, Willerton, Clymer, MacDermid, & Weiss, 2008). Military spouses are asked to embrace the mission as the first priority in their life; often the mission must come before their family's needs. Like the service member, the spouse may experience physical and mental health consequences due to military culture and lifestyle. Spouses not only have the ability to impact the well-being of the service member during times of separation but also the well-being of the children (Verdeli et al., 2011). Therefore, their mental health is of equal importance when considering the military's mission in which the soldier needs to be able to focus on his or her mission versus worrying about the family.

When the service member transitions to veteran status, this transition occurs for the entire family. The spouse is often used to being the sole and consistent caregiver for the home and its occupants and may therefore struggle in losing this independent role. Spouses during this transition time must also work to create a new identity in the home as well as in the civilian world while supporting the family through this process. Counselors may need to intervene to support spouses through this transition independently or as a family unit (Arcuri et al., 2016).

Children

The military lifestyle also impacts military children in similar ways to the military spouse; they must move and adapt during times when the service member is away. Given different stages of development, these children may experience consequences in their social life, emotions and behaviors, and academic success (Hall, 2016). Military children not only have frequent new homes but also new schools (Clever & Segal, 2013); specific impacts and severity are often contingent upon their developmental stage. Due to the numerous relocations, establishing and maintaining friendships may be difficult. Additionally, engaging in extracurricular activities may be challenging as relocations do not always align with sign-ups and tryouts. Another factor is schools across the United States do not have a streamlined curriculum. Therefore, children may excel in some schools while struggling to catch up at others. Due to some curriculums, classes offered during one grade vary, and therefore children may find themselves with a schedule adjustment that leaves them with students of different ages.

During times of deployment, military children are affected based on (a) their developmental stage; (b) the stay-behind parents' ability to cope and the mental health status of both parents when the service member is back home; and (c) resilience, risks involved, and the family's access to resources (Bello-Utu & DeSocio, 2015). Leaving the military lifestyle may be confusing to military children, who are used to moving frequently and having parents separated. When moving into the civilian world, they learn of a life that is more permanent in terms of surrounding people and places. They may struggle with this new understanding of life and family and therefore need help processing their thoughts and emotions through counseling resources more specific to children (Arcuri et al., 2016; Wadsworth et al., 2016).

MILITARY-SPECIFIC MENTAL HEALTH ISSUES

The military culture impacts individual's willingness to receive mental health services when issues occur, given the perception that negative consequences will occur if such action should be taken (e.g., fear of losing job or being seen as weak) (Acosta et al., 2014; Greenberg et al., 2007). For instance, if service members admit to having emotions that may distract them from fulfilling their duty to complete a mission, they can be deemed unfit for duty, which can cause them to be forced to separate from the military. This alone enforces the stigma of avoiding seeking mental health services among this population. This may be a reason why there are so many more veteran programs in comparison to active duty opportunities.

Commonly seen mental health issues in the military population for the service member and veteran include mood disorders, trauma/post-traumatic stress disorder, sexual assault, suicide, addiction, adjustment issues, and relationship concerns (Exum et al., 2011; Tanielian, Jaycox, & RAND Corporation, 2008). Other issues facing the military population are physical disabilities, the criminal justice system, homelessness, financial difficulties and career concerns, unemployment, and violence (Tanielian et al., 2008). Commonly seen mental health issues in military spouses and children are mood disorders, trauma, adjustment issues, and relationship concerns (Pincus et al., 2001; Tanielian et al., 2008). Nature-based counseling interventions are applicable for the service members/veterans and their spouses and children, as well as family unit as a whole to address these mental health issues.

When considering why mental health issues are different for this population, we must first consider the work service members do and that veterans previously did. The overall mission received by these individuals when swearing in for duty is to safeguard the country from enemies at all costs. Individuals who enlist raise their right hand and swear in for service by committing to the following statement:

> I, _____, do solemnly swear (or affirm) that I will support and defend the Constitution of the United States against all enemies, foreign and domestic; that I will bear true faith and allegiance to the same; and that I will obey the orders of the President of the United States and the orders of the officers appointed over me, according to regulations and the Uniform Code of Military Justice. So help me God.

In times of peace, these individuals train to be able to defend the country. In times of war, they defend the country. Their job contracts do not include guarantees for safety. As they take this oath, the individuals commit to the understanding that at times their life may be put in danger. This reality is known by their family. The family members are left to wonder and hope that their service member is safe whether training or defending, sometimes for short amounts of time, like days or weeks, and for others much longer, as in months.

Counseling a service member, spouse, child, or family is not drastically different from counseling those outside of this culture (Hall, 2016). Theories and techniques will be similar depending on the presenting issues. For example, if you are treating a service member for anxiety, the techniques (e.g., cognitive behavioral therapy [CBT]) that you use will not be much different from the techniques you use with another client outside of this culture. The big difference is that you understand the client and/or the family's unique military culture, and its implications, and treat the client in a culturally sensitive and appropriate way (American Counseling Association [ACA], 2014, A.2.c., E.8.; Exum et al., 2011; Hall, 2016; Pryce et al., 2012).

COUNSELING MILITARY INDIVIDUALS USING NATURE-BASED INTERVENTIONS

The literature includes research using nature-based interventions with military veterans; however, there is little information on nature-based interventions with service members and their spouses and children. For service members, inadequate research exists concerning nature-based therapy's impact on the individual. Perhaps this is due to the stigma associated with mental health treatment for this population, especially since nature-based therapy occurs in nature, where treatment may be visible to others.

To understand how the military culture embraces nature-based interventions, research efforts must be broader. Seeking the discovery of mental health interventions when working with this population leads to the identification of numerous activities that occur in nature. For instance, wilderness-based experiences have been noted as being therapeutic. Additionally, recreation sport participation, including adaptive sports, have proved to be therapeutic (e.g., Wasatch Adaptive Sports: Veteran's Program). Programs are available to both male and female veterans and consist of activities held in nature spanning the four seasons (e.g., Sierra Club: Military Outdoors). Animal-assisted therapies (AATs) have reported profound therapeutic effects for service members in the field and combat and wounded veterans (e.g., Heroes and Horses and Soldier Ride). Some activities appear to test the limits of nature more than others. For instance, veterans reported therapeutic progress when climbing mountains and fly-fishing. Others found reward in team running events (e.g., Team Red, White, and Blue [Team RWB]. All of these resources have the intention to treat mental health concerns of this population while exposing them to nature.

There is little information on nature-based interventions with active military and spouses and children outside the mention of *specific programs* that are available that are designed with nature elements. For instance, Hike it Baby is a hiking club organized for spouses. Various camps are available for children that focus on completing activities that embrace nature and intend to offer children a safe place to foster their well-being (e.g., Camp Corral, Purple Camps, and Military Teen Adventures). Couple retreats are also available with the intention of fostering the well-being of the couple as a unit and process how their disconnection from their normal world when placed into a natural environment can help them identify their emotions. The family as a whole can participate in Team RWB together or with events specified for just them (i.e., children or service member). Other programs such as the Cape Fear Botanical Garden (2016) and the Brave Heart Program have the intention of allowing a safe place for the separate roles within the family as well as the family as a whole to process the stressors associated with current military life or the residual emotional factors left still to process and navigate as a veteran family.

All of these programs embrace nature and operate in accordance with Buzzell's (2016) perspective of level 1 nature-based therapy, a human-centered approach in which nature in general or a connection with nature improves mental and physical health. Analysis of our experiences in nature such as how nature affects our emotions is the baseline to explore our emotions in general along with how the absence of the natural world in other avenues of our life looks and formulates perspectives of our lives. However, first and foremost, the focus is initially exclusively the well-being of the person; this can even occur without any conscious effort.

For any client, counselors have an ethical duty to do research about the client's unique experiences (ACA, 2014, A.2.c.). With this notion, a counselor must understand that even when a client indicates his or her background stems from a specific culture, the counselor must understand that each person's experience within that culture varies. When working with the military population, the counselor is tasked with understanding the client's background culture in addition to the military culture. For instance, consider an example of client information collected during an intake. A male client presents indicating that he is 32 years of age, married, the father of two biological children, a practicing Roman Catholic, and a U.S. Marine. The client is not just a U.S. Marine nor is he just a father, spouse, or man in his 30s. All of this information is important to consider when working with the client, in addition to numerous other variables (e.g., socioeconomic status, previous trauma experience, strengths and resources). These considerations, plus many more, influence how clients perceive their world.

Taking time to understand the client as a whole is imperative to understanding the client's worldview (Quinn, 2012). Understanding what aspect of their life clients consider their *main culture* versus their *subculture* will impact how counselors can effectively provide treatment. Implementation of evidence-based treatments should align with the needs of the client (ACA, 2014, C.7.). Counselors can adapt these services to include evidence-based nature interventions to treat similar symptomology with different cultures (ACA, 2014, C.7.b). To further highlight this notion, cases are explored in this chapter with respect to the application of two nature-based interventions. The first nature-based intervention explored is an in-depth application of a horticulture approach, and the second intervention focuses on an AAT equine therapy approach.

A Horticulture Approach to Working With Military Families

Horticultural therapy is a therapeutic technique that involves gardening; it provides clients with an opportunity to examine their well-being in regards to nature's most basic elements (i.e., soil and weather) (Wise, 2015). Horticultural therapy, as applied to the military population, helps give the client a simple task that is semi-structured and relaxing in nature while also providing room for the development of trust within the therapeutic relationship. Trust is particularly important with veterans because seeking counseling has been stigmatized as a weakness. Horticultural therapy is helpful in particular when a veteran may not be ready to talk at first (Wise, 2015); instead, the veteran and therapist can work together in the garden, allowing for time and simple trust-building conversations to occur. After engaging in horticultural therapy, such as building a garden, veterans report an increased sense of purpose, skills, and wellness (Wise, 2015). When gardening in a group, research has found participants report an increased ability to engage in other social activities. For veterans, nature provided them with the opportunity to fill a void; Veterans discussed always being connected to their weapon and now without it often felt lost (Poulsen et al., 2018). Nature is one option for filling that void.

Horticultural Case Application

Brian has voluntarily sought counseling services for his family. For the past nine months, Brian indicated he was having a heightened feeling of anxiousness. He specified that when his wife would begin conversations with him about what they were going to do next after he retires from the Navy, his chest would feel tight and he would struggle to catch his breath. About eight months ago, he thought he was having a heart attack. When his wife took him to the hospital, he was diagnosed with a panic attack. He said that, after that experience, he knew the stress of leaving the Navy was getting to him. Brian shared that, despite this knowledge, he no longer shared his symptomology with others and tended to withdraw because he was not willing to risk the timeline of his separation from the military as a retiree. Now that he is fully retired from the service, he is still struggling with these pains and is experiencing a great deal of conflict with his spouse and children about what is next for the family. This is what finally made him decide it was time to seek family counseling.

Brian and his family separated from the military approximately 2 months ago. Brian is struggling with deciding his and his family's fate regarding their future. He describes himself as only knowing life as a sailor and life at sea, with very little consistent time stateside with his family. He shared that he struggles with understanding who his wife is and what she expects from him as a man, a father, and a husband. He also struggles with knowing what his children like and don't like. Brian says that he feels his family seems distant from him on a everyday basis. He worries about how his family will adjust to their new lifestyle as civilians.

Brian is a 49-year-old male. He had 20 years of service in the Navy. He describes himself as a Puerto Rican and Italian with "some other things mixed in there," but he mostly connects with his Puerto Rican culture. His wife, Sara, is a 38-year-old Caucasian female. She has been married for 20 years to Brian. Brian and Sarah have four children; all are their biological children. AJ is their 20-year-old son who lives at home and attends community college; Jessica is a 17-year-old female graduating from high school at the end of this school year; Sean is a 12-year-old male who loves sports and dislikes academics (Sean shared that he only tries so hard in school so he can play sports); and Joey is their 7-year-old son who is very attached to his mother.

As the counselor, I met with this family for eight sessions. My primary theoretical orientation stemmed from a CBT approach. Therefore, the style in which I approached the case stemmed from that mindset while using the intervention of nature.

The first session consisted of the entire family meeting with me. Each family member had the opportunity to discuss how he or she felt about the current experience of separating from the military and now being a civilian family. Each member, other than Joey, shared many fears concerning civilian life. Joey was very shy at first and sat very close to his mother while holding her arm and sometimes hiding his face behind her. As the counselor, I normalized many of their fears for them and commended them for coming in as a family to try and manage some of these fears. Each family member agreed the main purpose for counseling was to navigate what to do next as a family and try to find ways to make the house more functional. Each member shared there was a lot of conflict in the household. They were having a hard time trying to identify where the conflict was stemming from and how they could fix it. The family shared how this can be difficult to put into words sometimes, because there is so much going on in everyone's life. I provided psychoeducation concerning the importance of getting in touch with one's five senses as a way that they as individuals, as well as a family, could best navigate the presenting issues that were creating difficulty for them. I also provided some psychoeducation concerning how nature can offer them an opportunity to step outside of their normal, busy life and practice using their five senses. I explained that people tend to do their best thinking when they step outside of the business of their daily lives. Furthermore, I demonstrated what the five senses were, to ensure everyone understood, including Joey. I continued by connecting how their recent role changes within the family can impact their five senses. Each client was asked to make an "I" statement regarding one of their senses concerning their role in the family. As each family member began to share, I helped them find a common theme, and everyone discussed roles in respect to when Dad is gone. Bringing this to the family's attention was a necessity, as was discussing the goal of the family reorganizing their responsibilities so Dad is included.

I highlighted the idea of environmental changes with the use of a visualization of a garden. I then placed a large live plant in the center of the group and explained that, some days, an outside plant's soil is moist because of rain, while other days it is dry and the plant wilts due to the heat, and still other days the leaves look healthy and bright. The plant's keeper must adjust how he or she cares for the garden while taking into consideration these factors. I gave some examples of how gardeners would have to adjust how they cared for their garden based on factors beyond their control (e.g., the weather) while then transitioning the conversation to link how as a family; just like gardeners, they have had to each adjust many times to account for changes in their life because of the obligations to the armed services. I then concluded by sharing that, even though the family is changing, they can continue to use some of the skills that worked for them during military life to adjust to life without the military affiliation. I concluded this metaphor with the following statement: "Just like the plants weathered the storms, so has your family and you can do it again, but this time it will just look a little different." This was intended to explain how families, just like gardens, can be resilient. Then, while asking the family members to touch a part of the plant, I asked them to share how it impacts one of their senses. Joey jumped right in and said he felt a hole and pointed to the hole in a leaf. Joey's selected leaf appeared as if it had experienced some damage. Joey said, "But it is okay because the other leaves look good." Jessica shared that it smelled like a rainy day. Sean noted the bark was strong. AJ shared that the branch felt rigid where a branch appeared to break off. Brian said the leaves were thick. Sarah said when the wind blows in, the leaves sounded like distant wind chimes. I thanked all of the family members for being present in the moment, which is such an important aspect. I summarized their observations and reiterated that both the family and the gardeners have to work for success.

I followed this summary with the idea of having the family create their own garden to help them learn new roles for the family as a whole now without the military having a strong presence in their life. At first AJ was not on board with helping the family construct the garden, as he declared he was hoping to be away more from home. After discussing how his future plans can be represented in the garden, he agreed to partake as it might be beneficial for the family to understand what he hopes to happen with his future. Once all members of the family agreed to the creation of a family garden, I asked them to help me get a better sense of their family by hearing from them what their garden may include. Each family member named places they have lived as well as fruits and vegetables they enjoyed from each area. Each family member was asked to bring up on their cell phone a picture of a favorite tree, plant, or landscape they have lived by. Children and parents were able to google them using their iPads and smartphones. I then wrapped up the session by noting some of the differences and similarities in favorites chosen. The family and I then discussed how raising a garden takes work and, if they had a family garden, some members may be in disagreement about some of the items planted or how they took care of them. Furthermore, I shared that with their future being a bit unknown right now, for homework, they were to each individually create a garden which they wished would represent their future. Each member of the family had to note how they would like their future to be and draw an image of what their garden would look like to represent this. Each client was directed to bring this drawing to his or her next scheduled session, since I planned to meet with each member of the family individually and allow them to process their garden. (The developmental levels of all the clients were noted. Some chose to incorporate collaging and use of iPad drawing apps.) I encouraged the family members to create this visual while being outside to heighten their senses for nature and asked them to write down how they wanted their garden to affect their senses. For instance, would they like their garden to have thorns or be soft to touch?

During the second session, each family member met with me for a 25-minute individual session in which their garden was explored along with how it relates to their hopes for their future outside in the courtyard at the counseling center. AJ and Sean chose to sit under the tree. Sara, Brian, and Jessica chose to walk and talk, and Joey described his perfect garden in a sandbox with objects (e.g., sticks, leaves, flowers, and buckets for water). Each family member was asked how they felt being outside right now: what did they feel, see, smell, hear, and taste (the five senses)? Both Sara and Brian (i.e., the husband and wife as well as mother and father) noted hearing the simple things. Sara shared that at home she often has a headache since all of the children and Brian tend to be fighting for her attention. She shared she could not remember the last time she actually heard the birds singing like she does now. She indicated it feels like an escape today. She explained her garden has a very strategic layout. She wants the plants to be easy to get to and not get in the way of another plant's growth. Very similar to his wife, Brian said he actually feels like he can breathe right now. He shared that at home tension has been so thick that he feels like he is suffocating in everyone's fears of their future. Brian's garden visual was also very strategically set up. He explained the garden needs to be structured so it doesn't become overwhelming. AJ indicated that at home he feels like a prisoner to his parent's wishes. He indicated that I was the first person not telling him what to do but asking him what he wants. He noted that in this space right now he can feel hope because he doesn't feel confined. Furthermore, his garden had a lot of space between each plant. Jessica was happy to be outside. She pointed out how blue the sky was. Jessica's garden visual was very bright in color but also had distinct space between plants. Sean said he was hot and would prefer to sit in the shade. He said the breeze felt good when it came. Sean's garden was very small because he explained he does not have a lot of time to take care of it. Joey was quiet at first but then began to talk when he saw a bird land nearby the sandbox. He pointed out how sometimes birds are in gardens. He explained that he would want his garden to be nice for the birds but also give him some food. Joey's garden had a lot of color, and all of the plants were very close. It was difficult to tell which plant was which. He demonstrated how the garden could look in the sandbox. After each member met with me separately, the whole family met together for a 20-minute session.

When the whole family came together, I shared some of the similarities and differences they saw between the garden visuals. There seemed to be an overwhelming need for structure and space by many of the family members. The family members were explaining that when it is structured it is easier to move around in the garden. The discussion of size then came up. AJ was adamant that if he participates it cannot take much time because he has a lot going on. Sara seconded this notion along with Jessica. Joey was eager and said that he would like a big garden. Brian than shared the idea of each family member picking out one plant to grow in the family garden. The family members agreed that would be a reasonable and good starting point. The family then created some ground rules for their garden. They noted that each person was responsible for their own plant. Sara suggested that even though each person had their own plant, they can ask for help if needed. When Sara suggested this, she looked at her youngest child Joey. The other family members agreed that would be fine. The family came to a consensus to respect each other's plant and not invade in their space. Another rule consisted of if something is wrong with someone else's plant, they needed to tell the family member. The family agreed that they would begin to create the garden that weekend. They agreed on a place in their backyard to start it and what time the family would need to be available on Saturday to begin the project. Homework for each member was to report back concerning how the garden project went. I again encouraged the members to journal about their senses experienced when completing this project. The family was also encouraged to take pictures and/or videos of their experience.

At session three, there appeared to be a bit of tension between AJ, Brian, and Sara. When I inquired about how the experience went, Joey said that the family didn't finish and AJ didn't want to do it. AJ rolled his eyes at Joey and then stated that he had better plans with his friends and he had to leave at 5 PM but everyone got upset with him and didn't appreciate that he was helping out from the very beginning in the morning. AJ shared he got up early to help his dad clear the grass in the area where the garden was going to go, but no one cared that he did that, just that he had to leave early. Brian said that he was grateful for his help but it would have been nice to have the whole family plant their own plant together. AJ immediately snapped back at his father and shared that he has no right to want to be around now when for most of his life he was never around. AJ continued to raise his voice and share that all other house projects around the house usually consisted of him helping his mom while he was gone. AJ yelled at his Dad that he has "no right coming home now and pretending like he is this big family guy." Sara jumped in trying to deescalate a screaming match between the two. All of the other children began to withdraw in their own seats. Jessica and Sean shared they agree with AJ because when their dad was gone they relied on AJ for a lot.

Next, I had the clients explore what went well for the family during this experience. Everyone shared that they all found a plant successfully but there was some confusion if they could have the same plant. As a group they decided if anyone wanted the same plant as another it would be fine but if they can find two different kinds that would be better. For instance, if both wanted a pepper plant, one could choose a jalapeño plant and another a green pepper plant. This ended up being the case with tomatoes. Joey chose grape tomatoes and Jessica selected bigger tomatoes. They shared that this conversation went pretty well and everyone was calm during the experience at the nursery. Sara indicated that AJ and Brian were great at getting the garden prepped for the start. When I inquired about what the rest of the family was doing during the prep work, everyone other than AJ and Brian began to withdraw. Jessica said she was still sleeping. Sean said he was also sleeping. Joey said in the morning he was watching TV. Sara shared she was doing laundry and cleaning around the house. When the counselor inquired how Brian and AJ decided they would be the ones to do the prep work, Brian said it was because it would make it easier for the family to begin to plant if the grass was cleared. Brian shared that he usually does the outside work so it felt right to do. AJ shared that he actually usually does the outside work around the house and he knew if he could get it started, he could then get to his friend's place on time later that day. Jessica then began to share that she didn't want to get dirty before going to the store. The counselor explored why it was okay for AJ and Brian to go to the store dirty. Jessica shared she guessed it wasn't fair. Sean, Joey, and Sara then also began to display guilt for not helping from the start.

When I inquired about their senses involved in the process, Brian and the children all shared they chose a plant that tastes good. Sara said she chose basil because she loves the smell. The family explained that they made sure the spot had sunlight but some shade too. Jessica said it was nice to be outside in the sun planting. They explained that, after the store, AJ left but the rest of the family went in to their garden together and stood at the spot that gave others room. They all dug a hole for their plant at the same time and planted at the same time. Joey said his mom helped him make his hole bigger and that it was funny watching his sister when a worm climbed over her foot. Jessica started cringing. She explained how it felt so gross because it was so slippery on her bare foot since she was wearing sandals. All family members besides AJ laughed at this moment. Sean said he didn't realize the soil was so dry and that he had to make a lot of trips to the hose to fill up the bucket to have his cucumbers actually sink into the ground and not tip over. Sean said he was surprised how much concentration it took. When inquiring about when AJ will plant his plant, he said that night after the session.

The family then processed what it was like to be out in the garden together. The family shared how it was actually exciting to see their plant in the ground and hope that their plant really thrives. There appeared to be a bit of competition among all members about who will have the most vegetation. When processing this competition, they shared how they can make their plant be better than the others. As they discussed ways in which they can address the weather elements, they began to give each other ideas that could be helpful and shifted away from the competition. Sara shared it felt rewarding to be with her family away from to-do lists, phones, and computers; she was happy to simply strategize together. She shared that her children were listening to each other and being helpful without distractions of toys and gadgets. There was some acknowledgment from everyone that this was true for them as well. To conclude this session, I commended them for being so open as what they put into the sessions will ultimately help direct what they get from the sessions. For homework, each member was asked to journal about their experience with the garden and their senses over the next week; pictures and videos were also encouraged.

Session 3 began with AJ sharing that he planted his squash. He shared that the family left him a good space and everyone came out to watch him plant. During this time, they decided to water their plants together. They took turns with the hose and checking their plants. Jessica said she spotted some weird bugs on hers and said the leaves were getting brittle. Her mom then jumped in and said it has been very hot so the soil was dry. Jessica said it felt like gravel. Sean shared that his plant was really hanging on Monday and Tuesday and thank goodness his dad watered his plant a bit because it would have died. Sean said he was away for a track meet and completely forgot when he got home Tuesday. His dad had shared a picture of what it looked like Monday night. Joey said that after school he comes home and inspects everyone's plants and gives everyone updates. Sara said that her and her daughter had a nice conversation in the garden the other day. Jessica shared that it was nice to have some just her and Mom time. Sara shared how it was nice to talk with her daughter without TV in the background or cell phones ringing. Jessica agreed that she felt like it was good quality time. Each family member shared how they actually had a quality conversation with another family member in the garden. They were all in tune to their surrounding environment as well as the reduction of distractions in that space. They were assigned the same homework as previous sessions at the conclusion of session 3.

During session 4, the family members continued to share stories of the quality time they spent in the garden. They were very in tune to their surroundings as well as their emotions of themselves and others. During this session, there was some processing regarding how the garden has impacted family roles. All members unanimously agreed that the garden is a shared venture and one in which they enjoy spending time with one another. During this time, family members indicated they had some great talks about what their future may look like. AJ said that he had a good talk with both parents. He said he actually spoke with them both while in the garden. He shared it was the first time he felt like he had true leverage when talking with his father. He explained how he feels like he is mature and ready to venture out on his own. Both parents shared how they discussed some of their concerns but also shared how they only want the best for him. Together they decided that next semester he will try living on campus. The parents both indicated that they also spent time with each child finding out a little bit about what they would like in their future as well as what they call home. The parents noted that this time was spent with each child outside in the garden. They indicated that the space allowed them to listen fully to each other without other distractions. The family appeared at ease with the idea of possible changes, knowing that they have each other as support. During this session the family seemed a bit closer and warmer.

For session 5, Joey brought in his first tomato. He was so proud. He said that it was a lot of hard work but the tomatoes are looking great. He explained that his tomatoes taste so sweet. During this session the family continued to discuss the serenity they felt outside with one another away from the distractions of technology and other responsibilities. Jessica said she actually spent some time tanning in the backyard and saw so many beautiful butterflies paying the garden a visit. She said she didn't notice this ever before. She shared how it reminded her that butterflies change over time and become more and more beautiful. She said it gave her a strange sense of hope.

Session 6 was very similar to session 5. Discussion concerning their personal reactions to their process thus far was explored. Personal as well as whole family and subsystem (i.e., siblings, couple) cognitions and behaviors were explored for similarities and differences. A CBT ABC model was applied. The family analyzed their (a) activating events, their (b) belief/thought surrounding the event, and their (c) emotional and behavioral consequence surrounding the belief surrounding the activating event (Sharf, 2012).

During Session 6 I visited the family's garden. The session was conducted right next to their garden. There seemed to be an overwhelming easiness among each member. The clients shared how it is much more peaceful to discuss their hopes and dreams in their backyard versus the counseling office. Each family member had 15 minutes with me individually to process their experience thus far, and then everyone came together as a group. Each family member showed me what they do in their role for the garden and explained any work that needed to be done together as a subsystem and/or whole family. Discussion about their individual feelings regarding the process occurred. Discussion about each member's thoughts for their personal and their family's future were explored also, as they were working in the garden.

The family members were proud of their trials and tribulations as well as the teamwork it took to keep the garden alive. All of them seemed much clearer in their desire for the future. When coming together as a group, the clients shared they appreciate structure for their family and feel like before their garden they felt a bit unorganized and lost. They indicated that their focus on the garden has allowed for a great deal of quality time to be spent together without the distractions of their busy lives.

In session 7, I visited the garden again and facilitated the family session around the garden. We discussed the impact of the family garden and personal reactions to the process. We discussed role responsibilities and how these were symbolized by the garden in reference to their futures (i.e., thriving plants versus those that were struggling). I reminded the family that the next session would be their last, so any unfinished business they believe they needed to address should be journaled.

Session 8 was the last session for the family. I once again went to see the garden and we had a 120-minute family session around the garden. We discussed where they started and where their garden was now. Each member had the opportunity to discuss any unfinished business regarding their garden and future aspirations for themselves individually as well as for the family as a whole. We discussed moving forward and devised a plan they could all agree on concerning their garden. The family was encouraged to dialogue openly about future goals and aspirations as well as what that process may look like for individuals as well as subsystems and the family as a whole. Each member of the family was encouraged to utilize symbolism from the garden to help explain themselves when having difficulty expressing their desires.

The family as a whole appeared very calm. AJ noticeably had a better relationship with his father. What once appeared as tension between the two was now a relaxed atmosphere in which both felt comfortable joking with one another. Joey was a bit less attached to his mother and more closely connecting with his siblings. Jessica and her mother indicating that they had so many great talks together about life, wishes, hopes, dreams, and desires. They said they would like to continue spending quality time together away from the distractions of life. Sean was still very active with his school sports, but he indicated that he has been appreciating the trails he runs so much more since working in the garden. He explained that he never really knew how lucky he was to be able to run so many new places and see new things. Rather than using ear phones during practices, he said he embraces the environment now. Conversation between the family members appeared to flow much more easily and without the hesitation of offending one another. All attributed their change to the fact of being able to step away from distractions in life.

Seeing the change within this family as they worked in a garden was remarkable. With so many subsystems to consider, the ability for each family member to step into an equal playing field with a common goal was vital, and through their experience of the removal of distractions, truthful conversations about fears as well as desires were able to prosper.

Animal-Assisted Therapy

AAT occurs when animals are introduced into the healing process. Animals have been found to improve various aspects of a person's functioning whether it be social, emotional, or cognitive, and therefore they have been used in treatment of physical and/or psychological disabilities (Altschiller, 2011). For example, studies have shown that playing with a dog can reduce aggression or agitation in some populations. Depending on the animal used in therapy, this takes on a specific form such as canine-assisted therapy, equine-assisted therapy, and dolphin-assisted therapy (Altschiller, 2011; Chandler, 2017). In counseling, AAT can be applied to the various popular theories (e.g., CBT and Gestalt), processes (e.g., diagnosis and treatment), and populations with special needs (e.g., hospice and incarcerated clients) (Chandler, 2017).

AAT is another area growing in research with the military population. This is especially true for veterans who have experienced combat and trauma (Owen, Finton, Gibbons, & DeLeon, 2016). Research is looking at how animals help clients and have shown some positive links to decreasing mental health symptoms, as the animal is there to provide support and keep the individual active (Beck et al., 2012; Fike et al., 2012; Lanning & Krenek, 2013). This same research has elements of nature-based therapy because service members must be active outside in order to take care of the animal (e.g., walking, hiking, or jogging with a dog). Many researchers in the field of AAT find it hard to distinguish between the natural environment and the counselor's role, seeing the animal, nature, and the counselor as a triadic relationship (Hinds & Ranger, 2016).

Policy Trends

Recently there has been an increase in the number of counseling clients requesting letters of support from their mental health providers to allow them to have their animals with them in places where there may be restrictions (Masinter, 2017). In January 2016, the DoD released instructions regarding guidance on the use of service dogs by service members. This instruction (number V1300.27) indicates that active duty recovering service members who have medical conditions that require the assistance of a service dog for activities of daily living may utilize service dogs on DoD installations. However, each military department retains the authority over installation access, control, and domiciling for all animals other than service dogs, including therapy animals. The Commandant of the Marine Corps on July 14, 2014, discussed breed restrictions for animal assistance dogs and referred to them as companion dogs in Marine Corps Order 11000.22 (Department of Defense [DoD], 2014). These documents indicate that active duty members do indeed have animal-assisted animals, yet there is no research to document the effectiveness.

Research is growing to help support the notion that AAT for the military population is evidence based, specifically related to equine-assisted therapy and new ways to assess this (e.g., Ferruolo, 2016; Voelpel, Escallier, Fullerton, & Abitbol, 2018). Given such efforts, the U.S. House of Representatives, in June 2018, passed HR 5895 (the Military Construction and Veterans Affairs Appropriations Act), which proposed an amendment to increase funds for equine-assisted therapy as part of the Veterans Affairs' Adaptive Sports Grant Program (Committee on Rules, 2018). This increase in funding will promote the development of additional services that utilize equine-assisted therapy and mental health treatment to veterans and provide researchers more opportunity to examine how and why the approach works. This will continue to build off what is known related to the positive benefits equine-assisted therapy has been linked to for this population, such as increasing one's ability to trust, confidence, and communication skills and reducing one's anxiety and feelings of isolation (Lanning & Krenek, 2013), in addition to helping both the individual and the group become self-aware and resilient for the future (Gehrke, Noquez, Ranke, & Myers, 2018). These themes can be seen in the following example below.

Animal-Assisted Example

For understanding of this intervention's application, consider the story of Han, who is working with a counselor concerning primarily depression symptomology. Han was adopted from China at the age of 3 by an American Caucasian couple. He shared that growing up was hard for him and he never felt that he belonged in the culture he grew up in. He described his parents as loving but when he shared thoughts and feelings surrounding "not belonging," "feeling isolated by peers," and "having a hard time connecting to others," they reminded him of how lucky he was to be in the United States, in his school, and in his family. As he continued to grow up, these thoughts and feelings increased. At the age of 12 his parents got a divorce. His mother left him and his father to start a new life with a man that she had met at work. His father tried his best to take care of him, but it had been his mother who took care of both of them before that. His father grew overwhelmed in his single-parent role and began working more. By age 14, Han was taking care of himself. He had little contact with his mom because he recognized her as living a happier life without him. He wondered if she really had wanted to be a mother. This plagued him with feelings of sadness and worthlessness. He saw his mom again for the first time in two years at his high school graduation and was surprised when she showed up with her new husband and stepdaughter.

After Han graduated high school, he once again felt lost in the world. He considered college, but, given lack of finances and direction, he decided against it. Instead he worked "mediocre part-time jobs" at Best Buy and Quaker Steak for a couple of years. He continued to share a home with his father who he saw occasionally when they were both off of work. He considered his dad to be his only real friend. Han was never successful in establishing relationships with others. He was able to maintain work friends, but all romantic relationships ended given his trust issues, feelings of insecurity, and lack of emotional intimacy. Aside from working, he enjoyed alone time hiking outdoors and exercising at the gym.

One day while shopping at his local mall, Han was approached by an Army recruiter who asked him if he would be interested in learning more about military service. He was honest in that he had never thought about it as he had no prior exposure to the military. In the recruitment meeting he learned the position of an enlisted soldier and that he met all the general requirements to become an enlisted soldier in the U.S. Army. After looking more into what the military had to offer him, he decided it would be good for him. It would allow him an avenue to escape his current life and give him needed benefits of healthcare and schooling.

A year later, Han had successfully completed basic training and Air Assault School, which was physically and mentally demanding. As an Air Assault soldier, he needed to be skilled in working with heavy equipment and performing dangerous jobs under exceptionally stressful conditions. He earned his wings as an Air Assault Soldier and continued training for operation missions until he was deployed to Afghanistan to help support Afghan forces in their fight against the Taliban. During his deployment he grew close to the many other soldiers in his platoon. He enjoyed his new sense of purpose in life and finally felt like he was where he belonged. Six months into his nine-month deployment, Han was involved in a fall where he suffered a moderate spinal cord injury that started the process of him being brought home to the United States and discharged from active duty military status. In his platoon's next mission during the deployment, when Han was already back stateside, several soldiers died in an accident. Han found himself experiencing the loss with a variety of negative associated feelings such as extreme guilt over the fact that he was not there, anger, sadness, hopelessness, and physical consequences of insomnia, fatigue, and chest pain.

Han was discharged from the military and, during the several months following the accidents, engaged in multiple unsuccessful counseling relationships. He continued to struggle with issues such as (a) not often leaving his home due to loss of interest in all things he enjoyed before the military and his injury and (b) a desire to go to sleep one night and not wake up as he is, tired of fighting his chronic pain and thoughts of those he left behind who are no longer on this earth. He had admitted to his primary care provider that he wanted help but that "help has not seemed to help him," and he became discouraged. The primary care provider educated him on additional resources that the VA has to offer, aside from the current counselor he was seeing who was ineffective.

Han now finds himself in a new psychotherapy program that is equine-assisted and provides services to veterans through TRICARE insurance coverage. Most of the staff are veterans themselves and understand common situations that the clients are going through. Additionally, Han has the opportunity to work with a therapy team where he meets with an equine specialist instructor, a counselor, and a horse during treatment. This is done in a group setting. Therefore, the general structure of the program is counselor check-in, work with horse and equine specialist instructor (known as "Instructor") in group, and then staying to process anything individually if needed after the group session. Han was originally drawn to this place as it is no longer the "typical office setting that made him feel uncomfortable" because "when the door closed he became center of attention." The therapy works to allow him time with the horse and to be completely present with it in order to build a bond. Building a bond after trauma and loss with someone is often expressed as one of the hardest things; however, when this is done with the horse, it can then be translated to other relationships. Additionally, a variety of therapeutic interventions are infused into the equine program; Han also learned that equine-assisted therapy has been used as a therapy for those with physical challenges and can work to improve muscle strength and mobility, which he struggles with since his injury. He agrees to continue with the 5-month program, which meets weekly, and is hopeful this will turn into something great, "killing two birds with one stone," though he remains somewhat pessimistic that it will provide him with all the positives promoted in the introduction to the program.

In the first session, Han interacted with the horses in a limited manner. The instructor paired him up with a male named Major. The instructor shared with Han that he needed to begin to learn appropriate saddling and handling, the language of Major, and building a trusting relationship with him. Han and Major were distant from each other. Major tended to lean toward the instructor and ignore Han. Han was rather stand offish as well. After the first session Han was asked to journal about the experience and his thoughts and feelings related to it. This journal would be used to help note changes over time and possible adjustments to be made. Journaling was a familiar technique for him. Assessment of Han occurred each week by the counselor and instructor based on Han's self-reporting and their observations.

In the second session, after the counselor and Han explored his journal reflection, Han indicated that he believed Major was not interested in working with him. The instructor posed the question: "How did you show Major you were interested in working with him?" Han did not have an answer. The instructor explained to Han that a relationship with Major is just like any other relationship he seeks. Han and Major joined the other participants and their horses in the ring to engage in a trust walk; Han had to stay present and accustomed to Major through an obstacle set up and led by the instructor. The counselor helped process the activity when it was over and was always there for support when something trauma triggering occurred. Major would not jump over the stick, and he kept raising his left front leg, kicking his hoof, and retreating backwards while shaking his head. Major began to snort but Han continued to try to pull Major's rope forward. Han was angry in his tone and demanding Major to "come on," "move," and "go." When Han tried to pull Major forward with all his might using both hands on the rope, Major raised on both hind legs made a long and loud squeal and ripped the rope from Han's hands, sending him to the ground. Han quickly got up, offering Major space, and started to change his tune with Major. Rather than commanding Major to jump, he began to sooth Major by telling him "it is okay." Slowly approaching Major's rope, Han retained eye contact with Major. The instructor watched and stood by closely but did not interject; a trusting relationship was in its formation stage. Once Han got closer to Major, he continued to tell Major it would be okay and that they were okay. There appeared to be a deep understanding between the eye contact between Han and Major. For the remainder of the session, Han and Major disregarded the challenge requested of them by the instructor and instead stood quietly together as Han brushed him and talked to him. Han journaled that evening that he felt bad for Major because the instructor was trying to make him do something he is obviously afraid of. When Han came back for his third session, he shared his frustration regarding this with the instructor.

At the third session, the instructor shared that she was proud of Han for being so in tune to Major's needs. Han still did not understand why she would push Major. The instructor indicated, "I didn't; you were." Han became angered by this statement. He told her that he did no such thing. The instructor simply relied, "You were pulling the rope, not me." Han fell silent and then said, "But you told me to." The instructor explained that she told him that he and his horse had to overcome the obstacle in their path together but he chose how he wanted Major to do it. Following this conversation, Han went to visit Major in the stable. As Han brushed Major and was getting him ready to come out to the ring for another instructor-led trust exercise, he talked to Major and asked him how his day was. Han was encouraging Major that together they were going to do great in the ring. Han was sensitive to any flinching Major did and would then go softer, rubbing in those areas. When Han took the rope, Major easily followed his lead. When Major and Han got out to the ring and began the activity, Han took a moment to encourage Major that they are a team. As they together, side by side approached the stick, Major began to snort again. Han quickly turned to Major and began to brush his mane and soothe him. Han then gave the rope some slack and himself edged toward the stick. After Han took about six steps, he gave the rope a bit more slack as he saw Major was not coming and was standing firmly his ground. Han then moved the rope into his right hand and slowly began to bend down and reach out with his right hand toward the stick. Major snorted again. Han immediately stopped reaching and with a soothing tone told Major it is okay. Han then turned back to the stick and started to touch the stick. Major began to take a few steps forward. As Han continued to touch the stick, he looked back at Major and said "it's okay." Major continued to take steps forward and was finally by Han's side, leaning toward the stick and smelling it. Both Han and Major stood here together for the remainder of the 30-minute exercise. During the fourth session, Major followed Han right up to the stick. Major again snorted. Han gave the rope some slack and bent down to touch the stick while keeping eye contact with Major, telling him it was okay. Major followed by smelling the stick. Han then slowly rose, gave the rope even more slack, and then slowly put one foot over the stick, followed by the other careful, not to pull Major's rope. Han then reached to brush Major's mane and began to tell him he was okay and it was okay. Han then slowly stepped across to the other side of the stick and then continued to sooth Major by brushing his mane. Han then tightened his grip of the rope a bit and got to the side of Major. Together they took tiny steps forward. Han then loosed his grip a bit with the rope and slowly took one step over the stick. He looked back at Major and asked for him to join him. He slowly tightened his grip on Major's rope until he moved right up to the stick. Han then put his other foot over the stick and turned immediately to look at Major. Han again asked Major to come with him and ensured him that he would be okay. Han slowly took one step back, tightening his grip on the rope, and then slowly Major crossed the stick and joined Han on the other side. Once Major had all four legs over, Han congratulated him and began stroking and hugging Major.

In Han's journal entry that evening, he shared how proud he was of Major. Han also shared that he believed that Major finally trusted him and that he never thought about the trust Major needed in order to follow him when he first started working with him. He also shared that he noticed that Major responded a lot better when he asked Major to do something rather than commanding him to do it.

In the fifth session, Han excitedly reunited with Major. As Han got Major ready to join the group in the ring, he told him about his day and paid close attention to where Major appeared to enjoy the brushing, as areas that were not as enjoyable. When Han and Major joined the group, each participant was with their assigned horse by their side with space between the pairs. During this session, narrative writing was used to share emotional experiences among the group. Han was asked to bring a situation, in writing, that was emotionally challenging. He decided to talk about the guilt he carried over the loss of his friends. Horses remained close to each group member as they read their story and shared feelings. Horses' behaviors were noted as they responded to the expressions of the group members. As Han shared his story, he leaned in closer to Major when words were difficult to share. Major was open to and allowed Han to lean on him for support.

Over the next several weeks, Han continued meeting weekly with the treatment team and members of the group, sharing noteworthy changes to domains of his well-being. The instructor addressed questions, concerns, and comments Han had about the horse and occasionally led them both in activities. The counselor continued to address Han's psychosocial and physical domains with check-ins and debriefings as well as ran guided visualization, meditation, and other interventions for growth. As time went on, Major grew more responsive to Han's breathing and emotions as well as vice versa.

After the seventh session, where Han closed his eyes and was guided around by Major, he noticed that the slow rhythm was promoting relaxation and healing. Also, the slower his breath, the slower the movements of Major. The more fluid breaths also resulted in more fluid movements of Major. In his follow-up counseling session, Han reported to be experiencing positive changes to his mood and sleep in normal everyday living, as the work he did with Major helped him to better understand his emotions and reduced his feelings of isolation.

After the 16th session, Han reported that the therapy had helped to increase his self-esteem, ability to trust others, and physical and mental well-being. He pulled out his journal as proof to show that it had been almost 3 months since he held thoughts related to suicidal ideation. His depression symptoms overall seemed to be decreasing.

Over the last couple weeks, Han continued to learn about himself, Major, and the rest of his group as they engaged in the equine intervention program. By the end, all had learned about emotional triggers and ways to self-regulate skills and techniques learned. Han felt ready to move on in his life by (a) finding a job that would provide him with the accommodations that he needed and (b) trying to build relationships with others without the same past fears of "losing them" or "not being good enough" holding him back. Han continued to visit the equine center after being discharged from the program and to work individually with a counselor for support throughout his new life transitions, knowing that the infusion of nature-based techniques were what worked for him in conjunction with talk therapy.

MOVING NATURE-BASED THERAPY FORWARD WITH MILITARY/VETERAN POPULATIONS

Nature-based interventions can be incorporated into counseling military veterans, service members, spouses, children, and the family as a whole unit to promote psychological healing in their relationship with nature (Buzzell & Chalquist, 2009); often this intervention will be attached to stressors directly linked to issues related to military life. Veterans tend to like to be involved with nature in different direct activities, such as sports or horticulture. These activities moves veterans out of the counseling setting into a place that gives them time to reflect and be comforted by the surroundings of nature. With this space, veterans may feel less threatened by the therapeutic exchange, as it helps remove the traditional stigma associated with receiving mental health care. Stigma for this population comes with being seen in mental health settings and has created barriers to help-seeking given fear of social repercussions (e.g., being weak) (Zinzow, Britt, McFadden, Burnette, & Gillispie, 2012). Research has provided evidence to support changing the counseling delivery format to be more fitting for this culture such as telehealth and virtual reality, which is more interactive than traditional talk therapy (Zinzow et al., 2012). This fits with the goals and benefits of using nature-based interventions, which breaks the rules of typical office-setting counseling.

While it appears that nature-based therapies have been used with the military population over time, research on their use and effectiveness is limited. Counselors may want to use nature-based therapies but may be limited due to ethical guidelines practice/organization standards (liability issues against things such as taking clients outside for walks), funding (e.g., for equipment and space), and understanding (advocacy and research can help increase use as an intervention) (Hasbach, 2013; Reese, 2016). Sometimes when nature-based therapies are used they may not be documented as the focus of the intervention. Anecdotally, it is known that nature-based therapies are being used with the military population, including veterans, service members, spouses, and children. There are a variety of ways to incorporate nature into the counseling session, and there are many nature-based therapeutic opportunities for the service members/veterans and spouses, as well as their children. The horticultural therapy intervention, described previously, is only one such example of an approach that can be used when working with families, and the animal-assisted equine therapy example is just one example of an approach that can be used with the veteran.

We encourage interested counselors to volunteer with preestablished programs to gain insight about how each program draws the population toward the treatment and their therapeutic process within the program. As the counselor, you can gain professional development in using nature as an intervention. By infusing such nature-based therapeutic interventions in your own treatment planning with this specific population, you too can yield positive therapeutic outcomes for your clients.

REFERENCES

Acosta, J. D., Becker, A., Cerully, J. L., Fisher, M. P., Martin, L. T., Vardavas, R., . . . Schell, J. L. (2014). *Mental health stigma in the military*. Santa Monica, CA: RAND. Retrieved from https://www.rand.org/pubs/research_reports/RR426.html

Altschiller, D. (2011). *Animal-assisted therapy*. Santa Barbara, CA: Greenwood.

American Counseling Association. (2014). *ACA code of ethics*. Alexandria, VA: Author.

Arcuri, N. M., Forziat, K., Erb, C., Schmouder, S., & Jensen, B. (2016). Active duty to civilian: Family transition to veteran status. *Journal of Military and Government Counseling, 4*(1), 90–117. Retrieved from http://acegonline.org/wp-content/uploads/2013/02/JMGC-Vol-4-Is-2.pdf

Beck, C. E., Gonzales, J., Florie, Sells, C. H., Jones, C., Reer, T., & Zhu, Y. Y. (2012). The effects of animal-assisted therapy on wounded warriors in an occupational therapy life skills program. *U.S. Army Medical Department Journal, 2012*, 38–45. Retrieved from http://www.cs.amedd.army.mil/FileDownloadpublic.aspx?docid=73e8d2aa-1a2a-467d-b6e3-e73652da8622

Bello-Utu, C. F., & DeSocio, J. E. (2015). Military deployment and reintegration: A systematic review of child coping. *Journal of Child and Adolescent Psychiatric Nursing, 28*(1), 23–34. doi:10.1111/jcap.12099

Blaisure, K., Saathoff-Wells, T., Pereira, A., MacDermid Wadsworth, S., & Dombro, A. L. (2012). *Serving military families in the 21st century* (1st ed.). New York, NY: Routledge.

Buzzell, L. (2016). The many ecotherapies. In M. Jordan & J. Hinds (Eds.), *Ecotherapy: Theory, research, practice* (pp. 70–83). New York, NY: Palgrave Macmillan.

Buzzell, L., & Chalquist, C. (2009). *Ecotherapy: Healing with nature in mind*. San Francisco, CA: Sierra Club Books.

Castaneda, L. W., & Harrell, M. C. (2008). Military spouse employment: A grounded theory approach to experiences and perceptions. *Armed Forces & Society, 34*(3), 389–412. doi:10.1177/0095327X07307194

Chandler, C. K. (2017). *Animal-assisted therapy in counseling* (3rd ed.). New York, NY: Routledge.

Clever, M., & Segal, D. R. (2013). The demographics of military children and families. *The Future of Children, 23*(2), 13–39. doi:10.1353/foc.2013.0018

Committee on Rules. (2018). *H.R. 5895—Energy and Water Development and Related Agencies Appropriations Act, 2019 [Energy and Water, Legislative Branch, and*

Military Construction and Veterans Affairs Appropriations Act, 2019]. Retrieved from https://rules.house.gov/bill/115/hr-5895

Cordova, J., Miller, J., Leadbetter, G., Trombetta, S., Parks, S., & O'Hara, R. (1998). Influence of the National Disabled Veterans' Winter Sports Clinic on self-concept and leisure satisfaction of adult veterans with disabilities. *Palaestra, 14*, 40–43. Retrieved from http://ezaccess.libraries.psu.edu/login?url=https://search-proquest-com.ezaccess.libraries.psu.edu/docview/213163914?accountid=13158

Department of Defense. (2012). *Military deployment guide preparing you and your family for the road ahead*. Retrieved from http://download.militaryonesource.mil/12038/ Project%20Documents/MilitaryHOMEFRONT/Troops%20and%20Families/ Deployment%20Connections/Pre-Deployment%20Guide.pdf

Department of Defense. (2014). Marine Corps Order 11000.22. Department of the Navy: Headquarters United States Marine Corps. Retrieved from http://www.mcrdpi.marines.mil/Portals/76/Docs/Pet-Policy.pdf?ver=2017-02-22-073739-017

Department of Defense. (2016). *Department of Defense Instruction Number 1300.27*. Retrieved from http://warriorcare.dodlive.mil/files/2016/03/DoDI-Guidance-on-the-Use-of-Service-Dogs-by-Service-Members_1300.27.pdf

DeVoe, E. R., & Ross, A. (2012). The parenting cycle of deployment. *Military Medicine, 177*(2), 184–190. doi:10.7205/MILMED-D-11-00292

Drescher, K. D., Foy, D. W., Kelly, C., Leshner, A., Schutz, K., & Litz, B. (2011). An exploration of the viability and usefulness of the construct of moral injury in war veterans. *Traumatology, 17*, 8–13. doi:10.1177/1534765610395615.

Drummet, A. R., Coleman, M., & Cable, S. (2003). Military families under stress: Implications for family life education. *Family Relations, 52*(3), 279–287. doi:10.1111/j.1741-3729.2003.00279.x

Exum, H. E., Coll, J. E., & Weiss, E. L. (2011). *A civilian counselor's primer for counseling veterans* (2nd ed.). Deer Park, NY: Linus.

Faber, A. J., Willerton, E., Clymer, S. R., MacDermid, S. M., & Weiss, H. M. (2008). Ambiguous absence, ambiguous presence: A qualitative study of military reserve families in wartime. *Journal of Family Psychology, 22*(2), 222–230. doi:10.1037/0893-3200.22.2.222

Ferruolo, D. M. (2016). Psychosocial equine program for veterans. *Social Work, 61*, 53–60. doi:10.1093/sw/swv054

Fike, L., Najera, C., & Dougherty, D. (2012). Occupational therapists as dog handlers: The collective experience with animal-assisted therapy in Iraq. *U.S. Army Medical Department Journal, 2012*, 51–54. Retrieved from https://habricentral.org/resources/690/ download/fike_najera_dougherty-occupational_therapists_with_dogs_iraq.pdf

Gehrke, E. K., Noquez, A. E., Ranke, P. L., & Myers, M. P. (2018). Measuring the psychophysiological changes in combat veterans participating in an equine therapy program. *Journal of Military, Veteran and Family Health, 4*, 60–69. doi:10.3138/jmvfh.2017-0015

Gooddale, R., Abb, W. R., & Moyer, B. A. (2012). *Military culture 101: Not one culture, but many cultures*. Retrieved from http://www.citizensoldiersupport.org/lib/resources/ ORNC%20Military%20Culture%20101%20 Workshop%202014%20Sep%2012.pdf

Greenberg, N., Langston, V., & Gould, M. (2007). Culture—what is its effect on stress in the military? *Military Medicine, 172*(9), 931–935. Retrieved from http://

ezaccess.libraries.psu.edu/login?url=https://search-proquest-com.ezaccess.libraries.psu.edu/docview/ 217059096?accountid=13158

Hall, L. K. (2016). *Counseling military families: What mental health professionals need to know* (2nd ed.). New York, NY; London, England: Routledge.

Hasbach, P. H. (2013). Moving therapy outdoors: Techniques, challenges, and ethical considerations. *Voices: The Art and Science of Psychotherapy, 49*, 37–42. Retrieved from http://www.northwestecotherapy.com/wpcontent/uploads/2014/02/Voices_Spring_2013_Hasbach.pdf

Hays, D. G., & Erford, B. T. (2014). *Developing multicultural counseling competence: A systems approach* (2nd ed.). Upper Saddle River, NJ: Pearson Education.

Hinds, J., & Ranger, L. (2016). Equine-assisted therapy: Developing theoretical context. In M. Jordan & J. Hinds (Eds.), *Ecotherapy: Theory, research and practice* (pp. 187–198). New York, NY: Palgrave Macmillan.

Lanning, B. A., & Krenek, N. (2013). Examining effects of equine-assisted activities to help combat veterans improve quality of life. *Journal of Rehabilitation Research & Development, 50*(8), vii–xxii. Retrieved from http://ezaccess.libraries.psu.edu/login? url=https://search-proquest-com.ezaccess.libraries.psu.edu/docview/1492922139? accountid=13158

Laser, J. A., & Stephens, P. M. (2011). Working with military families through deployment and beyond. *Clinical Social Work Journal, 39*(1), 28–38. doi:10.1007/s10615-010-0310-5

Lester, P., & Flake, E. (2013). How wartime military service affects children and families. *The Future of Children, 23*(2), 121–141. doi:10.1353/foc.2013.0015

Masinter, M. R. (2017). Does OCR have authority to investigate emotional support animal housing complaints? *Student Affairs Today, 19*(12), 6. doi:10.1002/say.30310

Owen, R. P., Finton, B. J., Gibbons, S. W., & DeLeon, P. H. (2016). Canine-assisted adjunct therapy in the military: An intriguing alternative modality. *The Journal for Nurse Practitioners, 12*(2), 95–101. Retrieved from http://dx.doi.org.ezaccess.libraries.psu.edu/ 10.1016/j.nurpra.2015.09.014

Pincus, S. H., House, R., Christenson, J., & Alder, L. E. (2001). *The emotional cycle of deployment: A military family perspective.* Retrieved from http://www.hooah4health.com/deployment/familymatters/emotionalcycle.htm

Poulsen, D. V., Stigsdotter, U. K., & Davidsen, A. S. (2018). "That guy, is he really sick at all?" An analysis of how veterans with PTSD experience nature-based therapy. *Healthcare, 6*(2), 1–20.

Project Cohort. (n.d.). *Project Rebirth.* Retrieved from http://www.projectrebirth.org/project-cohort/

Pryce, J. G., Pryce, D. H., & Shackelford, K. K. (2012). *The costs of courage: Combat stress, warriors, and family survival.* Chicago, IL: Lyceum Books.

Psychological Health Center of Excellence. (n.d.). *Psychological health effects of deployment.* Retrieved from http://www.pdhealth.mil/clinical-guidance/deployment-health/psychological-health-effects-deployment

Quinn, A. (2012). A person-centered approach to multicultural counseling competence. *The Journal of Humanistic Psychology, 53*(2), 202–251. doi:10.1177/0022167812458452

Reese, R. F. (2016). EcoWellness & guiding principles for the ethical integration of nature into counseling. *International Journal for the Advancement of Counselling, 38*(4), 345–357. doi:10.1007/s10447-016-9276-5

Sharf, R. S. (2012). *Theories of psychotherapy and counseling* (5th ed.). Belmont, CA: Brooks/Cole Cengage Learning.

Tanielian, T. L., Jaycox, L., & RAND Corporation. (2008). *Invisible wounds of war: Psychological and cognitive injuries, their consequences, and services to assist recovery*. Santa Monica, CA: RAND.

Today'sMilitary.com. (2017). Becoming a military officer. Retrieved from http://todaysmilitary.com/joining/becoming-a-military-officer

U.S. Department of Veterans Affairs. (2014). *Understanding military culture*. Retrieved from http://www.mentalhealth.va.gov/communityproviders/military_culture.asp#sthash.94aOe2V0.dpbs

Verdeli, H., Baily, C., Vousoura, E., Belser, A., Singla, D., & Manos, G. (2011). The case for treating depression in military spouses. *Journal of Family Psychology, 25*(4), 488–496. doi:10.1037/a0024525

Voelpel, P., Escallier, L., Fullerton, J., & Abitbol, L. (2018). Interaction between veterans and horses: Perceptions of benefits. *Journal of Psychosocial Nursing and Mental Health Services, 56*(5), 7–10. doi:10.3928/02793695-20180305-05

Wadsworth, S. M., Cardin, J., Christ, S., Willerton, E., O'Grady, A. F., Topp, D., . . . Mustillo, S. (2016). Accumulation of risk and promotive factors among young children in US military families. *American Journal of Community Psychology, 57*, 190–202. doi:10.1002/ajcp.12025

Wise, J. (2015). *Digging for victory: Horticultural therapy with veterans for post-traumatic growth*. London, England: Karnac.

Zinzow, H. M., Britt, T. W., McFadden, A. C., Burnette, C. M., & Gillispie, S. (2012). Connecting active duty and returning veterans to mental health treatment: Interventions and treatment adaptations that may reduce barriers to care. *Clinical Psychology Review, 32*(8), 741–753. doi:10.1016/j.cpr.2012.09.002

CHAPTER 7A

FROM COMBAT TO CALM: EQUINE THERAPY WITH VETERANS

Brooke Lichter

Therapeutic horseback riding is a program that teaches children and adults with cognitive and physical challenges how to ride horses. I have witnessed firsthand how amazing the effects of this work can be; I have worked in this field for many years as well as witnessing my own brother's transformation while riding in the program. Therapeutic riding lessons brought such joy to my brother as well as the development of new skills. There is immense power in the healing bond between person and horse. I know for myself, when I ride or even just spend time near horses, the hustle and bustle of everyday life washes away. My worries or thoughts that weigh heavily on my mind leaves, and I am completely focused upon the horses. Riding allows me always to acquire new equitation skills, but I also simply love being with the horse, absorbing my surroundings. Listening to the birds, watching the leaves move in the trees, smelling the grass; in combination, it created a sense of peace.

I am a Licensed Social Worker with a concentration in clinical practice with families and children. I am dually certified through the Professional Association of Therapeutic Horsemanship (PATH) International as an Equine Specialist in Mental Health and Learning, and through EAGALA (Equine Assisted Growth and Learning Association). I have always had a deep passion for animals. This passion has led me on many amazing journeys. The first journey began at a young age when I volunteered at the Monmouth County SPCA, and for a therapeutic equestrian center and later employed by that therapeutic horseback riding center for several years. I have also been fortunate enough to intern at the Walt Disney World's

Animal Kingdom. During this journey, I realized that I wanted to combine my love of animals and helping people by integrating Animal Assisted Therapy into therapy. Upon graduation, my dream became a reality as I aided in the establishment of a non- profit organization, Serenity Stables. At Serenity Stables we provide free equine assisted therapy to Veterans, active duty members, and their families through a program called "From Combat to Calm." I guide all therapy sessions with compassion, patience, creativity, and view clients through a strengths perspective. Through this experience, I offer you a glimpse of the amazing work we do at Serenity Stables.

It was a beautiful sunny day at the barn and it was my favorite day of the week, Wednesday. Wednesday—the day that a group of ten veterans living in an addiction recovery center visit from New York City. Living in an environment full of noise, sirens, and much hustle and bustle, most of them told me how much they enjoy the mere peacefulness of not hearing the birds and being surrounded by nature. My goal each week was for the veterans to develop a relationship with the horses and incorporate the lessons learned during the sessions into their daily lives.

Today, a marine veteran named David had returned for his fourth session at the barn. The theme for the day was mindfulness. I led the veterans through a silent mindfulness exercise with the horses. I asked each Veteran to approach the horse with whom they felt the most connected. During this activity, I led the veterans through connections concerning all five senses with the horse: listening to the horse's breathing and trying to match their breath with the horse's; listening to the sound of the horses eating their hay, the sound of birds chirping, and to feel the wind on their face and the horses hair in between their fingers. As I led them through this, I could see the horse's body language telling me that they were relaxed. Some of the veterans even closed their eyes. It was amazing to watch them fully drop in and connect with their horses.

At the conclusion of the session, I gave them each a piece of their horse's tail for grounding. I told them that when they returned to the city and feel stressed, they can hold their horse's tail, close their eyes, and be able to bring themselves back to this peaceful time and reproduce the relaxed feeling that they have had with their horse. I directed the group to gather in a circle in order to share any thoughts about what they had just experienced. I told the veterans that they have helped the horses to relax and feel loved just as much as the horses have helped them; it was a mutually beneficial experience. As everyone took a turn around the circle, David had a serious look on his face. Finally, it came his time to share, and he offered the following:

> Living in the house with all the guys, I used to find entertainment and enjoyment when one of them would fall and get hurt, when someone would start using drugs again, and would hope for fights to breakout. But I don't feel that way anymore. Now I want to help my fellow housemates, see them succeed, and be a leader in recovery for them. Do you know who taught me that? The horses. The horses have taught me love, compassion, patience, understanding, and empathy. If it wasn't for them, I would not have changed my outlook. I thank God for these horses and all they have taught me so far.

Hearing this was surprising and heartwarming and I had chills up my arms. David's reflection on what the horses had taught him was a reminder for me of what I too gain from this experience, connection, peace and fulfillment. To me, all this would be impossible to accomplish in a traditional in-office therapeutic setting. I have always known the

Figure 7.1 The incredible bond between an equine therapist and her horse.

positive impact that horses have made upon my life, but to share this with someone with very different life experiences than myself and for them to take something so important away from this experience meant the world to me. What a great reminder that the touch of horse can change the course of a life.

CHAPTER 8

◦⋀◦

Ecospirituality

JOANNE JODRY AND MERRITT REID

Ecospirituality is a manifestation of the spiritual connection between human beings and the environment. Ecospirituality incorporates an intuitive and embodied awareness of all life and engages and engages a relational view of person and planet, inner to outer landscape, and soul to soil.

—Lincoln (2000, *p.* 227)

SPIRITUALITY, COUNSELING, AND NATURE

On April 22, 2009, the United Nations adopted a resolution to designate "Mother Earth Day" citing that "in order to achieve a just balance among the economic, social and environmental needs of the present and future generations, it is necessary to promote harmony with nature and the Earth" (UN General Assembly, 63/278).

According to Darwin's (1859/2003) theory of evolution, the human consciousness that we know today has evolved from a single source that began on the planet Earth. "Analogy would leave me to one step further, namely, to believe that all plants and animals are descended from one prototype" (Darwin, 1859/2003, p. 502). If so, the evolution over the past 4.5 billion years has moved from that one source of existence to a human consciousness that dominates all other species across the planet. Therefore, this single prototype potentially has spawned from Earth itself. In essence, we are nature's children evolved over many, many generations to our current human form. In our earlier existence, hunters and gatherers were able to maintain life from the nurturing Mother Earth that fed her children. In return, the early humans treated her with love and reverence they knew she merited. If the widely accepted theory that Darwin postulates is true, the earth, precisely, is the collective mother of all existence, meaning, she not only is the one true source of all humans but is also a progenitor to all species of flora and fauna alike.

Considering spirituality is such an individual experience, it is often elusive in definition. For the purposes of our discussion, spirituality is a phenomenological personal experience that helps one to organize, define meaning, and create significance in one's life. Spirituality is a way of organizing an individual's intrinsic beliefs to make sense of the world and his or her place in the world. Many people have found spiritual guidelines in religions that have attempted to define meaning in the human existence. Religions have often interpreted holy scriptures and have explained lives of prophets or the concepts of gods in an attempt to define and confine spiritual experiences. Organically, before the formations of organized religions, people organized their meaning through interaction with their environmental surroundings and quest for survival. Therefore, the search for spirituality and human significance has a foundation in nature.

No matter how one understands one's own phenomenological spiritual development, there is a collective drive toward personal significance. Yalom (1980) states that all people share four ultimate concerns (death anxiety, freedom of choice and taking responsibility, fear of living a meaningless life, and fear of isolation) that permeate the human consciousness and underpin the individual quest for meaning. This existential drive can also be considered a spiritual quest to understanding the intrinsic self and its relation to the environment.

Although spirituality is a personal experience with various perceptions that can shape personal interpretations, some common threads to define spirituality are

- A fundamental quest to internally organize one's place in the world
- A search for answers to the mysteries of life and death
- A search for an explanation of the part of human consciousness that has no science to explain it
- Attempts to control or explain the unexplainable
- A sense of universal connection to each other and the environment
- A desire for community that supports one's spiritual understandings

Ecospirituality, therefore, is the organic connection between nature and spirituality. As previously stated, it was the original source of organizing human meaning and existence. There are therapeutic benefits to helping. Simply put, ecospirituality is one's search for meaning, finding personal significance, and organizing one's internal relationship to the world within nature. It is connecting to nature on a visceral level and being able to use that relationship to increase the personal meaning of life. Ecospirituality can exist within or without a structured religious context.

EARLY CONCEPTS OF SPIRITUALITY

To understand ecospirituality, it is important to understand some of the historical and developmental aspects of the human relationship with nature and the earth. As human consciousness developed and evolved, so did the complexity of the relationship between the earth, its creatures, and the meaning of human existence. In human attempts to master, understand, and relate to the environment, new ways of healing, worship, and rituals developed. Most of the traditions, hypotheses, and theories are grounded in spiritual underpinnings.

Mother Earth

James Lovelock and Lynn Margulis developed in 1979 the Gaia theory, which postulates that the earth is one self-regulating complex system that is interdependent and exists as one whole. Lovelock's (1979) progressive thinking has led to the concept that "[Earth] regulation, at a state fit for life, is a property of the whole evolving system of life, air, ocean and rocks" (p. 144). This is in contrast to earlier thinking that humans adapted to Earth. This would further Darwin's (1859/2003) ideas about evolution and human existence being created from a single source. Sisk and Torrance (2001) claim that whatever we do unto the earth we also do to ourselves. The source is a whole, working in consistency together as a symbiotic relationship.

According to the Smithsonian National Museum of Natural History (2018), many anthropologists would suggest that human consciousness began in Africa and then indigenous people began to migrate across the planet. Many native people and early primal worshippers carried a commonality of respect for Mother Earth, the elements, and other species also created from the earth. As human consciousness has developed throughout evolution, some people may have maintained a visceral recognition of the early connection to the life-giving planet. Many people are naturally drawn to open air and often feel their best in the sacred womb of the earth. Some even go as far as immersing themselves in nature as a way of communicating with the higher power.

The Mother and Her Creatures

In addition to the earth and all that is intrinsic to it, humans began to spiritually connect with animals as they rose in the ecological hierarchy. Gross (2017) also proposes that animals play a large role in "almost every area of religious expression, including myth and scripture, visual arts, cosmologies, dietary practices, and ethical systems" (p. 1). Animal worship and sometimes sacrifice were also part of the collective focus of much religious worship in the past and remain even today (Gross, 2017). The earliest worshipers stayed reverent and humble to Mother Earth and the other plants and beings created by the earth. Gross (2017) argues that animals are an integral part of "religion and ecology" because in the whole environment "animals touch people in a more robust way" than other parts of ecology (p. 5).

Mother Earth and the Cycle of Life and Death

Early worshipers recognized the miracle that is birth and life. According to Van Voorst (2013), the earliest form of religion centered on Earth and women, connected by their feminine and reproductive attributes. Often, statues were made to depict the woman and their reproductive body parts, which were worshiped with a sense of mysticism, emphasizing the role of being a life-giver. The fetus, which later grows into a child, is dependent on its mother for life and growth. Likewise, the life cycle of the earth provides for all forms of life and growth. Perhaps the early people had a collective instinct of awareness for this life cycle being rooted in the earth, which may explain why some people today still feel grounded and spiritual in nature. Either way, many people seem to relate inherently to Mother Earth as both life-giving and essential for survival. Although it takes a different form today, many people may still sense the spirituality in nature and are drawn to it as a meaningful experience.

Nature has an annual death and rebirthing process as it goes through the process of the seasons: fall (preparation for death), winter (death), spring (rebirth), summer (growth). Likewise, humans have seasons throughout their lives as they age, grow, learn, and lose abilities until death finally comes to the body. All of the elements of Earth interact with each other to create part of the whole throughout this life and death cycle. Human consciousness also has seasons of change, which are known as developmental stages of life. These seasons of change allow humans to grow and continually rebirth physically, mentally, spiritually, emotionally, and consciously throughout their lifespan. Some of the mysteries of life (what happens at death, unexplainable suffering, etc.) may lie within the earth and the natural cycle of death and rebirth. This can be seen by the natural and instinctual burial processes that transcend religion such as burning, burying, or other forms of placing the human body back into the earthly roots of nature.

In summary, there is historical and cultural longevity that suggest the earth and its elements are connected. They offer potential knowledge, healing, roadmaps for the living, and spiritual interconnectedness with each other. At a minimum, they offer interesting thoughts around human commonality. The traditional symbolism of each element has spiritual properties that can be drawn upon to make the human suffering and existential meaning more appreciated. All of the elements are only found in nature.

FREUD, JUNG, AND SEARCH FOR MEANING

Religion, in short, is a monumental chapter in the history of human egotism. (James, 1901/1997, p. 381)

Freud, who focused his theory around the individual's unconscious, drives, and impulses, viewed nature as a force to be conquered since it was a great source of human suffering. Freud (1929/2010) suggested that there were three sources of human suffering: "The superior power of nature; the feebleness of our own bodies and the inadequacy of the regulations which adjust the mutual relationships of human beings in the family, and the state and society" (p. 57). He also suggested that nature could never be completely mastered and that nature would always play a larger part to the human existence than that of the individual will or ego. In other words, nature was greater than human consciousness.

Freud (1929/2010) believed that hostility within civilization could be traced back to "the victory Christendom had over heathen religions. For it was closely related to the low estimation put upon earthly life by the Christian doctrine" (p. 59). He may have been implying that being close to nature created an increased potential for happiness. Freud may also be suggesting that the creation of a human God moved human ego to a higher state of entitlement over other animals and earthly beings. This may have allowed humans to separate themselves from Earth and its creatures by declaring superiority with the concept of God in man's image. Perhaps, as the humans ego developed and narcissism took effect, there developed less of a need to take homage to the roots of Mother Earth.

Additionally, Freud (1929/2010, p. 65) suggested that as humans continued to conquer nature and animals through developments beginning with fire and tools, they began to move themselves to an omnipotent god position in the ego. As technology and science continued to grow, humans moved further away from the need for any gods (including nature). Freud suggested humans may be seeking the ideal power of mastering all nature (animals and the planet) and, hence, elevating themselves to the status of God.

Freud (1927/1961) suggested in the *Future of an Illusion* that as humans evolved through different phases of development and grew in consciousness, they began to ban/tribe/clan together, and civilizations were born. Of course, human beings instinctually wanted to exist individually (fight or flight, survival of fittest), but there was also a collective drive to exist as a species (Darwin, 1859/2003). Darwin suggested that the strongest and fittest would rise as leaders of the tribe. This was the beginning of hierarchies and weighted value among people. Working together and protecting each other allowed the earliest worshipers to gain a sense of control over nature and its elements (Freud, 1929/2010). Darwin further suggested that this forming of civilization led to the rise of power and coercion (and religion). In many indigenous people, shamans (healers) were often the leaders because they possessed spiritual communion with nature that allowed for community and individual healing. This ability allowed shamans great positions and privileges in groups as civilization developed.

Jung, who added a spiritual element to the unconscious and also theorized the concept of the collective unconscious, suggested

> For it is the body, the feeling, the instincts, which connect us with the soil. If you give up the past you naturally detach from the past; you lose your roots in the soil, your connection with the totem ancestors that dwell in your soil. You turn outward and drift away and try to conquer other lands because you are exiles from your own soil. . . . The feet will walk away and the head cannot retain them because it is also looking out for something. That is the Will, always wandering over the surface of the earth, always seeking something.
>
> (Jung, 2002, p. 73, as quoted in Sabini, 2002)

Jung believed in a universal connectedness and that all life was, in essence, connected. This included nature. Jung conceptualized, according to Sabini (2002), that humans were, in fact, part of nature and that nature was a part of humans, and to go against nature was spiritually harmful both individually and collectively: "Whenever we touch nature, we get clean" (p. 1). Sabini suggests that Jung postulated that being connected to nature, as well as respecting nature, promotes holistic well-being.

Despite the psychologically minded beliefs of Freud and Jung, religions continued to rise and thrive. The relationship and view of nature continued to suffer with the rise of industrial capitalism. Regardless of the movement away from nature toward human-based religions, many people still have the spiritual draw to the origins of the earth.

WORLD RELIGIONS AND NATURE

> By the sweat of your face
> You will eat bread,
> Till you return to the ground,
> Because from it you were taken;
> For you are dust,
> And to dust you shall return.
> (Genesis 3:19, New King James Version)

Traditional religions throughout the world have had deep-rooted connections with nature. Often in the founding stories and scriptures, nature is the essential component for people seeking spiritual awakenings. People trying to explain life, death, and mysteries related to unexplained human condition often sought refuge in nature and Earth.

Religion and Nature

Throughout the constructs of organized religions and their historical developments, there are many tales of seeking refuge, knowledge, and communing with God in nature. Many prophets and gods used the earth to find prayer and healing. For example, John the Baptist in the Christian tradition bathed people in the water as a means of cleaning away sins. The story of Mohamed included his retreat into a cave where the archangel, Gabriel, spoke to him and the Koran was born. Moses went to the mountains of Mount Sinai to receive the Ten Commandments from God. Examples can be found within Western religions' holy texts:

[Elijah] went into a cave and spent the night. And the word of the LORD came to him . . . a gentle whisper. (1 Kings 19:9, 12, New King James Version)

At once the Spirit sent [Jesus] out into the desert, and he was in the desert forty days, being tempted by Satan. He was with the wild animals, and angels attended him. (Mark 1:12–13, New King James Version)

Jesus went out to a mountainside to pray, and spent the night praying to God. When morning came, he called his disciples to him and chose twelve of them. (Luke 6:12–13, New King James Version)

Jesus took with him Peter, James and John the brother of James, and led them up a high mountain by themselves. There he was transfigured before them. His face shone like the sun, and his clothes became as white as the light. (Matthew 17:1–2, New King James Version)

Eastern religious philosophies, likewise, have intentional interactions with nature as part of the spiritual process of human growth. The Buddha took refuge in the forest and had significant relationships with trees in the forests as he moved toward enlightenment. As a young man, the Buddha wandered throughout the forests and finally sat under a Bodhi tree (which is now located in Bodhgaya, India) for 49 days as he became Enlightened. Kaza (2006) reported that the Buddha urged his followers to choose natural places for meditations. Examples can be found within eastern religions' holy texts:

It is Nature that causes all movement. Deluded by the ego, the fool harbors the perception that says "I did it." (Veda Vyasa, The Bhagavadgita, or The Song Divine)

Ether, air, fire, water, earth, planets, all creatures, directions, trees and plants, rivers and seas, they are all organs of God's body. Remembering this a devotee respects all species. (Srimad Bhagavatam, 2.2.41)

Contemporary eastern thoughts of His Holiness the 14th Dalai Lama (1992) suggests, "The elements (earth, wind, fire, water and vacuum/space) create an interrelationship between the environment and the humans living within it" .

Ego Versus Spirit

It is as though the earth had suddenly discovered that the sun was the center of the planetary orbits and of the earth's orbit as well.

But we have always known this to be so? I myself believe that we had always known it. But I may know about something with my head which the other man in me is far from knowing, for indeed and in truth, but did not live it. Any why did they not live it? Because of the bias which makes us all live from the ego, a bias which comes from the overvaluation of the conscious mind.

(Jung, *Collected Works*, Vol. 16, para. 107–108, as quoted in Sabini, 2002)

Humans have historically sought natural cures in medicine and have gone to nature for spiritual enlighten and refuge. Ayurveda, the science of life, is a Hindu medicine based on healing within the context of nature. The premise of this type of medicine includes being part of the environment and seeking natural solutions for wellness found in the environment.

Many children are told to "get out and get some fresh air." Parents for generations have been sensing the need to connect with the environment. There is an instinctual naturalness to the idea of sun, air, water, and playing outside are all good for children. As humans develop through life stages, social constructs (capitalism, patriarchal norms, etc.) shape our psychology and often move individuals away from spirituality. Many people in modern life find themselves sitting in offices for hours, some days never seeing the sun. Kaufman (2018) suggested that nature greatly contributes to wellness, yet humans are moving further from interaction with it. The adult culture in the West tends to focus on material acquisition, hierarchies of status, and, more recently, electronics and social media. The general Western culture leans toward personal satisfaction of the individual experiences and entitlements rather than cultural collective progress. In other words, the ego (the reality of one's existence) seems to matter the most to many people, which may lead to great suffering.

The influence that capitalism has had on the spiritual nature of people often seems to have conflict. Many people have woven religious beliefs with capitalistic beliefs to justify not loving neighbors, casting first stones, and so on. These are all ego-driven activities that are determined to keep the individual person's views of truth intact. These instincts within the Western culture allow people to destroy the environment if they are able to make money. These ego-driven lives are very different than spiritual purpose driven lives. The ego driven life is self-soothing at its core. It creates a small existence with the goal of self-satisfaction (or, as many people describe, happiness). The capitalist culture tends to promote ego-driven lives as successful journeys.

ECOSPIRITUALITY IN ECOTHERAPY

The purpose-driven life is existential at its core. Searching for a more meaningful existence and thinking past one's own desires allows for humanism to thrive. One goal of ecospirituality is to keep people grounded in the larger picture of the life and death cycle, existential meaning, and Gaia. Lincoln (2000) suggested that ecospiritual consciousness is associated in five ways to the human experience: (a) tending (intent/attending), which is being fully conscious and present in the moment.; (b) dwelling (being grounded and aware), which is being centered or focused thinking; (c) reverence (honor of mystery and earth), or discovering the mystery in beautiful sacred creations; (d) connectedness (to the whole), or unification with creation; and (e) sentience (sense of knowing), the visceral intuition of knowing and connectedness.

Another aspect of clinical ecospirituality within ecotherapy includes the addition of holistic application to the ecotherapy. Drawing spiritual connections to experiences allows the client to fill in the gaps between thoughts and behaviors. The spiritual mysteries of life can be discussed during the counseling experiences, and this may give some clients a fuller healing experience. Gendlin (1962) discusses how many clients do not use logic as the basis of their decisions or psychological processes but they use "felt meaning." Genglin suggests that experiences such as art and religions often leave people with a "felt sense" of the experience that is difficult to express in works. This "felt meaning" is where people often identify with spiritual experiences. The clinician who works with this may be able to aid more fully in the ecotherapy process.

CLINICAL APPLICATIONS OF ECOSPIRITUALITY

It is a general truth that the earth is the depreciated and misunderstood part, and so the unconscious regularly puts great emphasis on the chthonic fact. Nietzsche has expressed that very beautifully: "You shall become friends of the immediate things." And the immediate things are this Earth, this Life.... For quite long enough our ancestors, and we ourselves have been taught that this life is not the real thing, that it is provisional, and that we only live for Heaven. In the course of the centuries, man has repeatedly experienced the fact that the life that is not lived here, or the life lived provisionally, is utterly unsatisfactory. It leads to neurosis.
(Jung, *Interpretation of Visions*, p. 192, as quoted in Sabini, 2002)

The aim of this section is to allow counselors, no matter what theoretical counseling affiliation, to integrate ecospirituality techniques into clinical practice. The following are examples of how a clinician can work with clients in a spiritual manner and allow him or her to gain power by connecting to the original "Mother" nature.

Altars to Alter

According to the Oxford Dictionary, the word *alter* means, "Change in character or composition, typically in a small, but significant way" (Oxforddictionaries.com, 2018) Altars can be created in any location. They can be indoors in a corner of a room or outdoors below a tree. The key to a meaningful altar is that it is a place that is easily visited and has implications for the client. Working with a client on the existential meaning of life issues and what items might be placed on the altar to represent that can be accomplished in a counselor's office.

The client can use this sacred place that he or she creates to pray, meditate, or just be mindful. There can be a specific purpose to the altar, or it can just be for the general purpose of grounding and remembering the larger issues of life. Specific alters may help the client work on specific issues. For example, self-esteem, career goals, or family issues could be symbolized as reminders of who the client would like to be in different situations.

Many clients experience stress and unhappiness because they are dealing with issues of the ego and not the spirit. The purpose of this type of altar might be to allow the client to remember the larger picture of human existence, recenter his or her behavior from a more spiritual existential frame, and be mindful, pray, or meditate with a proper focus. Clients can attach any meaning they wish to any object, but, if help is needed, clinicians can assist in establishing archetypal or common existing meanings to the objects on the altar.

Examples of ecological items that might be placed on an altar include flowers, wood, crystals, and other objects from nature. In *A Dictionary of Symbols*, Cirlot (2002) suggests that specific flowers each have an individual meaning separated into two categories: the essence of the flower and the shape of the flower, which includes its color. Flowers may represent change, rebirth, or beauty. He also explains that, due to its shape, the flower is an archetypal representation of the soul. The significance is also adapted to the nature of the flower's color. For example, red is associated with fire, passion, blood, or animal life.

Additionally, Cirlot (2002) expounds that wood is a mother symbol that when burned represents wisdom and death. Various types of wood all represent specific symbolism and meaning. For instance, oak is associated with strength, wisdom, beauty, and long life; pine is associated with longevity, hope, and creativity; and olive is associated with peace, purification, fruitfulness, and victory.

Chevalier and Gheerbrant (1996) explain that crystals and gems are a symbol of wisdom and divination. Some examples of crystals are emerald, associated with intuition; amethyst, associated with temperance and protection from intoxication; and jade crystal, associated with protection and self-healing. Clients may choose to assign their own meaning to the crystal such as connections with birthstones.

Prayer Flags to Create Personal Energy

In many countries, it is not usual to see Tibetan Buddhist prayer flags flying in the breeze. Prayer flags are a way to promote compassion and strength to all people. The flags have prayers and auspicious symbols written on them with the belief that as the wind blows through the prayer, it will carry the intention to all people and spread the wish. Each of the Tibetan prayer flags is arranged from left to right in a specific order of color: blue, white, red, green, and yellow. Each color represents one of the elements: White symbolizes the air and wind; red symbolizes fire; green symbolizes water; yellow symbolizes the earth; and blue symbolizes space.

This concept could be used as a counseling technique while working with clients. The client can create his or her own prayer flags with the intention (s) that he or she would like to add to the world. Each flag would be carefully chosen for color and content. Clients could use the prayer flags to add goodness to the world or make the prayer specific to their household and/or individual intention.

Hanging the prayer flags also could hold significance to clients. They could hang the flags near their house or in other natural locations where the flags could be exposed to the wind on a regular basis and spread the client's messages. Ideas for creating the prayer flags include

- Prayers important to the client
- Symbols of empowerment (animals, nature)
- Words that hold concepts the client would like to become
- Mantras that clients want to live by
- Symbols of who the client would like to be in the world
- Wishes for others/self

One With Tree (Meditation)

Meditation is a spiritual, psychological, and behavioral antidote to anxiety and other disturbances to the psyche. Using meditation to connect with nature has clinical potential to help clients in grounding back to roots of safety and belonging. The following is a possible meditation that allows clients to use nature as their spiritual foundation:

> *Close your eyes and breathe deeply. Feel the air as it enters your body. Be grateful to the air for giving you life. As you breathe in the life-giving air and it leaves your body, recognize how you are one with the air. This interaction creates life.*
>
> *Imagine you are standing in a large open field. Look around the beautiful field. As your eyes gaze around the field, you see a tree. What does the tree look like? Does it have branches, leaves? Begin walking toward it. Walk very slowly toward the tree. As you get closer to the tree, look at the details. What is the trunk of the tree like? the branches of the tree, the details of the leaves of the tree, the color, the shape? As you continue to approach the tree, reach out and feel the bark of the tree. Is it rough? Is it smooth? Move your body up against the tree. How does it feel? Push your body gently to the tree and enter into the tree trunk. Be inside the tree and see how it feels to be one with the tree. Feel your arms as the branches and feel the leaves flying from your arms. Feel the comfort of Mother Earth. Breathe and enjoy the oneness of the womb of the earth.*
>
> *Take another breath and begin to move back out of the tree. Slowly begin to walk away from the tree. Take a few steps back to where you came from. Turn around and look at the tree. Give thanks for the unity with nature. Continue to walk back and sit down facing the tree. Notice if the tree is different from when you first saw it or if it now brings a different feeling. Breathe slowly three more times and open your eyes when you are ready.*

Finding a Sacred Spot

Finding sacred places to pray allows one to find peace any time it is needed. Although churches and holy sites are abundant, they are often shared with larger communities. Clients may benefit from finding a spot that is solely theirs, where they can go to reflect, pray, or just be.

Step 1: Where do you get your energy? Where do you feel best? (mountains, hills, water, valleys, deserts, forests, plains, oceans, lakes, etc.). When trying to decide this, consider where you breathe best, where your skin feels best, where you feel most at peace. You may also want to consider your astrology sign and consider that as a starting point to find where your energy is best. Step 2: Get used to being physically alone with

Figure 8.1 One with tree meditation.

no sources of noise or human relationship. If you are someone who does not like to be alone, practice this at home. Step 3: Go to different places in the environment that feel right to you. When you are in your scared space, reflect on:

- What am I doing with my life that will contribute to the whole (Gaia)?
- How did life begin? What do I believe, and what do I want to choose to believe? (This is a choice that will inform how you live.)
- Why was I born into my situation, and what shall I do with that?
- Is there a God, many gods, no God? What difference does it make to me?

Figure-Ground With the Environment (Context of Consciousness)

It is evident that in postulating figure/ground formation as a basic dynamic of awareness, we are addressing ourselves to the familiar issues of how accessible our experiences are to us and what composes the context for the events in our lives. (Polster & Polster, 1973, p. 45)

Along the lines of the Gestalt's "the whole" and the concept of figure-ground in therapy, often the environment moves into the background

Figure 8.2 Finding your sacred spot.

part of our experience, going unnoticed within the context of the prominent focal point of the whole situation. The figure (focal point) of a situation often arises due to the maintenance of the historical experiences, narratives that are grounded and identities that are formed for the individual client. In this exercise, we ask clients to challenge these figures (focal point) and ground (background) constructs in order to add the spiritual (unknown, mystery, the context of life meaning) to the ground.

As clients describe different situations, have them fill in the context of the environment and their spiritual connection to the environment. For example: There were trees in the background when you were fighting with your husband. What do the trees mean to you? What do you think the trees were experiencing? In the big picture of this whole world and your existence, how important was this fight, and why did your energy go to having this fight? These are often questions we do not ask in therapy. What was the weather like? How did you feel in the temperature of the day? What was around you that brought you comfort? What was around you that made you feel discomfort? Were there any noticeable smells? Paint a picture in your mind's eye without the figure; what do you see? Was there any background noise? How was your body feeling physically during this time? When you notice all of the background and you put the whole to your experience, how does it change spiritually? Looking at the larger picture, how does this even fit into your meaning of life and relationship to the mystery of life?

Going With the Floating

Floating in water and noticing how it will keep you moving by maintaining your buoyancy is yet another activity that combines nature with spirituality. The water is more powerful than you but can protect you. If you fight the naturalness of allowing the water to support you, you will sink. If you do not trust the environment, you will sink. There are many opportunities to float, but in all of them, mindfulness and learning the lessons of the water (and metaphor for the human experience) is the key to the spiritual experience of the float. While floating it is important to remember that the water is holding you up and protecting you. This is a good time to reflect on ideas of protection, asking for help, and the vast awesomeness of Mother Earth, staying mindful in every feeling of the movement or stillness, and reflecting when you move and why you move.

Opportunities for floating may include

- River tubing (understanding the river flow, like Chi, and not fighting it)
- Pool floating (manmade floating; keeps you more still than natural floating; stays in one place unless disturbed)
- Ocean floating (being rocked by waves coming in and out of shore [stable land])
- Floating with others (seeing how people can be still, and do nothing, versus yourself)
- Lake float (notice the life happening under you and around you and how you can be part of that whole)
- Float spas (floating in highly concentrated salt and feeling the healing properties on your skin; often in pods of sensory deprivation focused on complete relaxation)

CASE STUDY

Mark, a 45-year-old male client, sought marital counseling approximately eight months after 9/11. He had been working on Wall Street in the financial market at the time of the terrorist attack. Although he was not in the World Trade Center, he was working in a building close to the epicenter of the terror. He had experienced the trauma of people running, the dust flying when the buildings fell, and the loss of life with many people whom he had known. His wife was also fearful that day with her focus on getting him home and being worried that he would become one of the victims of that day.

The couple was seeking marriage counseling because Mark no longer wanted to go back to New York City to work, and he had a very large salary that supported the family. There was a large mortgage, three children in private schools, and a high cost of living that the family enjoyed. Mark's contemplating not going back to work was causing a tremendous amount of marital stress.

Mark stated that he had been questioning his career anyway because it was less than satisfying even before 9/11. After the terrorist attack took place, he felt more clarity about his life. He wanted to be with his family more, not commuting into New York City for 90 minutes each way daily, and he wanted to do something that brought him more fulfillment. All of the ideas around the future included him making less income for the family.

Melissa, his 42-year-old wife, expressed fear that if the children could not have the lifestyle they were accustomed to, it would affect them in a negative way. She initially related all of her fears through the eyes of the children. She initially said that if it was just her "she would live in a shack," but that it would destroy the children to not have the money and the social positions that currently existed.

The couple had no particular religious or spiritual practices with the exception of the commercialized Christmas and Easter. The children were not being raised in a context of religion, but both parents interacted with Christianity in childhood. Mark had been raised Catholic and went through all of the sacraments during his youth, but in the teenage years he grew away from the church and never returned. Melissa was raised in a liberal home that occasionally visited a local Methodist Church but never felt a connection to it. When asked where the clients felt their best and most grounded, Mark responded on hikes in the woods and Melissa said when she is running for exercise. Mark added that he had not hiked in years and Melissa runs almost daily (often with a personal trainer).

Mark said that he felt unloved and not understood by Melissa. The counselor decided to integrate spirituality through nature and the environment as part of the existential/spiritual intervention to help each of them find a root to the meaning of living. This decision was made because both clients felt most grounded in nature. Due to the existential nature of the events around 9/11, the counselor wanted to help give the clients a spiritual lens in an attempt to add a component of "felt meaning" (Gendlin, 1962) that could be discussed. The counseling process unfolded as follows:

Session 1: In a park, the clients were asked to throw a Frisbee or baseball back and forth for at least half an hour. Following this, the counselor sat them down to discuss their childhoods and what fun was like. What were their dreams when they were kids? What did they want to be when they grew up? Both of the clients had fun throwing to each other and cooperating with each other. The counselor then nudged them to talk about what they were taught regarding what life was as well as what they thought their purpose here on Earth was. The counselor also prompted discussion regarding their individual thoughts on religion and spirituality. They appeared to have a difficult time with these questions because "they had not really thought about them before." They grappled with the questions and were asked to take time out once during the week to discuss with each other what answers made the most sense to them. The counselor then inquired what was different now from how it used to be in their childhoods, and both of them seemed to show a commonality in thinking that they were no longer children who were carefree and were now tied down by societal expectations and financial commitments. It further led them to discuss their dreams, including traveling around the world and being free. Lastly the couple was asked to sit together without speaking and just feel what it was like to be a child sitting with your best friend. The goal of this session was to initially get the clients back into the child mindset where things may have been more simple and clear while also reconnecting with the outdoors. It was the beginning of a process intending to ground the clients in what was important in life and begin to pay attention to "felt meaning" (Gendlin, 1962).

Session 2: The clients were asked to take a walk in the woods together, holding hands. Melissa had to take the lead (because she was not the financial lead) and guide Mark through the hills and uneven terrain. She needed to keep him from falling, and he needed to let her. This was a marital metaphor, hoping that she was using her protective and empathetic nature to shield him. Discussions ensued around what they wanted to do with their lives and how far they were from those goals. During this walk, questions discussed included "What holds your marriage together?", "Would you call that a spiritual bond that you share?," "How can you help each other be your best selves?" Each one was assigned a task of finding something on their walk in the woods to give to the other person but not explaining the meaning behind the gift. Melissa picked a rock because she felt that Mark was like a rock solid force in her life and maintained strength in the family.

Mark also picked a rock and said that he needed her to be a rock right now while they were going through a transition. The couple were asked to sit together holding their rocks and feeling them. They were asked again to be together without words and holding hands with the rocks in each one. Contemplation questions were asked around the beauty of the earth, the formation of the rock, and where they fit into the whole picture of life. "Just like the rocks are a small part of the whole of nature, where does your life fit into the human existence?" Additional spiritual questions were contemplated around the creator of Earth. "Why and how does a 9/11 happen?" "Is there a God?" The goal of this session was to begin spiritual conversations of what the couple individually believed about the mystery of life. "What do bad things happen to good people?" "What happens in death?" The intention was to move the clients to more spiritual discussions that would allow them to discuss, think, and consider each other's thoughts as a team. It also served to have them move to spiritual existential thinking before making psychological and behavioral decisions.

Session 3: The clients were asked to go tubing together down a river. The tubes were tied together and the counselor took a passive role except to draw metaphors and begin existential topics. Discussions and metaphors were drawn to the power of the river and the flow of changes in life. The river is directional, and the moves you make depend on where you go. The couple worked together with a goal. During the floating times in the river, the couple reflected on human interaction with nature and how it feels to be part of the whole of the earth. The couple was asked to think about questions like "What part do you want to play while you are here on earth?" "How do you want to contribute to the earth and humanity?" "What are you currently doing that works or doesn't work with that goal?" The river trip allowed for a discussion of how society had shaped their personal beliefs of happiness and success, allowing for a redefinition if desired. At the end of the river, the couple sat and reflected that they had been living life in a nonspiritual manner and that they needed to make changes in their lives. The goal of this session was to move the couple to discuss and begin deciding what it would mean to live by choice in a spiritual/existential manner or if they would like to remain living in the social capitalistic manner.

Session 4: This session happened in the counselor's office. The couple discussed what they wanted to do with the rest of their lives and what changes would be required to do that. Although they had been married in a church, they decided that their "marriage agreement" had been based in capitalism idolatry rather than spiritual meaning. They decided to downside, and Mark decided to take a lower-paying job that brought him more meaning (he wanted to be a teacher). As supplemental income, Melissa decided to work in a nonprofit and go back to school to become a social worker.

The couple decided that they believed in God and that they felt God in nature, and they committed to having monthly interactions with nature and discussions around spiritual beliefs. These spiritual values that would remain at the center of the marriage were reevaluating the need for material items, needing less money to be happy; going places (nature) where they could feel grounded; and regular discussions around beliefs in God and what they were doing here on Earth to meet their decided life purposes.

The goal of the ecospiritual intervention was to ground the couple in their spiritual-existential humanness in relation to the environment and to realize the larger picture and the reality of their life cycle. Many interventions could accomplish this, but being in nature and getting in touch with the original source of life, "Earth," makes the counseling experience holistic and may have a greater impact on the experience and hence the outcome.

REFERENCES

American Federation of Astrologers. (n.d.). *History of astrology*. Retrieved from https://www.astrologers.com/about/history
Chevalier, J., & Gheerbrant, A. (1996). *The Penguin dictionary of symbols* (2nd ed.). New York, NY: Penguin Books.
Cirlot, J. E. (2002). *A dictionary of symbols* (2nd ed.). Mineola, NY: Dover.
Dalai Lama. (1992). *A Buddhist concept of nature*. Retrieved from https://www.dalailama.com/messages/environment/buddhist-concept-of-nature
Darwin, C. (1859/2003). *The origin of the species*. New York, NY: Signet Classics. (Original work published 1859)
Freud, S. (1961). *The future of an illusion*. New York, NY: W. W. Norton. (Original work published 1927)
Freud, S. (2010). *Civilization and its discontents*. New York, NY: W. W. Norton. (Original work published 1929)
Gendlin, E. (1962). *Experiencing and the creation of meaning*. Evanston, IL: Northwestern University Press.
General Assembly Resolution 63/278. (2009, May 1). International Mother Earth Day, A/RES/63/278. Retrieved from https://www.undocs.org/A/RES/67/97
Gross, A. S. (2017). *Animals and religion*. Oxford Handbooks Online. Retrieved from https://www.doi.org/10.1093/oxfordhb/9780199935420.013.10
James, W. (1997). *The varieties of religious experience*. New York, NY: Touchstone. (Original work published 1901)
Jung, C. G. (2002). *The earth has a soul: C.G. Jung on nature, technology, and modern life* (M. Sabini, Ed.). Berkeley, CA: North Atlantic Books.

Kaufman, J. A. (2018). Nature, mind and medicine: A model for mind-body healing. *Explore: The Journal of Science and Healing, 14*(4), 268–276.

Kaza, S. (2006). The greening of Buddhism. In R. S. Gottlieb (Ed.), *The Oxford handbook of religion and ecology* (pp. 184–206). New York, NY: Oxford University Press.

Lincoln, V. (2000). Ecospirituality. *Journal of Holistic Nursing, 18*(3), 227–244.

Lovelock, J. (1979). *Gaia.* New York, NY: Oxford University Press.

Moore, L. S. B., & TAKATOKA. (2018). Spirit guides & totems. Manataka American Indian Council. Retrieved from https://www.manataka.org/page291.html

Oxford Dictionaries. (2018). Alter. Retrieved from https://en.oxforddictionaries.com/definition/alter

Polster, E., & Polster, M. (1973). *Gestalt therapy integrated: Contours of theory and practice.* New York, NY: Vintage Books.

Sisk, D. A., & Torrance, E. P. (2001). *Spiritual intelligence: Developing higher consciousness.* Buffalo, NY: Creative Education Foundation Press.

Smithsonian National Museum of Natural History. (2018, September 14). *Introduction to human evolution.* Retrieved from http://humanorigins.si.edu/education/introduction-human-evolution

Understanding Science. (n.d.). Astrology: Is it scientific? Retrieved from https://undsci.berkeley.edu/article/astrology_checklist

Van Voorst, R. E. (2013). *RELG: World.* Instructor ed. Boston, MA: Wadsworth.

Yalom, I. D. (1980). *Existential psychotherapy.* New York, NY: Basic Books.

CHAPTER 8A

FROM THE DELAWARE TO THE GANGES RIVER

Jessica Colucci

I have always felt most connected to my spirituality and nature when I am close to water. From "Mommy and me" classes as an infant to swimming competitively as a Division I athlete at Northeastern University, water has been my safe haven. I began swimming competitively at the age of 6. Once I found water, I felt like I had found home. Although I was competitive, I always had a healthy relationship with water. When I was having a bad day, getting in the pool was my escape. Water helped me think, relax, and connect to something greater. While swimming, I experienced a time of self-reflection and release from the world around me. I was a swimmer for 17 years. Whether it be a pool, the beach, or a waterfall, I continue to feel most at peace in the water.

Whenever posed with the question, "What do you want to do with your lifetime?" my answer has always been the same: travel—more specifically, travel to places that lead me to bodies of water with which I can connect. To say "travel" as my answer to this question seems like a simple response. That said, there is a level of travel that always scares me. I asked myself: What if I get lost? How will I communicate with people when I don't speak the same language? Can I afford it? Will I be safe? Although these questions and worries flood my mind, I always feel the drive to experience the world and to be stronger than these anxieties. I know that once I get to where I am going, it will all fall into place.

I am lucky that my parents took me many places around the world. I have visited many places in the United States. I have been to Italy three times, and I have visited multiple Caribbean islands. When visiting Italy, I stay with family, and it is truly an immersive experience. Visiting Caribbean islands brings me close to water, which is always relaxing and peaceful. Although I have been blessed to be on these vacations, I always felt I wanted *more*. I was looking for a spiritual experience while surrounding myself in another culture. Enter the opportunity to go on a culturally immersive trip to India.

I studied clinical mental health counseling at Monmouth University in Long Branch, New Jersey. I had every intention of going into my master's program and completing my required coursework as quickly as possible. When I heard that Monmouth's program was two and a half years long, I strived to finish it in just two years. I had a goal in mind, and had every intention of sticking to it, until I found out about the opportunity to go to India. When I was in my third semester, I was in a class called Self-Exploration. I learned a lot about myself throughout this course and walked away feeling that I needed to take a break and slow down. I felt this most during a tubing trip down the Delaware River. While floating down the river with 13 students and a professor, I realized that there was no reason to be in a rush. I had finals and papers to write, but while out on the water all I focused on was being on the water. I felt connected to the earth that was around me. I felt connected to my peers. I reflected on my time in the counseling program and thought about what good it would really do for me to graduate a semester early. I realized: not much. Although there are aspects of being a student that are incredibly stressful, I recognized that I needed to take a deep breath and remember why I was in a counseling program and enjoy the ride.

During this class, when I first heard about the opportunity of a class going to India, I thought, "yeah, that probably won't happen" and pushed it out of my mind. Fast forward to that following fall semester, and it sounded like the trip to India was actually coming together. I heard the class was going to take place the following spring, and I thought to myself, "Well, I'll be graduated by then, so it doesn't matter." However, the more I learned about the trip, the more I wanted to go. It felt nearly impossible, as it meant all of my plans to graduate in two years would be railroaded. I would have to stay an extra semester, I would need to take out more student loans, and I would need to take two and a half weeks off of work. The reasons I *couldn't* go on the trip kept going by in my head. As I thought about it more, and spoke with supervisors and professors, the plans to *go* to India began to make more sense. I reflected back on my Self-Exploration class and the way I felt on the river that day. We watched the movie *Siddhartha* and learned about the Ganges River, where the Buddha was said to become enlightened. I pondered about how amazing it would be to visit one of the most sacred places in the world. It felt even more right for one reason: water.

I realized that it didn't matter which semester I graduated. It didn't matter that I had to ask off from work. Everyone was supportive, and plans began to fall perfectly into place for the trip to happen. Here it was—the opportunity I had so been longing for: a culturally immersive traveling experience, one that would lead me to a place that would change me for the better, and an opportunity to go work with children in an orphanage that needed help, help that I could provide. This was an opportunity to connect myself in nature and enhance my understanding of my own spirituality and what that means to me.

I decided to take the plunge and, for the first time, not follow the set-out plans I initially laid for myself. I was ready and willing to take the break I had been looking for to recharge and reset before entering the world as a counselor. The trip to India was not just a trip but a class. The class was set up so that we (students) were ready to enter into a world that was culturally and spiritually different than ours. We used our counseling skills to create treatment plans that could be used for the children of the orphanage who were suffering from disabilities. We read about and studied different cultural differences between what we experience in the United States and what we would experience in India. We visited temples of different religions in the United States to prepare for the various religions we would come across while in India. We were fully prepared to embark on this journey.

January 1, 2019, came, and we took off out of John F. Kennedy airport to New Delhi, India. When we arrived, I was beyond excited. I could not wait to experience this new adventure. On our first day, we visited the orphanage, One Life to Love, the reason we were in the class and on the trip. Walking up to the gates of the orphanage was overwhelming, to say the least. The children were waiting for our arrival with flowers and signs. The second our class walked in, it felt like a family reunion. We participated in activities with the children, and the day flew by as we sat with one another. All of my worries of traveling dissipated quickly. I felt at ease.

Our home base was always New Delhi and with the children of One Life to Love. Throughout our time in India, we also explored many new places. I felt the most connected spiritually and emotionally to Dharmshala and Varanasi. We went to Dharamshala, which is in the Himalaya Mountains. This city is where the Dalai Lama lives and many of his followers reside. When we first arrived and I took a look at the view, I was in awe. I felt completely connected to where I was and incredibly at peace. The weather was not on our side (it was very cold and rainy), which is something that normally would have me complaining. When I look back on those days in

Dharamshala, I don't even remember the weather. I remember doing yoga on the roof of our hotel, with a beautiful view of the snow-topped mountains, watching the sun rise. I remember visiting the Dalai Lama temple and praying with my classmates. I remember feeling no anxiety. I remember feeling like I could stay there for a long time.

Each day in India brought new light and understanding to my life. I experienced new food, a new culture, and many wonderful people. Toward the end of our trip, we visited Varanasi. This city is where the Ganges River is located. We took two boat rides on this river: one during the sunset and the next morning during sunrise. These boat rides were breathtaking. It is quite hard to put into words the beauty I saw and feelings I had when being out on the water. I felt at home, as being on and near water is always comforting. The evening prayer ceremony we witnessed during the sunset ride was unlike any other experience I had had in my short life. Hundreds of people gathered in the surrounding towns, as well as on the water, to be a part of the ceremony. The ceremony was an incredibly introspective moment, and I felt that I was surrounded by the spirit of my loved ones and my peer's loved ones. We all sat on the water, incredibly close to one another, yet we each had our own connection and experience to the ceremony. I felt overcome with emotion for myself and others I was with. It was a night of silence and prayer for many.

The ceremony consisted of music, fire, and chanting. The sounds reverberated through me. I closed my eyes and absorbed all that I was feeling through the vibrations. The light was enchanting and captivating. People on other boats passed us flowers with candles that in them that many people lit and placed on the water as a prayer for their lost loved ones. There was crying and laughing among our group. Although no one was talking much, it was evident that there was a heavy weight sitting upon all of us. I silently watched my peers experience the sensations that I knew I was experiencing in those moments. I prayed silently to myself. I felt a wave of calmness come over me. I felt connected to something that is not tangible on this earth but felt incredibly real.

The next morning, we went on a sunrise boat ride. We woke up early to make our way down to the water. The boat rides felt as though it brought everyone full circle. The intense emotion we all felt the night before seemed to be lifted the next morning. It was a cycle of grieving for the past and having a sense of closure for the future, all within a 12-hour span. It was intense but incredible. While out on the water in the morning, there was more conversation, laughing, and sharing of what we all felt the night prior. Although we all had our own experiences, we all shared something special together. We didn't have to speak to one another to feel it. I am not

Figure 8a.1 The Ganges River, India.

Buddhist, but I felt connected to the religion. I realized that it does not matter what religion a person is and that spirituality is grounded in nature and the people we are surrounded by.

My trip down the Delaware River in a tube ultimately led me to the Ganges River in a boat. India was an intense, amazing, and overwhelming experience. I had traveled in the past, but each place I visited in the past was unlike this experience. I was completely immersed in a new culture and a new way of life the entirety of the trip. The Ganges River was a turning point in the trip. I felt at ease and uplifted. I feel the trip impacted my mental health in a positive way. I took a chance on something that I was unsure of in the beginning. All of my questions around travel that were based in fear disappeared quickly. I interrupted "set" plans I had for myself. I disrupted my normal routine, something that would often be anxiety provoking. I am grateful I did all of these things, because it all brought me to where I am today. I feel engrained in India in some way. I plan on going back, but I have even more of a desire to travel and experience more of the world. I found healing in my experiences in India, and I know there is more work to be done elsewhere in the world as well.

CHAPTER 9

Ecotherapy Interventions

MAEVE HOGAN AND MEGAN E. DELANEY

An inherent connection to nature is embedded into the fabric of each human being. When recollecting the formative years for any individual, one is likely to notice the fact that the natural world plays an important role. So many of us were enlivened by the warmth and vibrant colors of a summer day and cradled to sleep at night by the light of the moon and natural sounds of the outside world. Even as adults, we can easily witness the curiosity and bewilderment of a child encountering aspects of nature for the very first time, with wide eyes fixed on the small caterpillar skulking its way across the garden floor. The intimate closeness with nature does not necessarily fade as we mature; it is merely too often forgotten by modern humans seemingly obsessed with a technological world. This disconnect is believed by many to contribute to the unsoundness of the mind in contemporary society.As mental health professionals, we can foster this reconnection with the natural world in our clients. Beyond the interventions described in the chapters of this text, there are other variations of ecotherapy. This chapter describes horticulture therapy, green exercise, forest bathing, animal-assisted therapy, equine-assisted therapy, and adventure immersion/wilderness therapy. Some of these variations may require additional training or certification (i.e., equine-assisted therapy, animal-assisted therapy, adventure-based counseling) beyond the scope of a counseling license. Other interventions (horticulture, green exercise, forest bathing) are more accessible to everyday clinicians.Horticulture Therapy

Horticulture therapy elicits the intrinsic harmony between human beings and nature. Through exposure to plant life and gardening, individuals are able to achieve therapeutic and rehabilitative outcomes (Chen, Ho, & Tu, 2013; Simson & Straus, 1998). This outlook on mental health treatment dates back to centuries ago, as professionals often sought natural resources to promote wellness in those afflicted by mental illness (Foucault, 2009; Monroe, 2015). When clients regain access to the natural world through gardening or cultivating plant life, they realign themselves not only with nature itself but with what it means to be fully human.

Many individuals, especially those in the mental health counseling field, may commonly associate horticulture therapy with those within the elderly population. This may be due to the fact that various studies show the positive benefits of introducing horticultural activities to those residing in nursing homes or suffering from dementia (Gigliotti & Jarrott, 2005; Yao & Chen, 2017). In particular, Gigliotti and Jarrott reported that individuals involved in a dementia treatment program increased engagement levels when participating in horticultural therapeutic activities. Furthermore, the older adult participants within the study often began as soon as materials were placed in front of them, without prompting or instruction. This suggests not only the effectiveness of the intervention but that participants truly enjoy the horticultural aspect. This notion is supported by the findings of Yao and Chen, who described an overall increase in happiness of group participants over an eight-week period. In addition to an increase in positive affect, interpersonal intimacy and levels of daily activity were also enhanced in those participating in the horticultural therapeutic group.

While there have been multiple studies concerning the positive benefits of horticultural therapy within the elderly population, this intervention is not limited to serving only one group of individuals. Research has shown that plant-based modalities can be useful in serving adolescents, women, and veterans (Beela, Reghunath, & Johnson, 2015; Kim & Park, 2018; Lehmann, Detweiler, & Detweiler, 2018). Increased self-identity and confidence to take an active role in cultivating personal health was a common result of the horticultural experience in each of these unique populations. Additionally, Kim and Park found that women experienced a decrease in depressive and anxious symptoms. Adolescents with physical disabilities improved in understanding of self-concept when tasked with the responsibility to tend to plant life (Beela et al., 2018). Lastly, veterans previously introduced to a gardening program that eventually failed due to logistical complications took it upon themselves to continue the horticultural activities, as they believed them to be useful mechanisms to stress reduction

(Lehmann et al., 2018). Overall, engagement with nature does not discriminate against any person in search of healing. The way of the natural world allows for reciprocal growth when cultivating and caring for the earth.

For the everyday practitioner, there are several ways that horticultural therapy can be a part of the practice. For example, with warmer weather and space permitting, a clinician can create a small garden near his or her office. The client and counselor can work and talk, if only to simply pull weeds. A counselor can also give a small piece of the garden to clients and help them to add and care for the plants, checking and caring for the greenery each week during their normal sessions. In addition, a counselor can integrate a simple horticulture into a session. For example, using a simple bell jar as a container, the client can decorate the jar (with paint, markers, or stickers) and add dirt, pebbles, and a small plant. This simple activity can relax a client, helping to facilitate an easy conversation. The client can bring the plant home to nurture and enjoy. Counselors can achieve larger projects but might need additional time, space, money, and coordination. An example of a horticulture therapy project for clients suffering from eating disorders is described in detail at the end of this chapter.

GREEN EXERCISE

As previously mentioned, it is not necessarily required for those who seek to practice ecotherapy to maintain further credentials or training. Allowing clients to take a break from life indoors has the potential to provide extremely beneficial results. This informal practice is coined in the research as *green exercise*, which is succinctly stated as any activity conducted in the presence of nature (Barton & Pretty, 2010). Most often, this area of nature therapy consists of guiding individuals on a walk throughout an outdoor setting. Barton and Pretty explain that green exercise can be conducted in all green environments and will maintain positive effect even when consisting of only 5 minutes. Ideally, the nature activity is not excessively physically demanding. Those reported to benefit the most from green exercise are individuals struggling with mental health concerns (Barton & Pretty, 2010). Thus the attention of clinicians ought to be concentrated toward prospective implications for treatment.

Various studies have found both physiological and psychological outcomes of green exercise with those seeking mental health treatment (Barton & Pretty, 2010; Christie & Cole, 2017; Fuegen & Breitenbecher, 2018; Iwata et al., 2016; Jordan & Hinds, 2016; Korpela, Stengård, & Jussila, 2016; Pretty, Peacock, Sellens, & Griffin, 2005). Frequent reports of significantly increased positive mood and self-esteem have been associated with clients participating in green exercise activities (Barton & Pretty, 2010; Fuegen & Breitenbecher, 2018; Iwata et al., 2016; Pretty et al., 2005). Korpele et al. pointed out that the depression ratings of participants decreased after partaking in a treatment intervention that utilized nature walks. Furthermore, a healing component was associated with the green exercise that did not exist within the therapy conducted within indoor settings. Not only does this treatment modality allow for mental well-being to improve, exposure to outdoor settings may beneficially impact physical wellness. Pretty et al. discovered green exercise to be impactful in improving scores pertinent to cardiovascular health, particularly when compared to exercise alone. Therefore, it would be most advantageous for an individual to perform physical activity in a pleasant outdoor setting if he or she seeks optimal health benefit. Although simple in tactic, it is undeniable that this natural activity provides the metal health field with a powerful and accessible treatment modality for overall well-being.

While it is valuable to identify the multiple psychological improvements that result from green exercise, perhaps it is even more crucial to explore what exactly clients experience when confronting the natural world as a part of treatment. Iwata et al. (2016) reported that individuals involved in therapeutic forest exploration expressed feelings of calmness and relaxation. The natural environment provided a quiet escape much different than the atmosphere of everyday life. Furthermore, participants encountered the many awe-inspiring, beautiful elements of nature.

Jordan and Hinds (2016) outlined the experience of individuals inclined toward stress-related mental disorders. Participants in a green rehabilitation program experienced feelings of awe when meandering through the natural world. This, in turn, allowed the clients to detach themselves from the worries of everyday situations. Christie and Cole (2017) explain that one of the main components involved in the natural enhancement of mental health reported by all participants is the tranquil and healing nature of the environment. As therapists, it is clear that a common goal is to introduce a sense of serenity into the frequently chaotic worlds of our clients. Accordingly, it would be a senseless blunder to forgo the natural aid provided by Mother Nature herself.

FOREST BATHING

While green exercise allows for direct contact with the outside world in a somewhat casual manner, some individuals may desire a deeper immersion into the natural environment. Shinrin-yoku, also known as forest bathing, is a practice utilized to fully experience the abounding wonder of a thriving forest setting. "Naturalistic outdoor environments in general remain some of the only places here we engage all five senses, and thus, by definition, are fully, physically alive" (Williams, 2018, p. 23). Created by the Japanese government nearly 40 years ago, forest bathing, based on Buddhist and Shinto ideals, essentially means taking in the elements while walking in the woods (Williams, 2018). While it originated in Japan, anyone can shinrin-yoku in natural settings and receive the benefits involved (Morita et al., 2007).

Immersing oneself into the depths of the forest environment is advantageous for both the body and the mind (Hassan et al., 2018; Lee et al., 2011; Mitchell, 2013; Morita et al., 2007; Ohtsuka, Yabunaka, & Takayama,1998; Williams, 2018). The ambiance of the forest acts as an all-natural stress reliever, lowering both blood pressure and salivary cortisol levels (Hassan et al., 2018; Lee et al., 2011; Ochiai et al., 2015; Williams, 2018). Some may propose that these effects manifest as a result of simply taking a break from the chaos of day-to-day life. However, Lee et al. (2011) state that those exposed to natural stimuli display significantly lower levels of salivary cortisol than those experiencing urban environments. Perhaps our bodies are not intended to function within the artificial and highly stimulating modern society we have grown accustomed to. The natural environment may be the only setting in which we can truly find peace. Not only does forest bathing benefit our physical well-being, but it produces various mental health benefits as well. In fact, Mitchell (2013) identified that those who regularly use natural environments for physical activity are at a lower risk for poor mental health. Additionally, Morita et al. (2007) reported that participants engaging in forest bathing saw decreased levels of depression and hostility. More interestingly, these decreases were significantly stronger for those who entered the forest when compared to separate groups instructed to participate in favorable activities. This suggests that the forest environment in and of itself dramatically influenced the beneficial outcome.

The ability to relax has become an increasingly more difficult task for modern individuals. Even when finding the time to decompress, it is sometimes challenging to slow down racing thoughts that sometimes swirl within our minds. Morita et al. (2007) identified the chronically stressed as those benefitting the most from forest bathing. Repeatedly, participants express the relaxation element of shinrin-yoku with words such as "comfort," "natural," and "relaxed" when relaying the experience of forest bathing (Hassan et al., 2018; Morita et al., 2007; Ochiai, 2015).

Physical measurement of brain waves also shows the effects of relaxation. In measuring the alpha waves of the brain—those associated with alertness, calmness, and mental coordination—individuals engaging in forest bathing experience show an increase in power of alpha. This suggests that exposure to the forest setting allows for an increase in relaxation and mental focus (Hassan et al., 2018). It is undeniable that the forest setting offers a sense of stillness not often found within the bustling surroundings of contemporary civilization. If we seek to quiet our minds, we may consider becoming one with the stillness and immersing our senses into the depths of the natural world.

ANIMAL-ASSISTED THERAPY

So far we have discussed interventions that every therapist interested in a natural orientation may employ. Animal-assisted therapy, however, frequently requires specialized training in order to work with both clients and animal professionals. In understanding the merit of the technique itself, clarifications on the theoretical tenets of animal-assisted therapy must first be explored. Specific distinguishing factors differentiate animal-assisted therapy from other therapeutic interactions with animals, such as animal-assisted activity (Chandler, 2012; "The IAHAIO Definitions for Animal-Assisted Intervention and Guidelines for Wellness of Animals Involved" [IAHAIO Definitions], 2014). Animal-assisted activity involves the social interaction with a therapy animal for the purpose of educational or recreational benefits. Animal-assisted therapy, on the other hand, requires the human–animal bond to serve a therapeutic purpose within the scope of treatment planning (Chandler, 2012; IAHAIO Definitions, 2014.) Chandler and Masini (2010) explain that animal-assisted therapy may be encompassed within the pre-existing theoretical orientation that the mental health counselor maintains. Further, one particularly useful aspect of animal-assisted therapy is the fact that human beings have a natural inclination toward the nurturing relationship with the nonjudgmental, genuine nature of the animal they work with. Therefore, trust—a vital ingredient within the counseling relationship—is naturally established within the therapeutic setting.

Animal-assisted therapy is often associated with therapy dogs. Although often confused, therapy dogs are different from service dogs. Service dogs are trained to help with very specific tasks. These tasks aid their handlers with everyday responsibilities, such helping a blind person navigate in a seeing world, assisting a person with severe allergies sniff out life-threatening ingredients, or working with a police office to locate explosives or drugs. Typically, these dogs maintain a no-pet policy, discouraging individuals of the general public from distracting the animals from their work. Therapy dogs, in contrast, undergo training to provide psychological or physiological assistance to people other than their handlers. Therapy dogs are gentle and easygoing and are encouraged to interact with people. These special animals can provide individual care for those who are in need. For example, clients who experience high levels of anxiety may experience calming effects provided by therapy dogs. Additionally, these therapeutic canines can assist in larger groups such as patients in hospitals, nursing homes, or hospice, for example. Besides dogs, cats, guinea pigs, rabbits, birds, and even pigs can be therapy animals. It is important, especially for ecotherapists, to consider the well-being of any animal working in the capacity of service or therapy to humans. Animals should not be used but rather receive as much nurturing as they are providing.

EQUINE-ASSISTED THERAPY

Horses are one of the commonly associated animals within the field of animal-assisted therapy. Equine-assisted therapy, guided by a trained therapist, involves the relationship and bond a client experiences with a horse that helps facilitate healing and change. Horses are highly sensitive creatures, hyperaware of their surroundings and constantly alert. Horses communicate through body language and are very sensitive to the nonverbal behaviors of humans. As such, a human's interaction with a horse must be intentional and calm (Maclean, 2011). Equine-assisted therapy is especially beneficial to those who have experienced trauma, have difficulty with trusting others, and/or have numb themselves to feeling. A client working with a horse learns, through the guided interactions, a mutual trust. The client must also tap into and learn to manage feelings, especially if they become agitated or angry, in order to establish a bond with the horse (Earles, Vernon, & Yetz, 2015; Maclean, 2011.)

In relating to the horse, the client is able to understand more fully the inner workings of their own human psyche. The therapist and client process the interaction after each encounter (Masini, 2010). While equine therapy may be particularly beneficial to those who are reluctant to counseling, it is helpful for various populations and groups (Masini, 2010). Borgi et al. (2016) found that children with autism spectrum disorder improved in social functioning, decision-making skills, and speed for problem-solving tasks after participating within a six-month equine-assisted therapy program. Schultz, Remick-Barlow, and Robbins (2007) demonstrated an increase in the global assessment functioning of children with a history of intrafamily violence and substance abuse after experiencing equine-assisted therapy. Veterans suffering with posttraumatic stress disorder also experience a decrease in symptomology with treatment involving equine assistance (Romaniuk, Evans, & Kidd, 2018). An additional interesting finding associated with this research study was the notion that those veterans who participated in a couple's equine therapy program maintained restorative outcomes for a longer time period than those involved in the individual program. In understanding the unique and somewhat mysterious impact that animals have upon the mental well-being of humans, Chandler (2012) calls attention to the innate desire of human beings for social connectedness. The ease in bonding with a living being outside of our own species points directly to the cohesion of the natural world.

ADVENTURE IMMERSION OR WILDERNESS THERAPY

Up until now, the various interventions discussed have ranged from easily accessible to training necessary for utilization. Adventure therapy falls on the latter end of the spectrum, as it is imperative for all professionals involved to secure the safety and overall well-being of those participating in the process. The actual definition of wilderness therapy has been a source of debate and may change considerably depending on the particular framework of the professional conducting the therapy (Gass, Gillis, & Russell, 2012; Russell, 2001). However, various key elements are essential in order to present a clearer picture of this modality. Primarily, the intervention is therapeutic, occurs within a natural setting, and encourages the use of natural consequences, metaphors, and rites of passage within the wilderness experience (Tucker et al., 2016). Responsibility of the participants is stressed, as clients are put in charge of their own outcomes and are impacted by natural consequences within the environmental setting (Gass, Gillis, & Russell, 2001; Tucker et al., 2016). In wilderness/adventure-based therapy, interventions often involve an immersive experience in a remote natural landscape. Typically participants backpack or even canoe or kayak for multiple days or weeks. At the core of this type of therapy is the intense wilderness exposure.

Adventure therapy is predominately used as a treatment option for adolescents, and research has shown that this intervention is especially effective in reducing recidivism rates for juvenile offenders (Neill, 2003; Williams, 2000). Outcomes for adolescents who participate in wilderness therapy include an enhanced sense of self and increase in coping and relational skills, particularly helpful for children emerging from broken and abusive homes (Hattie Marsh, Neill, & Richards 1997; Russell, 2001). The researchers also found in through follow-up surveys that there was considerable evidence that this change persists over time. One of the best-known wilderness programs is Outward Bound (www.outwardbound.org). For over 50 years, Outward Bound has been providing wilderness experiences for teens and adults in a variety of settings across the globe. Outward Bound is not the only outdoor adventure company; the breadth and width of programs vary with population served and the needs of participants. It is important, however, to do extensive research on any wilderness-based or adventure company to ensure that the organization is experienced, insured, properly staffed, and capable.

Remarkably, readiness to change is not essential for success within these therapeutic environments (Bettman, Russel, & Parry, 2013). A somewhat magical effect is seen in various participants when they endure the natural elements involved in adventure therapy. Williams (2018) partially credits this phenomenon to the *awe* frequently experienced in environmental immersion. For something to be awe-inspiring, it must be expansive and vast and must make us pause to take in the immensity of it all, such as an incredible sunset or an expansive mountain range. This feeling of awe inspires various positive human behaviors, such as curiosity and social connection. Full submersion into the natural world offers the possibility to inspire and reawaken the potential of a person who is feeling lost and alone. It allows the individual to develop a self-understanding deeply connected to nature—one of strength, responsibility, and inspiration.

Very few people will have the time, resources, ability, or even desire to participate in a full wilderness emersion program (although I highly recommend them). That said, the sense of awe and a deeper connection to the wilderness might not be that out of reach. An early morning sunrise at the beach can ignite that sense of awe, as can a long walk in the woods. Exploring places that are less crowded or at off-peak hours can allow, even if just for a short time, a sense of connection to a wilder world that still encompasses almost half of the planet (Mittermeier, Mittermeier, Pilgrim, Fonseca, & Konstant, 2002). It is just a matter of getting out there.

FLOWERS FOR CHANGE: A HORTICULTURAL INTERVENTION FOR CLIENTS WITH EATING DISORDERS

This intervention is intended for those clients who are struggling with eating disorders. The age of the client may range from adolescent to adult.

Ideally, this would be practiced in an inpatient program; however, it could be utilized in various settings.

Rationale

Many individuals who have developed eating disorders struggle with the need for control and perfection (Boone, Soenens, & Luyten, 2014; Dalgleish et al., 2001). In nature, there is an abundance of beauty and life; however, there is no concept of conforming to an ideal appearance. A flower simply grows, without fear of matching the image of its surroundings. By gardening, the client is able to get his or her hands dirty and maintain a safe space free from the perceived pressure to maintain perfection. The therapist should encourage and affirm clients that throughout the process, pointing to the beauty and unpredictability of growth.

An additional phenomenon often associated with eating disorders is a lack of developed identity (Cruzat, Díaz, Escobar, & Simpson, 2017; Stein & Corte, 2007). Clients regularly report that they experience the eating disorder itself as an identity due to the fact that it consumes every thought and dictates behavior. With many years of attending to an eating disorder, it is easy to lose sight of the true defining characteristics that an individual upholds. Constant attention paid to eating habits or avoidance does not leave room for the establishment of individuality. Caring for a garden allows the client to extend beyond this idea and develop his or her natural identity. If nothing else, the activity may potentially provide a break in the day from the thought-consuming reality of what it is to wrestle with disordered eating.

A fear of change, particularly physical change, is common among this population. This is especially evident with those suffering from anorexia nervosa (Linardon et al., 2018). Providing an opportunity for clients to follow the growth of each plant may foster an alternate outlook on transformation. Allowing oneself to grow may be seen as beautiful rather than terrifying. Furthermore, it might become evident that change is a slow process and that much patience is required. This depiction may possibly counteract the black-and-white mindset that many struggle with.

Lastly, the importance of nurturance is a major theme within this intervention. Just as humans, plants cannot grow unless they are nurtured. Individuals with eating disorders adhere to a scheduled meal plan in order to maintain health (Wisniewski & Kelly, 2003). Providing regular upkeep for the plant life models this kind of regimented self-care. The clients are able to have an active role in providing care and nutrients to the garden in order to allow the plants to become what they were meant to be.

Materials

- Outdoor area for gardening
- Soil
- Various flower seeds
  - Easy to grow: sunflower, marigold, cosmos, sweet peas, pansies
- Gardening tools
  - Watering cans, gloves, rakes, hand trowel, gardening fork, shovel, etc.

Length of Activity

This intervention is intended for those in a long-term recovery program. Each session consists of 20 to 30 minutes of gardening. The group then processes the experience for an additional 30 minutes with the therapist, talking about thoughts and feelings.

Instructions

Session One

In the first session, introduce the concept of gardening. Some participants will have some experience and some will have none. Take the time to talk about what plants you will be working with, how to plant the seeds, what to wear while gardening, and taking sun precautions. Explain the characteristics of each plant provided. Process any reservations about participation.

Session Two

Allow each member to choose a seed that he or she identifies with or is drawn toward. It may be helpful to pick hearty flowers, perhaps perennials so that the flower grows and blooms each year. Discuss the identification: What about the plant is relatable? Process the concept behind a small shell holding the potential for life. Allow each participant to choose a spot to plant his or her seed. Process what it was like to experience nature directly. Discuss mindfulness in gardening.

Figure 9.1 The garden planted by ecotherapy participants.

Session Three

Allow each participant to choose a spot to plant his or her seed. Process what it was like to experience nature directly. Discuss mindfulness in gardening.

Sessions Four and On

Spend time in the garden. Allow the participants to provide care and check on their flowers. It is helpful if the garden has some other growth (plants, herbs, etc.) that the clients can also attend to, such as pruning, weeding, watering, and so on. The counselor can also direct participants to talk to their flowers. The act of talking to a plant may seem odd at first, but encourage the clients. Flowers do not talk back; they do not judge and, obviously, can keep secrets. Clients can also explore natural themes or metaphors that occur such as transformation, growth, lack of control, fear, necessity for nutrients, sense of accomplishment, and so on. The metaphor of a flower may resonate with clients coping with eating disorders. Flowers are delicate and need care and nourishment or they will wither and die. Flowers are also resilient and can come back stronger with the proper care and attention. At the end of participants' time in treatment, they are encouraged to pot the flower and take it home with them to their own gardens as a reminder of their hard work and capacity to grow.

REFERENCES

Barton, J., & Pretty, J. (2010). What is the best dose of nature and green exercise for improving mental health? A multi-study analysis. *Environmental Science & Technology, 44*(10), 3947–3955.Beela, G. K., Reghunath, B. R., & Johnson, J. (2015). Horticulture therapy for the improvement of self concept in adolescents with locomotor and hearing impairment. *Indian Journal of Physiotherapy & Occupational Therapy, 9*(4), 57–62.

Bettmann, J. E., Russell, K. C., & Parry, K. J. (2013). How substance abuse recovery skills, readiness to change and symptom reduction impact change processes in wilderness therapy participants. *Journal of Child and Family Studies, 22*(8), 1039–1050. https://doi.org/10.1007/s10826-012-9665-2.

Borgi, M., Loliva, D., Cerino, S., Chiarotti, F., Venerosi, A., Bramini, M., . . . Cirulli, F. (2016). Effectiveness of a standardized equine-assisted therapy program for children with autism spectrum disorder. *Journal of Autism & Developmental Disorders, 46*(1), 1–9.

Boone, L., Soenens, B., & Luyten, P. (2014). When or why does perfectionism translate into eating disorder pathology? A longitudinal examination of the moderating and mediating role of body dissatisfaction. *Journal of Abnormal Psychology, 123*(2), 412–418.

Chandler, C. K. (2012). *Animal assisted therapy in counseling.* New York, NY: Taylor & Francis.

Chen, H. M, Ho, C. I, & Tu, H. M. (2013). Understanding biophilia leisure as facilitating well-being and the environment: An examination of participants' attitudes toward horticultural activity. *Leisure Sciences, 35*, 301–319.

Christie, M. A., & Cole, F. (2017). The impact of green exercise on volunteer's mental health and wellbeing: Findings from a community project in a woodland setting. *Journal of Therapeutic Horticulture, 27*(1), 17–33.

Cruzat, M. C., Díaz, C. F., Escobar, K. T., & Simpson, S. (2017). From eating identity to authentic selfhood: Identity transformation in eating disorder sufferers following psychotherapy. *Clinical Psychologist, 21*(3), 227–235.

Dalgleish, T., Tchanturia, K., Serpell, L., Hems, S., Silva, P. D., & Treasure, J. (2001). Perceived control over events in the world in patients with eating disorders: A preliminary study. *Personality and Individual Differences, 31*(3), 453–460.

Earles, J. L., Vernon, L. L., & Yetz, J. P. (2015). Equine-assisted therapy for anxiety and posttraumatic stress symptoms. *Journal of Traumatic Stress, 28*(2), 149–152.

Foucault, M. (2009). *History of madness*. New York, NY: Routledge.

Fuegen, K., & Breitenbecher, K. H. (2018). Walking and being outdoors in nature increase positive affect and energy. *Ecopsychology, 10*(1), 14–25.

Gass, M., Gillis, H. L., & Russell, K. (2012). *Adventure therapy: Theory, research, and practice*. New York, NY: Routledge.

Gigliotti, C. M., & Jarrott, S. E. (2005). Effects of horticulture therapy on engagement and affect. *Canadian Journal on Aging, 24*(4), 367–377.

Hassan, A., Jiang, T., Guo, L., Jiang, M., Aii, L., Zhihui, J., . . . Chen, Q. (2018). Effects of walking in bamboo forest and city environments on brainwave activity in young adults. *Evidence-Based Complementary and Alternative Medicine, 2018*, 9.

Hattie, J., Marsh, H. W., Neill, J. T., & Richards, G. E. (1997). Adventure education and Outward Bound: Out-of-class experiences that make a lasting difference. *Review of Educational Research, 67*(1), 43–87. https://doi.org/10.3102/00346543067001043.

Iwata, Y., Dhubháin, Á N., Brophy, J., Roddy, D., Burke, C., & Murphy, B. (2016). Benefits of group walking in forests for people with significant mental ill-health. *Ecopsychology, 8*(1), 16–26.

Jordan, M., & Hinds, J. (2016). *Ecotherapy: Theory, research and practice*. London, England: Macmillan.

Kim, K., & Park, S. (2018). Horticultural therapy program for middle-aged women's depression, anxiety, and self-identify. *Complementary Therapies in Medicine, 39*, 154–159.

Korpela, K. M., Stengård, E., & Jussila, P. (2016). Nature walks as a part of therapeutic intervention for depression. *Ecopsychology, 8*(1), 8–15.

Lee, J., Park, B., Tsunetsugu, Y., Ohira, T., Kagawa, T., & Miyazaki, Y. (2011). Effect of forest bathing on physiological and psychological responses in young Japanese male subjects. *Public Health, 125*(2), 93–100.

Lehmann, L. P., Detweiler, J. G., & Detweiler, M. B. (2018). Veterans in substance abuse treatment program self-initiate box gardening as a stress reducing therapeutic modality. *Complementary Therapies in Medicine, 36*, 50–53.

Linardon, J., Phillipou, A., Castle, D., Newton, R., Harrison, P., Cistullo, L. L., . . . Brennan, L. (2018). The relative associations of shape and weight over-evaluation, preoccupation, dissatisfaction, and fear of weight gain with measures of psychopathology: An extension study in individuals with anorexia nervosa. *Eating Behaviors, 29*, 54–58.

Maclean, B. (2011). Equine-assisted therapy. *Journal of Rehabilitation Research and Development, 48*(7), ix–xii. doi:10.1682/JRRD.2011.05.0085

Masini A. (2010). Equine-assisted psychotherapy in clinical practice. *Journal of Psychosocial Nursing & Mental Health Services, 48*(10), 30–34.

Mitchell, R. (2013). Is physical activity in natural environments better for mental health than physical activity in other environments? *Social Science & Medicine, 91*, 130–134.

Mittermeier, R. A., Mittermeier, C. G., Pilgrim, J., Fonseca, G., & Konstant, W. R. (2002). *Wilderness: Earth's last wild places* (No. 333.782 W673w). México City: CEMEX.

Monroe, L. (2015). Horticulture therapy improves the body, mind and spirit. *Journal of Therapeutic Horticulture, 25*(2), 33–39.

Morita, E., Fukuda, S., Nagano, J., Hamajima, N., Yamamoto, H., Iwai, Y., . . . Shirakawa, T. (2007). Psychological effects of forest environments on healthy adults: Shinrin-yoku (forest-air bathing, walking) as a possible method of stress reduction. *Public Health, 121*(1), 54–63.

Neill, J. T. (2003). Reviewing and benchmarking adventure therapy outcomes: Applications of Meta-Analysis. *The Journal of Experiential Education, 25*(3), 316–321. https://doi.org/10.1177/105382590302500305.

Ochiai, H., Ikei, H., Song, C., Kobayashi, M., Miura, T., Kagawa, T., . . . Miyazaki, Y. (2015). Physiological and psychological effects of a forest therapy program on middle-aged females. *International Journal of Environmental Research and Public Health, 12*(12), 15222–15232.

Ohtsuka, Y., Yabunaka, N., & Takayama, S. (1998). Shinrin-yoku (forest-air bathing and walking) effectively decreases blood glucose levels in diabetic patients. *International Journal of Biometeorology, 41*(3), 125–127.

Pretty, J., Peacock, J., Sellens, M., & Griffin, M. (2005). The mental and physical health outcomes of green exercise. *International Journal of Environmental Health Research, 15*(5), 319–337.

Romaniuk, M., Evans, J., & Kidd, C. (2018). Evaluation of an equine-assisted therapy program for veterans who identify as "wounded, injured or ill" and their partners. *PLoS One, 13*(9).

Russell, K. C. (2001). What is wilderness therapy? *Journal of Experiential Education, 24*(2), 70–79.

Schultz, P. N., Remick-Barlow, G. A., & Robbins, L. (2007). Equine-assisted psychotherapy: A mental health promotion/intervention modality for children who have experienced intra-family violence. *Health & Social Care in the Community, 15*(3), 265–271.

Simson, S. P., & Straus, M. C. (1998). *Horticulture as therapy: Principles and practice*. Birmingham, NY: Food Products Press.

Stein, K. F., & Corte, C. (2007). Identity impairment and the eating disorders: Content and organization of the self-concept in women with anorexia nervosa and bulimia nervosa. *European Eating Disorders Review, 15*(1), 58–69.

The IAHAIO definitions for animal-assisted intervention and guidelines for wellness of animals involved. (2014). In A. H. Fine (Ed.), *Handbook on animal-assisted therapy* (pp. 415–418). New York, NY: Academic Press.

Tucker, A. R., Combs, K. M., Bettmann, J. E., Chang, T., Graham, S., Hoag, M., & Tatum, C. (2016). Longitudinal outcomes for youth transported to wilderness therapy programs. *Research on Social Work Practice, 28*(4), 438–451.

Williams, B. (2000). The treatment of adolescent populations: An institutional vs. a wilderness setting. *Journal of Child and Adolescent Group Therapy, 10*(1), 47–56. https://doi.org/10.1023/A:1009456511437.

Williams, F. (2018). *The nature fix: Why nature makes us happier, healthier, and more creative*. New York, NY: W. W. Norton.

Wisniewski, L., & Kelly, E. (2003). The application of dialectical behavior therapy to the treatment of eating disorders. *Cognitive and Behavioral Practice, 10*(2), 131–138.

Yao, Y., & Chen, K. (2017). Effects of horticulture therapy on nursing home older adults in southern Taiwan. *Quality of Life Research, 26*(4), 1007–1014.

CHAPTER 9A

THE CYCLE OF THE GARDEN

Jonathan Yellowhair

My name is Jonathan Yellowhair, and I am from Flagstaff, Arizona. I am an avid enthusiast of alleviating mental health disparities in marginalized communities. I am also a member of the Navajo Nation, a U.S. Marine Corps veteran, and a graduate of Northern Arizona University (NAU). NAU gave me the opportunity to become educated, but it also encouraged me to be involved with various projects that benefitted my local community. It was through my communal projects that I recognized my passion for working with kids, youth, and young adults who come from homes and environments that hinder growth due to circumstances beyond their control. Working with students from my home community, and recognizing the pressing need for someone to invest in their emotional and spiritual well-being, helped shape the trajectory of my future work. I had fallen in love with my work but had also married the woman of my dreams. I learned valuable lessons from my family, the Navajo culture, and diverse mentors: now it was time to see if this knowledge was transferrable to our new home in Georgia.

When I moved from my home in Arizona to Atlanta, I felt professionally stagnant. I decided to take a year off to explore prospective graduate programs that catered to my future ambitions of becoming a counselor, but my time searching left me feeling abeyant: It was difficult for me to have not yet found an outlet for my passion. Serendipitously, I was forwarded an opportunity to work as a fourth-grade academic coach at an after-school program in the lower-income part of Atlanta. Even though I worked with young Native and Hispanic students in Arizona, I never was immersed in a culture quite like that of Atlanta's young African American students.

The children I met were full of life and happiness. I soon recognized the disparities in this neighborhood that paralleled those on the Navajo Nation, including food deserts, poverty, undereducation, and presenting historical and complex trauma. Also, much like Navajos, these students were extremely resilient. Many came from dire circumstances and troubled homes but still maintained the ability to survive and succeed. Unfortunately, subduing and pushing through their anxiety, their depression, and their stress can be detrimental to the current and future mental health and stability of children. With these circumstances in mind, I was ecstatic when I was asked to start up a garden project with students in the spring. I was excited about the opportunity to learn and to grow in this garden with these students.

Traditionally, Navajos grow all our own food, and this practice is still alive and well today. The planting, caring, and harvesting of crops is filled with lessons and teachings that are beyond words. It is a time for teaching and more importantly a time for learning no matter what age. In Atlanta, I had about 20 students that ranged from first grade to fifth grade. The very first day we gathered all our tools, gloves, and water and headed down to the garden. We set everything down, and I began to wonder how I would go about motivating these students to begin our garden on this particularly hot and sticky Georgia morning. I led with a half-baked motivational speech and started designating jobs for the students. "All right, let's go!" I said emphatically, but as I turned around and started walking, I realized I was the only one moving.

I figured they wanted to stay in the shade because of the heat, and so I walked back up to the shade and asked what the holdup was. I was surprised when a student told me that it was all because "there was a bee by the boxes." I told the student that the bee was not there to hurt them, to which the student responded, "But Mr. Yellowhair, don't you know? All black folks are allergic to bees!" This was a great lesson for me, because I had never heard this before. True or not, as an adult it is my obligation to respect the knowledge and intuition of young minds. I simply conveyed my ignorance and said, "Huh, I didn't know that," and then worked to ease their minds with the fact that I was CPR certified and had done first responder training in the Marines. It was not my job to tell them what was right and what was wrong; I figured that they got enough of that.

I used the bee as my first teaching point and conveyed to these children what I was told when I was very small. "Bees can agitate you and sting you, but they only do so out of fear when you provoke them and don't respect their space. In life, you cannot lash out at everything and everyone that agitates you, because you must live side by side with people and respect their space. Unfortunately, there will always be those that will agitate you, but only you can give them the power to sting you by responding in the way that they want you to. The outdoors is the bee's home. We are guests here, and if you are respectful of their space, they will help you build your garden." The students took to this lesson well, much better than my half-baked speech earlier. It also segued the conversation into a plethora of questions about bees that allowed me the space to describe the importance of bees and aspects of growth and pollination. We were now ready to work.

Children are not too fond of tilling dirt and weeding in the humid Georgia summer. I was enjoying being outdoors again, but my fellow gardeners began to question why all this work was being done and why their efforts were so strenuous. I told them that gardening, like life, is a lot of work and that sometimes you do not see the immediate fruits of your labors. Eventually, you learn that the hard efforts and time invested are fruits themselves. Speaking these words also struck me to my core, realizing that my current work with these children was a blessing in itself and that I needed to be patient with my academic search as well as life's other endeavors.

After tilling and preparing the soil, we were ready to put down some plants. The children loved this part, as they were able to plant and to learn about succulents, Roma and Cherokee tomatoes, cucumbers, squash, bell peppers, strawberries, jalapenos, peppermint, and basil. We also planted white, red, yellow, and purple Navajo corn that I brought from back home. I put an emphasis on the importance of this phase, as it is "when the plants first meet you." Puzzled, the students asked, "How can a plant meet you?" I told them that we must "treat plants as the living beings that they are" and that "these little plants you are holding are just babies and must be cared for as such. Be nice to them and treat them with respect, talk to them and tell them your hardships and about all the great things that are happening in your life. This helps alleviate stress while simultaneously making the plants grow strong, as they feed off your energy. Life can be frustrating, and you don't always get to show your stress, anxiety, and sadness but here in this garden, you can be as frustrated as you want, this is the place where you can express that safely."

There was anxiety from staff about particular students who had a history of violent behavior or who had come from violent homes because we were going to be using tools like shovels, rakes, and spades. I recognized the potential harm but, to me, these tools were a physical representation of trust. I couldn't write off these students, and so I gave them the opportunity to have their space and to do their work while being supervised. I know what it is like to be written off simply because of people's perception of you, your past, your family, or your culture, and so I refused to do the same with these children. I talked to them and told them that I trusted them, but if they began to feel frustrated to a point of outright anger, they needed to put their tool down safely and walk to the shade or come talk to me. Hearing these children's frustrations and trials reaffirmed my desire to become a counselor and help people on this journey through life. These children dealt with issues far beyond their years and comprehension—yet they had the fortitude and patience to cope in a way that was unfamiliar to them. We went the entire planting season without a single incident.

I have worked in numerous gardens, but I have never seen such a prosperous one. The cucumbers were near the size of melons. There was such an abundance of food that we started giving it away to the community. The students also had a plethora of questions when they started seeing vegetables and fruits of all different colors. They had never seen different and multicolored bell peppers and tomatoes. All of this tantalized their imaginations. When it was time, I gave the very first ear of corn to a student to open. As he tore back the husks, he was startled by the sight of the corn. "Purple!" he shouted as he nearly dropped the corn, stating, "Mr. Yellowhair, it is rotten!" I asked him to hand me the corn, explaining to the students that this is what plants are supposed to look like. Our whole lives we have been told that beauty is supposed to look a certain way, and that deviating from this projected image somehow makes you different, strange, or insufficient in some capacity. I told them that the diverse colors among the corn are what truly makes them special. It is okay to be different; in fact, we grow different kinds of corn because it is beneficial to have diversity. The corn grown for eating is different than the corn we grow for our ceremonies, which varies from the corn that we grow for bread. It is okay to be unique and special and to serve a purpose that deviates from the traditional path. At the end of the day, all corn came from the same place and can grow side by side while still giving space to recognize just how special each individual ear is.

This opened the space for discussion on healthy diets and lifestyle choices regarding food but also about their contributions to society. So often children are stigmatized as being a burden or simply as being consumers. Seeing their hard work come to fruition, I told them that the plants were a living testament that they are not just consumers in society but avid producers that can grow their own food and food for others. For Navajos, children are just as important as any other piece in the family constellation; they are the future of our people, and, as such, it is our job to guide them while also respecting them and honoring the lessons that they can teach us.

Figure 9a.1 A young girl holds her prized purple corn!

I also had to trust the students to make mistakes, because making mistakes also forwards the opportunity to learn and to grow. When we began harvesting, one of the second graders came up to me and said, "Mr. Yellowhair! This strawberry was ready to pick so I picked it myself!" and there she stood, with an entire strawberry plant, roots and all, with only one strawberry on it. I smiled and told her good job, then proceeded to ask her if she would be nice enough to teach me how we put the plants in the soil like we did when we first planted. She put it back and we patted down the soil. After doing this she stated that this was "way too much work" and that next time she'll just pluck the strawberry off by itself. It was nice to be her student that day. Children have the capacity to learn on their own without delegation; we just need the humility and patience to give them the space to do so. We foster autonomy by working alongside them, not over them.

Throughout our time together, I would remind students of the power and energy that they have within them. Many students thought of the word "power" meaning money, or strength but had never thought of power as existing within themselves. As Navajos, we are taught that our bodies contain medicine that is applied to everything we do. This medicine can be good or bad; it is our daily choice to delegate how it is utilized. Our relationships with people and the earth transmit and receive this energy and allow for growth or, when neglected, encourage decay. When I was younger, I was taught that Africans and African Americans have particularly strong medicine, as they are direct descendants of the first people of this world. I told my students of this medicine and how powerful they truly are. In a fenced-in garden built across the street from a park that no on goes to because of the crime, I told these students that they had the power to do whatever they want in the future. Their garden at full fruition, I could now reflect on the process with them and tell them how proud I was of them for reclaiming agricultural knowledge that was taken from them and abused for so long.

When the plants started to wither and die due to the end of their cycle, I used it as an opportunity to convey my final teaching point. In our time together, these plants were a physical representation of how my students and I had grown in our relationship together. I only worked with the fourth graders while in the actual classroom, and so the initial phases of this garden were very much the planting phases of our relationship. Like these plants, many things in life come to an end, and it is an absolutely valid emotion to be sad about those endings. It is important to feel this emotion as it is a representation of friendship and empathy.

Ultimately, I was accepted into my first choice master's program and would not see the children as often, and so we were all in mourning of the end of our time together in this garden. Some of the students reacted in the only way they knew how, in anger. They lashed out and showed me that they were in fear that I was abandoning them. I was transparent with them, as they deserved respect and I told them why I was leaving. I reminded them of everything that they had accomplished this season. I encouraged them to look in retrospect and see the place that they had built and remember the people they had fed and the friendships they built in a place where nothing was supposed to grow. They became excited at the thought of being able to teach new students about the garden next season, but little did they know that they were already teachers all along. Looking back, this was one of the greatest experiences I have ever had, and I think of and pray for my students daily. I was sad departing, but I was happy that I was leaving this garden in more than capable little hands. I will truly cherish this garden for the rest of my days, and I will tell my own grandchildren about it as I teach them to garden as well. Ahehee' (thank you).

CHAPTER 9B

THE HUMAN-ANIMAL CONNECTION

Jill Elizabeth Schwarz

They communicate without speaking, offer love without conditions, and forgive freely. Animals impact our lives in so many meaningful ways. Most of us can recall a relationship or encounter with an animal that influenced us in some sense. Perhaps the memory that comes to mind is the comfort you felt from a beloved childhood pet, or the awe you experienced seeing dolphins jump and swim through the ocean waves, or maybe a beautiful myriad of memories of animals throughout your life.

From the time I was a young child, I was drawn to animals. I felt connected to them and possessed what seemed to be an innate compassion for them. I also felt comfort and joy *from* them and eagerly sought out interactions with all different types of animals. I remember seeing puppies outside of the grocery store when I was four, in an enclosure behind a sign I couldn't quite read yet. My older siblings could read it though, and soon I learned that these puppies would be put down later that day if they weren't adopted. After pleading with my mom, she let us adopt a puppy that was supposedly a Beagle mix who "wouldn't get very big," which in reality turned out to be a Doberman mix who grew quite big.

I spent my childhood loving that big dog, and he gave me much love in return. A few months after being away at college I had a dream that my dog was telling me that he was sick (he actually was able to talk and articulate what was wrong in the dream). I told my college roommates, who were all drawn in by the detailed dream but assured me that of course it was just a dream and my dog was perfectly fine. I couldn't shake the feeling that something was wrong though. I was supposed to visit a friend at another college for the weekend, but, before I left, I knew I needed to call home (these were pre-cell phone days) to check on my dog. When my mom answered and I asked, "Is Boots okay?" She was flabbergasted. She responded immediately with "Who told you? I told them not to tell you!" My heart racing, I responded, "Tell me what? I had a dream that he was sick and needed me." My mother, still shocked, went on to explain to me that the dog was indeed sick, but they didn't want to worry me while I was away at college. I asked to come home immediately and was able to be with him later that night. In the meantime, my mother had taken him to the vet, who shared that Boots didn't have much time left, and we should say our goodbyes that weekend.

I slept with Boots on the living room floor the whole weekend and noticed that although he was very sick when I arrived, he seemed to be getting closer and closer to his normal self as the weekend progressed. On Monday when it was time for his appointment, the vet was no longer recommending putting him down but instead said that he had never seen such a miraculous recovery. "What changed?" he asked my mom. "His favorite person came home for the weekend!" she responded. There was a total change in him after that. Boots went on to live another two years until the age of 16.

I had always experienced a deep reciprocal empathy with animals throughout my life. This was the first time I had such a tangible experience, however. Others (especially those college friends who heard the details of the dream before any of us knew what was happening) were intrigued, and conversations about human–animal connections continued. People told stories of cats, dogs, horses, guinea pigs, and sheep. Some were about formal supports such as service animals, while others were individualized personal accounts of the impact of animals on people's lives. Humans rescuing animals, animals rescuing humans . . . the possibilities for people and animals to connect and support each other seemed endless.

After college, I continued to graduate school to become a counselor. Helping people had always been part of my passion, and I felt blessed to pursue a career focused on that very purpose. The more I learned about the importance of empathy, connection, intuition, safety, and trust in the therapeutic relationship and counseling process, the more those stories of human–animal connections came to mind. As I began to work with children and adolescents in schools and support them through grief, divorce, abuse, and other traumas and challenges, I thought how difficult it must be for them to trust yet another adult with their vulnerability. I found myself wondering how the presence of a loving animal could impact their comfort and sharing and began to look into the practice of animal-assisted therapy.

I decided to pursue dog parenthood as an adult and picked a pup with the "therapy dog" idea in mind. Thankfully, I had a principal who was an animal lover and open to the idea of allowing a dog to visit the children in the after-school program. Yankee, my Goldendoodle, seemed to instantly change the energy in the room of students who were tired after a long day of sitting inside in rows of desks and were now tasked with a couple of more hours of sitting inside doing homework. They lit up with smiles and enthusiasm, many eagerly rushing forward to pet him, while others smiled from across the room. Even those who had a fear of dogs didn't take long to warm up to him, with one student explaining, "I could see he was kind by the way he looks at you with his eyes." During this same time when I was serving as a school counselor, I was also supervising and teaching counseling students at a local college. One graduate student requested that I bring the "therapy dog in training" to her supervision sessions. She had been experiencing a difficult semester in many ways, and she explained that the dog helped her to feel comforted, grounded, and more easily able to express her emotions.

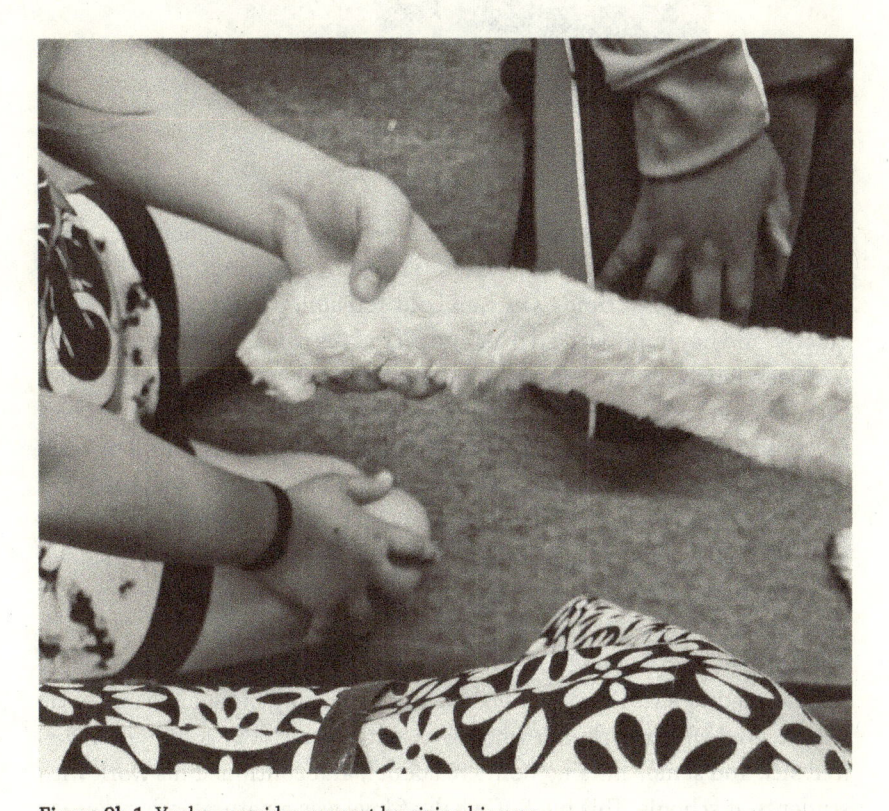

Figure 9b.1 Yankee provides support by giving his paw.

Figure 9b.2 Yankee the therapy dog.

I taught Yankee many things, and he was a quick learner; however, some things were just part of who he was, not a result of training or teaching. I'll never forget the first time I saw him hold someone's hand. She was crying quietly, and he simply walked over and placed his paw on her hand. Now he had been taught to "give his paw" for a treat and things of that nature, but there was no treat-seeking happening here. He didn't just give her his paw for a moment but left it there in her hand for 20 minutes until her tears subsided. At one point she held onto his paw and he actually "squeezed" her hand in return. We were both blown away by this unexpected show of empathy from this young dog. Hand-holding became a signature expression of empathy and comfort for Yankee—something that had never been taught or modeled, but that he seemed to just know on his own.

I realized this dog had love to give beyond what I had even imagined, so I decided to share him with others outside of my immediate circle. He volunteered with my church when we went out into the community, visited sick and senior nursing home residents, and continued his work with students at schools. This big fluffy ball of love was a natural icebreaker for people to start talking and connecting. Students who were having difficulty reading gained confidence by reading to a nonjudgmental listener who did not interrupt. One older gentleman at the nursing home who was nonverbal released silent tears when Yankee sat next to his wheelchair and held his hand. His adult daughter came to find us an hour or so later and asked if we could come back to her father's room. "We haven't seen that kind of emotional reaction or light in his eyes in years," she explained with her own tears. "Something about that dog woke up something inside of him." And so it seems to be for many of us. Animals intuitively sense what we need, picking up on our emotions and being willing to meet us where we are with unconditional love. They are natural therapists who are more than happy to assist when needed.

CHAPTER 10

Integrating Ecotherapy Into Counselor Education

MEGAN E. DELANEY

Although I am a professor, I am not a fan of lecturing. If I do lecture, I have a relentless internal dialogue. "Does what I am saying even make sense?" "Is anyone really listening?" "That student is smiling and looking at her computer while I talk about quantitative methodology. Clearly she is on Facebook." As such, I try to lecture as little as possible and still provide the course content as completely as I can. My methods are more experiential, often including discussions, group work, role-play, and student-led activities as often as possible. I find that, with creativity, students are often more engaged, are more connected with me and with each other, and better absorb the content of the course. Nevertheless, this is not always the case, especially with computers in front of faces in sterile, windowless classrooms. The first benefit of teaching unconventionally is that it takes the students outside of their comfort zone (the seat they assign themselves for the semester, the comfort of their open computer, the availability of bathrooms and snacks, the ability to zone out during the lecture or, worse, check in on social media). The second benefit is more obvious: We are learning in nature.

As discussed in Chapter 6, there are physical, emotional, and psychological benefits of teaching in the natural world. Students show improved cognitive abilities and focus, as well as a greater level of engagement in the educational content and process (Blair, 2010; Chawla, 2015; Li & Sullivan, 2016; Rios & Brewer, 2014). In addition, there is evidence that the natural world can improve creative and critical thinking (Berezoiwitz et al., 2015; Chawla, 2015; Williams & Dixon, 2013). Yet most of this research has been conducted in K-12 settings (Barnes, Cross, & Gresalfi, 2011; Benfield, Rainbolt, Bell, & Donovan, 2013). There is little research on the application of working in nature in other educational settings, especially in higher education.Furthermore, a recent review of the literature found only a handful of articles applying nature to counselor education settings. Of the few studies, students reflected that the experience of learning in nature helped with group cohesiveness as well as an enhanced connection to nature (Davis & Atkins; 2004, 2009; Schimmel, Daniels, Wassif, & Jacobs; 2016). My colleagues and I (Duffy, Springer, Delaney & Luke, 2019) have recently conducted a research study exploring student experiences in which nature themes and experiences were included in a "typical" course, in this case Human Development. The overarching themes found include

- interpersonal impact where students discussed the interplay and interdependence between people and nature;
- intrapersonal impact in which the students reflected on the experiences and their own personal growth; and
- counselor skill and development including ways in which the students plan to integrate nature-based activities with future clients.

One student reflected about her experience in a class that was taught at the beach:

> it was just kind of a moment of calm and quiet—we all just sat there and took it in. I can't think of another word except for cathartic. It was just this moment that it was so quiet and finally for a moment, my brain wasn't going 50 miles per hour about what I have to do for work, what I have to do for school. What needs to be done. It was nice just to sit there and be in that moment and listen to the waves and connect with nature and not worry about anything else . . . it's so hard for all of us to kind of take a moment of clarity. [This experience] forced us into that.

More recently, my colleagues and I have been exploring the experiences of students enrolled in my Ecotherapy class. Data analysis is still ongoing, but the overarching themes seem similar. Early data findings hint that students express a strong, rekindled connection to the natural world and an explicit desire to use the techniques learned in class in their future work as counselors. There is a potential bias to the data due to self-selection (those who enroll are more likely to be nature lovers), yet there are always a few who know nothing about ecotherapy before the first class. One such student reflected at the end of the class:

> Taking this class has been one of the most rewarding experiences of my college career. Not only have I become equipped with a new scheme of techniques and options for facilitating healing in others, but I have learned of ways to help myself as well. . . . Part of everything we have learned explains that ecotherapy is not just about what we can take from nature, but what we can give back.

Another stated:

> This class has been career and life altering for me. I am convinced that ecotherapy is not only a modality that therapists can utilize in their practice; it is also a way of life.

Many students talked about the curative benefits they received themselves just for coming to class. Students were able to be present, in the moment, aware of their heightened senses and their reduced heartrates. They reflected on how the worries of their daily lives and the stress of school slipped away during our three hours of class and how truly their connection to nature intensified.

> The class helped me connect with the natural world by encouraging me to truly take notice of what I observed visually and the textures I felt. It also made me realize how we can relax and forget our worries and fears by immersing ourselves in nature.

This is important because we must train our future counselors to take care of themselves, not just others. Therefore, incorporating ecotherapy into the counseling curriculum might just have a trifecta effect—the enhanced learning environment supplied by being in nature, the reconnection and rekindling of our inherent (and maybe lost) association to the natural world, and the therapeutic benefits of being outside. So how do we do implement this change?

ADDING NATURE TO EVERY CLASS

As with almost every application of ecotherapy we have discussed so far, the easiest way to include nature in your class is to take the students outside. This might pose some logistical challenges but is well worth the reward. Depending on your institution, the choices might vary. So many institutions have beautifully landscaped campuses. There might already be an outdoor location dedicated for classroom use. If not, you can pick a piece of the lawn or sit underneath a tree. Some obvious considerations are be sure the location is not in the middle of a highly trafficked area that may be distracting. Scope out a place that is relatively quiet and comfortable in advance of class. Also, in advance, give your students ample time to prepare. You might encourage them to bring a lawn chair and/or a blanket. They may also need a notebook or a charged laptop. Consider class size and topic. Nature's acoustics are wonderful but not necessarily for a class size of 30. In addition, due to our profession, sensitive topics may come up and confidentiality can be an issue. I regularly have my practicum and internships class on the beach but during the off-season, when the crowds are gone. We start the class with a meditation and a toe-dip in the ocean. This grounds the students, and I have found that discussions are richer and more meaningful. Students also feel good at the end of the class, perhaps from the Vitamin D and the fresh air alone.

Figure 10.1 Ecotherapy student dipping their toes in the ocean.

If you work in a city or an urban campus, you can still find your space, but you might need to be a bit more creative. I meet regularly with my classes at sites off campus. This comes with a few accommodations. First, my university requires students to sign an off-campus waiver form, so check with your institution and the legal department to see if off-campus is an option for you. Ask students about accessibility. This semester, for example, I had a student with limited mobility. We accommodated her by choosing convenient, accessible locations. Logistics is another factor to consider. For example, some of my students carpool to sites together so when necessary I leave time at the end of class for those students to get back to campus for their next scheduled class. Recently I have found a hidden arboretum literally around the corner from my campus. It has plenty of parking and is a quiet, less visited spot, which is difficult to find near our bustling and busy (where three major highways convene) intersection. Students love this spot because it is isolated and helps us, even just for the time of the class, forget where we are.

These spaces make class different and interesting. One week we might be at the beach, the next in the woods. You might have to find your space a subway ride away or a town next door, but as long as you give your students ample notice and time, they might be up for it.

Figure 10.2 F. Bliss Arboretum in Eatontown, NJ. A tiny oasis among busy highways.

Teaching outside takes away our tech-savvy classrooms. As a result, we have to be more creative. Sometimes it requires rearranging lesson plans for outdoor classes. I can still use my PowerPoint slides to support my content delivery. Students either bring a charged tablet or laptop or (less environmentally friendly), they may print the PowerPoint and use it to take notes. Video clips normally shown in the classroom I assign in advance. We take the time to discuss aspects of the video during class time. I also love to use podcasts in my teaching. With smartphones and Bluetooth speakers, playing a podcast is easy to do out in nature. Mostly I come prepared with discussion questions and activities. Anecdotally, I find that, in the classes that I hold outside, the students participate more. My hunch is the power of nature helps to ground and focus my students. My other hunch is there is less technology to distract them.

If traveling outdoors for every class is not an option, and most likely it isn't, another possibility is to plan a few lessons outside. For example, my colleague Jason Duffy and I both transformed our Human Development courses (at different campuses) to include a few relevant outdoor experiences. For one class, we ventured outdoors (a wooded area or grassy area with vegetation) where each student, individually, was told to do his or her best to sketch a picture, using a notebook and pencil, of a plant, catching as much of its uniqueness as possible. The students were also told to write down words or phrases that came to mind as they look at, touch, or smell the plant. Students then were instructed to go online before the next class to attempt to find the name of the plant and to figure out its growth/development cycle (What does it need to grow? How long does maturation take? What is needed for its developmental process?) During the next class, each student shared information on his or her plant. The parallel, of course, is that all living things have a developmental cycle that is similar in many ways and different in others. It also connects the students to place, time, and the natural world. As one student reflected:

> Our classes at the gardens, where we drew a picture of a plant we chose and then researched it, was helpful in reminding me that there is a story behind nature. For instance, you can see a flower and find it aesthetically pleasing but then finding it in a book or learning more about that flower and where it came from or how it grows was a way for me to connect with nature which I had never thought of before. Now, when I see that flower again, I will be reminded of where I first saw it and connect those memories.

For classes that involve group work or the importance of group dynamics, there are many outdoor activities we can borrow from adventure

Figure 10.3 Students sketch trees to research its lifecycle.

education such as the human knot (try it: it's fun) or trust walks. For this activity, you need a blindfold and some trust. One student is blindfolded and the other is the guide. The guide leads the blindfolded partner to a place close by (e.g., in a wooded area I tell students to lead their partners to trees). Once they are there, the blindfolded student tries to use his or her senses (other than sight) to try and garner a memory of the place or tree. The guide leads them back to the starting point still blindfolded, then the blindfold is removed, and the person tries to find the place/tree/rock using his or her memory of that place. This is a good activity for trust building but also for enhancing awareness and sensitivity.

These are just examples, and the possibilities are limitless with imagination and a willingness from the instructor and the students to partake in some experiential education.

TEACHING ECOTHERAPY—A 14-WEEK CURRICULUM

I work at an amazing university that has allowed me to create and offer a specific course called Ecotherapy: Applied Ecopsychology. It has quickly become a favorite among the students. One of the draws? None of the classes are held

Figure 10.4 Ecotherapy students in a trust walk.

on campus. None. In fact, the reserved classroom set aside for our normal meeting time and place remains empty for the entire semester. With some trial and error, I have found that offering the course in the fall semester during the day (1–4 PM) works best for activities. I based this on sunlight, temperature, and availability of activities. The following is an overview of projects that I incorporate into the class. This course is a labor of love and a work in progress.

Course Description

Ecotherapy is the application of the theory of ecopscyhology. Ecotherapy is defined as contact with the outdoors and nature as a method or element of therapy (Clinebell, 1996) and addresses the critical fact that as humans we are interwoven with the natural world (Buzzell & Chalquist, 2009). We will learn the theory of ecopscyhology as well as ways that we can apply these concepts in ecotherapy, or the work we do with clients that involve the natural world. Our relationship with nature is an important component of our mental and physical health. This class will explore your own relationship with nature as well as guide to you in the ways that you may be able to integrate nature in your future work as a counselor.

Learning Objectives

1. Introduce the relationship of humans and the natural world with a comprehensive overview of the current research conducted linking mental and physical health and nature. Provide evidenced-based connections regarding the benefits and therapeutic power of nature and provide at least ten resources for students to obtain additional information and techniques from reliable sources.
2. Provide an overview of theoretical concepts of ecotherapy from the current literature. Link theoretical concepts to individual, group, and school counseling in diverse populations.
3. Outline and describe at least five specific ecotherapy techniques to use with each client type and counseling medium (such as individual work, work with children, group work, school counseling) including examples and case conceptualizations. Ethnicity, race, culture, sexual orientation, gender, age, and ability will be considered throughout the course.

Book Recommendations

The following are some of books we have used in class. There are many others, including seminal texts (Buzzell & Chalquist, 2009; Clinebell, 1996; Roszak, Gomes, & Kanner, 1995); often I assign readings from several of these texts as well. In addition to the theoretical texts from the leading researchers on the subjects, my students and I enjoy reading the well-researched and narrative style of writing from journalist Florence William and her book *The Nature Fix* as well as Richard Louv and his prolific writings on the topic of nature deficit disorder" and Vitamin N. Assigned reading for the course typically includes:

> Hinds, J., & Jordan, M. (2016). *Ecotherapy: theory, research and practice*. New York, NY: Palgrave Macmillan.
> Kahn, P., & Hasback, P. (2012). *Ecopsychology: Science, totems and the technological species*. Cambridge, MA: MIT Press.
> Louv, R. (2008). *Last child in the woods: Saving our children from nature-deficit disorder*. London, England: Algonquin Books.
> Williams, F. (2017) *The nature fix: Why nature makes us happier, healthier and more creative*. New York, NY: W. W. Norton.

In addition to these texts, we examine research that supports the theoretical foundations of ecotherapy found in counseling, environmental psychology, ecopsychology, and conservation journals. While the foundational work is of paramount importance, it is woven into experiential activities each week.

Class Topics and Activities

The first three weeks of class is devoted to theory and research. Each week, I assign the students specific readings from texts and journal articles and tell them to be ready to participate in meaningful, related discussions. I also assign specific research articles to individual students who are responsible for summarizing the main findings during class time. This way we can cover multiple articles each week. We study seminal works and foundational pieces in week one along with a global overview of the related concepts (Hinds & Jordan, 2016). The concept of ecowellness is part of our reading (Reese & Myers, 2012; Reese, 2016), as is the idea of rewilding (Kahn & Hasbach, 2013) and ethical considerations (Hooley, 2016; Reese, 2016).

Each week we meet in outdoor places (the beach, a park); students bring chairs, blankets, notebooks, water, sunscreen, and anything else they need. During this time, we start to practice walking and talking, just to get the feel of the work. We debrief that exercise, paying attention to the verbal and nonverbal cues, sensations, sights, and smells. We talk about what it feels like as the counselor as well as the client. Students are often surprised that it is both easier and harder. They note that the dialogue comes easier and attribute that to the forward momentum of walking, the lack of direct eye contact, the fresh air and sunshine, and the peacefulness of the surroundings. The lack of eye contact and the constant movement also can feel difficult. Some students remark that it is a challenge to read nonverbal behaviors because they are not able to directly see the other person's face. We strategize techniques and practice some more.

The following few weeks of class is a series of experiential activities combined with associated readings. The activities are scheduled and confirmed, as necessary, before the semester begins. The following list is what has worked for my class and is not exhaustive:

- **Forest bathing or shinrin-yoku.** During this week, we go to a local natural park and practice the art of forest bathing, or a silent meditative walk in the woods. We stop for silent contemplation and time to experience nature with all of our senses. At the end of the hour-long silent walk, we debrief and discuss.

Figure 10.5 Ecotherapy students participating in forest bathing.

- **Paddleboard**. One of my good friends and fellow ecotherapists Kristen Huber utilizes paddleboards in her ecotherapy practice, taking her clients out at a local, beautiful river. She leads my students in a group lesson—teaching them the skills of paddle boarding and talking about her ecotherapy practice. Paddle boarding requires people to use their bodies to find the balance to stand and maneuver the board. This forces even the most anxious people to trust their own capacity to balance and at the same time takes them into their body and out of their head. The students have some fun on the paddle boards as well as learn valuable real-life experiences from a practicing ecotherapist.
- **Adventure-based therapy**
  - **Ropes course**. This activity requires access to a certified ropes course and trained personnel (and usually requires a per person fee). A ropes course is a team-building and personal development activity done with low and/or high elements. Each element requires the group to brainstorm together on the best (or most efficient) way to complete the challenge. It is a wonderful group-building experience but requires some trust and comfort. I like to do this activity a few weeks into the semester to challenge and hopefully enhance group dynamics.

Figure 10.6 Ecotherapy students doing counseling role plays while paddle boarding.

Debriefing the ropes activity is critical to acknowledge individual and group experiences and maximize learning.
- **Rock climbing**. Similar to the ropes course, a rock-climbing experience requires a licensed facility or site and professional assistance (and likely a fee). Rock climbing requires that an individual attempt to climb up a natural or manmade rock face. There are many factors in play when rock climbing. Often people have fears of height, doubt their ability, and get frustrated. Rock climbing also brings great rewards, including a sense of accomplishment for trying something new and challenging, reaching literal and figurative heights. The group plays an important role in the process, providing encouragement and praise for individual achievements.
- **Equine therapy**. My university happens to be in an area surrounded by horse farms, many of which offer equine-assisted therapy programs. A local facility, Serenity Stables, provides a program they call From Combat to Calm. This program provides equine-assisted therapy to service members, veterans, and their families to help with emotional well-being and quality of life. Our class is able to visit the facility and talk to the therapists about their work. We give back to the program by mucking

Figure 10.7 The ecotherapy class giving back by "mucking" at a horse stable.

their fields, and our reward is interaction and practice with the therapists and their horses.
- **Nature-based art therapy.** Art therapy combines creativity and art-making in many different modalities (painting, crafting, drawing, sculpting, to name a few) to allow clients the ability to express themselves and their emotions through the artistic process. A trained art therapist can interpret and apply the psychological and emotional subtexts of the art (Atkins & Snyder, 2017). For this class we make masks with items we have collected from our local park. Masks are a therapeutic metaphor for the social disguises we may wear to manage interactions with others. The outside of the mask represents what we show the outside world; the inside of the mask is what our feelings really are. This is only one of many nature-based art therapy projects; the possibilities are limited only to one's imagination.
- **Horticulture therapy.** Similar to art therapy, horticulture therapy can encompass a number of different interventions. For our class we visit the memory care unit of a local senior home. With the residents, we use mason jars, dirt, rocks, and succulents to make a low-maintenance but pretty item they can keep in their rooms. The students take time to sit with the residents and try their counseling skills. We find touching the

Figure 10.8 An ecotherapy student greeting a therapy horse.

dirt and rocks prompts the seniors to share stories of their days of gardening, which leads to stories about families and friends. At a recent visit, one resident spontaneously broke out in song and we all found ourselves robustly singing along. Similar to art therapy, horticulture therapy has various modalities. Another possibility is getting students involved in a community garden, especially if there is an on campus option.

- **Restorative yoga.** Tying in the concept of ecospirituality, one class is devoted to restorative yoga in an outdoor location. With the help of a certified yoga instructor, this class starts with talking about the benefits of yoga and meditation, after which we spend time taking part in a yoga practice. Yoga is a wonderful way to connect to your body and ground yourself in the present moment. Many of the movements (or asanas) are connected to animals or nature. Whether it is the tree pose or sun salutation, yoga connects us to our surroundings and ourselves. Plus, we feel great at the end of the class.

It's advisable to leave a class open for rescheduling/make-up class in case the weather is so bad we cannot possibly go outside. This is rare. At the

Figure 10.9 Nature based art therapy—creating masks with natural elements.

outset of the semester, the students are told to be prepared for the weather (as an ecotherapist always should) and bring layers, rain gear, change of clothes, water, and snacks as needed. I always have the emergency contact list and a first aid kit with me. In sum, there are many different ways to integrate the concepts of ecotherapy into experiential lessons. These are just some of the few that have worked for me.

Assignments

As with the class activities, there are many meaningful options as assignments for this course. I have experimented with several and will likely try others in the future. For example, I ask the students to provide weekly journals, reflecting on the readings and their experiences with the activities. Students can journal in a variety of ways such as blogging each week or emailing Word documents. I have found, however, if I hand out journals at the beginning of the semester and ask the students to handwrite their reflections, they tend to be more meaningful. Some even draw pictures. I often give them time during the class to devote to journaling, when their thoughts and feelings are sharpest. There are specific parameters;

for example they must reflect on a certain amount of the reading in their journal, and this section is graded. The personal reflections are graded on whether they were done (i.e., more than one sentence). I have also done this assignment in another variation where journals are separate. In addition, the students have a midterm and a final writing assignment due based on questions formulated from assigned readings. Since I want to devote as much time to the class doing experiential activities, I give these writing prompts to ensure that students are still reading the research and literature relevant to the topics we discuss.

Another important assignment links the concept of reciprocity in ecotherapy. For this assignment, I ask students to do a service project of their choice during the semester. The actual activity of the service project is up to the student and done outside of classroom, but must involve some benefit to the natural world. Examples include trail maintenance, park or beach clean up activities, volunteering in a local natural space or an animal shelter, helping at a community garden, taking children outside to play; the options are limitless. I ask the students to document their activity by taking at least 5 pictures and journaling their thoughts and reactions. At the end of the semester, I have the students compile their pictures into a powerpoint presentation and bring it in to class. We share our activity and our experience with each other in class.

A new assignment I have been trying is what I call a creative book report. Students are allowed to choose a book related to the natural world, ecotherapy, or some variation of that topic - something they are interested in reading more about (above and beyond the assigned readings). For the assignment, students are asked to creatively present 5 findings from the book to bring to class to share with the other students. I leave the assignment vague on purpose and ask the students to tap into their inner artistic-selves. I am always in awe at the creativity, even for those who are the most wary of this atypical assignments. Students have painted pictures, created videos, made dioramas and book reports in a bag, wrote and illustrated animated cartoons—the originality and the innovation of the output is astounding. Students reflect that using their imagination helps to think and reflect more deeply on what they are learning.

The final assignment is my favorite. For this project, each student develops an ecotherapy intervention and/or group session. The student can choose the population and design the intervention using any ecotherapy modality he or she selects. Creativity is encouraged! The results are amazing, and I am frequently impressed with the level of originality and imagination. What I especially love about this activity is that students often choose a population for the intervention that is in line with the population they wish to serve. This reflects the versatility of ecotherapy, allowing the students to imagine ways of adapting or designing techniques that they can use with clients in a multitude of settings. Some of the interventions designed by my students include a horticultural project for a client and the family in hospice care; outdoor play therapy interventions for children; interventions using nature scents as a way to work through trauma; gardening with clients struggling with eating disorders; and a meditation for the moon, to name a few. At the end of the semester, I compile the interventions into a PDF and distribute it to everyone in the class.

This course is a work in progress. One component that has been gnawing at me is a way to include a more intensive wilderness experience, something that I think is missing from a course that meets one day per week. Other programs that offer courses and/or certificates in ecopsychology involve a wilderness immersive experience. I understand this requirement and truly wish all students could dedicate the time to share in that transformative experience. Yet, I know that is not realistic for everyone. In my desire to reach more counselors and teach them about ecotherapy, I have been searching for other techniques and interventions. Recently I listened to Florence Williams (2018) e-book titled *The 3 Day Effect*. Williams explores new research uncovering the ways in which

Figure 10.10 Ecotherapy written in the sand.

being in wild spaces improves our health, happiness, and creativity (if you can, listen to it: it is terrific). The research indicates that spending several consecutive days in the wilderness significantly improves cognition and creativity (Atchley, Strayer, & Atchley, 2012) compared to a control group (Ferraro, 2015). These findings are interesting to me as my own immersive wilderness experiences have lasted 15 to 60 days. A few days seems more doable for busy graduate students who could devote a three-day weekend to an immersive experience. I am developing a plan to implement this three-day immersion experience in future classes. Later, I would like to expand this idea into a separate class, offering students a completely immersive experience in a wilderness setting. I envision doing this by offering a semester-long class in the spring. The immersive component would take place over spring break, giving us time before and after to prepare and then debrief the experience.

Teaching ecotherapy is one of the highlights of my career thus far. I develop a more intimate relationship with my students than I have in a traditional classroom. We all reflect that being outside each week makes us feel good; coming to class is therapeutic and healing. I have a personal goal of creating an army of ecotherapists right here at the Jersey shore.

REFERENCES

Atchley, R., Strayer, D., & Atchley, P. (2012) Creativity in the wild: Improving creative reasoning through immersion in natural settings. *PLoS One, 7*(12), e51474. https://doi.org/10.1371/journal.pone.0051474

Atkins, S., & Snyder, M. (2017). *Nature-based expressive art therapy: Integrating the expressive arts and ecotherapy.* Philadelphia, PA: Jessica Kingsley.

Barnes, J., Cross, D., & Gresalfi, M. S. (2011). When does an opportunity become an opportunity? Unpacking classroom practice through the lens of ecological psychology. *Educational Studies in Mathematics, 80,* 249–267.

Benfield, J. A., Rainbolt, G. N., Bell, P. A., & Donovan, G. H. (2013). Classrooms with nature views: Evidence of differing student perceptions and behaviors. *Environment and Behavior, 47,* 140–157.

Berezowitz, C. K., Bontrager Yoder, A. B., & Schoeller, D. A. (2015). School gardens enhance academic performance and dietary outcomes in children. *Journal of School Health, 85,* 508–518.

Blair, D. (2010). The child in the garden: An evaluative review of the benefits of school gardening. *Journal of Environmental Education, 40*(2), 15–38.

Buzzell, L., & Chalquist, C. (Eds.). (2009). *Ecotherapy: Healing with nature in mind.* San Francisco, CA: Sierra Club Books.

Chawla, L. (2015). Benefits of nature contact for children. *Journal of Planning Literature, 30,* 309–317.

Clinebell, H. (1996). *Ecotherapy: Healing ourselves, healing the earth.* Minneapolis, MN: Augsburg Fortress Press.

Davis, K. M., & Atkins, S. S. (2004). Creating and teaching a course in ecotherapy: We went to the woods. *Journal of Humanistic Counseling, Education and Development, 43*, 211–218.

Davis, K. M., & Atkins, S. S. (2009). Ecotherapy: Tribalism in the mountains and forest. *Journal of Creativity in Mental Health, 4*, 272–282. https://www.doi.org/10.1080/15401380903192747

Duffy, J. T., Springer, S., Delaney, M., & Luke, M. (2019). Eco-education: Integrating nature into counselor education. *Journal of Creativity in Mental Health*, 1–14. https://doi.org/10.1080/15401383.2019.1640152.

Ferraro, F. M. (2015). Enhancement of convergent creativity following a multiday wilderness experience. *Ecopsychology, 7*(1), 7–11. doi:10.1089/eco.2014.0043

Hinds, J., & Jordan, M. (2016). *Ecotherapy: Theory, research and practice.* New York, NY: Palgrave Macmillan.

Hooley, I. (2016). Ethical considerations for psychotherapy in natural settings. *Ecopsychology, 8*(4), 215–221.

Kahn, P. H., & Hasbach, P. H. (2013). *The rediscovery of the wild.* Cambridge, MA: MIT Press.

Li, D., & Sullivan, W. C. (2016). Impact of views to school landscapes on recovery from stress and mental fatigue. *Landscape and Urban Planning, 148*, 149–158.

Louv, R. (2008). *Last child in the woods: Saving our children from nature-deficit disorder.* London, England: Algonquin Books.

Reese, R. F. (2016). Ecowellness and guiding principles for the ethical integration of nature into counseling. *International Journal for the Advancement of Counselling, 38*, 345–57. doi:10.1007/s10447-016-9276-5

Reese, R. F., & Myers, J. E. (2012). Ecowellness: The missing factor in holistic wellness models. *Journal of Counseling & Development, 90*(4), 400–406. doi:10.1002/j.1556-6676.2012.00050.x

Rios, J. M., & Brewer, J. (2014). Outdoor education and science achievement. *Applied Environmental Education and Communication, 13*, 234–240.

Roszak, T., Gomes, M. E., & Kanner, A. D. (Eds.). (1995). *Ecopsychology: Restoring the earth, healing the mind.* Berkeley: University of California Press.

Schimmel, C. J., Daniels, J. A., Wassif, J., & Jacobs, E. (2016). Learning the ropes: A creative orientation approach for counseling students. *Journal of Creativity in Mental Health, 11*(1), 27–38. doi:10.1080/15401383.2015.1095663

Williams, D. R., & Dixon, P. S. (2013). Impact of garden-based learning on academic outcomes in schools: Synthesis of research between 1990 and 2010. *Review of Educational Research, 83*(2), 211–235.

Williams, F. (2017). *The nature fix: Why nature makes us happier, healthier and more creative.* New York, NY: W. W. Norton.

CHAPTER 10A

ECOTHERAPIST IN TRAINING

Emmi McCauley

I learned of ecotherapy in my first year of graduate school. The course was being offered as an elective option, and I was intrigued. Before class, I Googled the term *ecotherapy* and the result said, "healing and growth nurtured by a healthy interaction with the earth." I was shocked that this term even existed. I felt instantly connected because nature has *always* influenced my own mental health. When in nature, I feel grounded, present, and at peace. When I feel stressed or overwhelmed, I either take my two rescue dogs on a trail in the woods or sit at the beach and listen to the waves crash and watch the sun set. I wanted to learn more about ecotherapy, so I enrolled in the class. After the first ecotherapy class, I immediately went to my professor because everything I had just learned aligned with my own beliefs. I felt pure joy and excitement! At that moment, everything clicked for me: I knew what I wanted to do as a future Licensed Professional Counselor (LPC).

One of our classes involved meeting with ecotherapist Kristen Huber, LPC, to learn more about her practice, Jersey Shore Ecotherapy. During class, Kristen took us out on paddleboards and demonstrated how she incorporates nature into her practice. While paddling, she explained to us how paddle boarding, in particular, has been a powerful way to work with her clients. Paddle boarding requires concentration, balance, and strength. It takes people out of their heads and into their bodies. With time, Kristen explained, clients become centered and focused, even the most anxious, and real conversation happens. That night, after paddle boarding, our class gathered around a campfire and she talked to us more in depth about

Figure 10a.1 Emmi, an ecotherapist in training.

ecotherapy. I fell in love with her private practice and knew it would be such an honor to do my practicum experience with her. I scheduled my classes so that practicum would fall during summertime and she could be my supervisor. I was thrilled when Jersey Shore Ecotherapy took me on as their intern for the summer.

Through my practicum experience, I had the opportunity to cofacilitate group paddle board sessions and conduct workshops held outdoors. I also had the opportunity to conduct ecotherapy with clients of my own under Kristen's supervision. My favorite part of this internship was being able to see firsthand the many benefits nature has on someone's overall mental health and well-being. I met with my first client in the office for eight weekly sessions, before she wanted to meet in an outdoor setting. Her case required crisis intervention counseling, so she requested keeping it structured and to meet weekly in the office to process what she was going through. The first time we met outdoors, we sat down by the water at the nearby lake. It was the perfect time to go, around sunset, just as the sky began to turn

Figure 10a.1 Continued

from orange-red to yellow and pink. The lifeguards had just gathered their belongings and were leaving while we entered. We sat down on some stairs in a private section of the lakefront. Sitting on the water's edge, we could see the little guppy fish swimming up to the surface. I began this session by explaining what the concept of ecotherapy was and ended it asking how she felt to have a session held outdoors. She said her body felt more *relaxed*. She also said that it felt more *natural* and *less pressured* to have a conversation with me since I was not sitting in a *therapist chair* across from her. Later she mentioned that she was at first skeptical that there would be a difference meeting outdoors versus indoors, but from that session on she requested to continuously meet at the lake weekly around sunset hours. We ended our session with the quote, "every sunset is an opportunity to reset."

Another client, a 13-year-old boy, immediately said how comfortable he felt meeting in an outdoor space versus the office setting. Part of the reason was that the setting was familiar, similar to a spot that he would go to with friends, a short bike ride away from his house. I could clearly see the difference in his level of anxiety the following week when we met in the office for the intake. At this meeting, he presented as more nervous than when we met outdoors. Another client whom I met on a paddleboard said how standing on a paddleboard forced her to stay present and grounded in the moment—mostly because she was focusing on trying not to fall off the board. This helped her mind stop her typical racing thoughts. One thing that Kristen taught me when incorporating ecotherapy with clients is nurturing the earth back. In ecotherapy, nature nurtures us, and, in return, we nurture nature. For example, with our clients on paddleboards we say, "Take three for the sea." When we are paddle boarding and notice garbage, we take three pieces and place it on our paddleboards to dispose of appropriately after our sessions.

The highlight of my summer internship experience was cofacilitating a wind therapy workshop on the importance of self-care. For this experience, we went sailing out on the bay in southern New Jersey. With us were six clients who had not met each other. The clients' occupations varied from being a teacher, sales representative, lawyer, employee at a store, mental health professional, and student. Before we sailed, we met at the picnic tables to introduce each other and sign paperwork. These six clients were all women ranging from 18 to 50 years old. Before we went onboard, we passed around the essential oil bergamot to place on the shen men point on our ears as well as inhaled it through our nostrils. Research has shown that the mental health benefits of this oil helps harmonize the spirit and mind, grounds you, and clarifies your thoughts.

Our first group activity was reading a daily meditation from Co-dependents Anonymous (2006), *In This Moment Daily Meditation Book:*

> *In this moment, I allow myself rest. Why is it so hard for me to recognize that I need rest? Rest is part of the natural cycle for all living things. When I'm overworked, overextended, or my emotions are raw, I deserve a break. For me, relaxing doesn't mean taking a long nap. It means doing those things that calm and soothe my soul, as well as my mind and body. Relaxing helps recharge me so that I'm more enthusiastic and effective. Resting when I need it is not selfish. It is self-loving.*

Following this reading, we started our workshop with some psychoeducation on the importance of self-care and then headed to the sailboat to have a light and healthy breakfast.

Stepping onto the sailboat was a bit nerve-wracking not only for some clients who have never been on a sailboat but for me as well. I was nervous because, as an intern, I did not know what to expect from this workshop. This then made me mindful of what the clients might be experiencing and helped me gain some perspective of their mindset. To get onto the boat, we had to walk up a couple steps, onto a stool, lift our leg over a rope, and hop onto the boat. The captain graciously helped each one of us get onto the boat safely. After he pulled the boat out of the marina and we were headed out toward the bay, we could feel the boat begin to roll from side to side. It was so serene to feel my hair blow from the wind, the sun falling gently on my skin, and to smell the ocean from the breeze. I felt happy and at peace.

It took the clients some time to open up; I could see that some of them were quicker to talk about themselves and others were more reserved and presented as anxious. Before sailing, while we were filling our plates with fruit and yogurt or buttering a bagel, we did an icebreaker so that all the clients could learn each other's names. We asked them to go around the circle, say their name, and tell how they were currently managing their stress. This helped us get a sense about whether they were coping with their stress in productive ways. It also helped encourage other members to share what was causing them stress and what they were doing to cope with it. I enjoyed being able to help facilitate the process of this by asking "Jane" how it felt to know that "Jessica" was also having a hard time managing the stress of working full time and taking care of her family. I guided the conversation of the importance of utilizing positive self-care practices in daily routines such as taking some time to yourself to read a book, having a cup of morning coffee by yourself, or other practices that bring peace. The best part of being a cofacilitator of this workshop was being able to watch the clients push out of their comfort zones. We were out on the water, so there were no cellphones or other distractions; we were living in the moment and truly connecting with each other. One client mentioned that she was nervous because she has social anxiety and this workshop allowed her to talk to other people. The feedback she received from the other members was that they could not tell she was "socially awkward," and she processed that this feedback made her feel happy.

Kristen guided a mindfulness meditation while sitting on the edge of the sailboat. She focused on sitting in an upright position, feeling ourselves sitting on the boat, aware of the movement of the waves, all while also focusing on breathing. After, we gave each client a journal to do some mindfulness reflection. Some questions and activities we included as prompts included:

1. Mindfulness exercise: name five things you see, hear, smell, touch, and taste.
2. If you could give yourself a medal what would it be for?
3. You are authentic! Write every positive quality, attribute, character trait that you could think of about yourself.
4. Unlike self-criticism which states *you're not good enough*, self-compassion asks *what's good for you?* So, what practices of self-care do you have now?
5. What else can you do that's "good" for you?

After doing this activity, one of the clients shared how beneficial this was for her because she rarely takes the time to do things for herself. These questions made her look inward instead of always worrying about other people. She shared how this workshop forced her to take three hours out of her day to focus on herself and her mental health. Other clients agreed with her after she shared this and realized how important it was to take some time to themselves.

Another client shared how this workshop was a challenge for her because she herself is a mental health professional. She has never been to therapy before and was unsure what her role would be at the workshop. She said it felt different to be a client. She also shared that her loved ones did not know she was attending this workshop; she processed what that would mean for her if they found out. We talked about the importance of self-care and that in order to take care of others, you must take care of yourself first. We also talked about normalizing therapy and the benefits of working with a therapist: even therapists see therapists. This client also expressed that she was always curious about ecotherapy and ways it could be utilized in everyday life. She said she felt so much better both personally and professionally after attending this workshop.

The best part of this day is when we asked the captain if we could stop the boat and jump into the water. It was so hot outside! The water felt glorious. This was such a memorable experience, one that I will forever cherish. Most of the clients jumped into the water. I loved watching the ripple effect of the water after the first person stepped to jump in; other people hesitated but after seeing someone else jump, they took the leap as well. It was so much fun! One client shared with us that she had not been in the water since she was 10 years old. Our swim lasted about 30 minutes, and we had fun in water, forgetting about life problems and feeling like kids again.

This experience was especially powerful because I witnessed all the clients, of different ages with different backgrounds and life experiences, being present together. We closed by asking the clients the one thing they would take away from the workshop. One particular client's answer stuck with me. She said, "Being out here on the water just puts in perspective how big our world is and how tiny our problems sometimes can be." All other clients agreed and made a promise to devote time to themselves daily. My heart felt so full.

What a blessing and amazing opportunity to work as a counselor-in-training at Jersey Shore Ecotherapy. I always gave my clients the option if they felt more comfortable meeting in the office or meeting outdoors. I enjoyed processing the difference in the client's interactions when we worked indoors versus outdoors. My observation is that I was able to build a therapeutic alliance more quickly with a client when we were outdoors. I expect this is because of experiencing something in nature with the client together and having the chance to process it together. For example, while paddling with a client along Cedar Creek, we stopped because we saw a family of turtles sunbathing on the rocks. This brought her back to a memory with her father she had when she was younger, and I learned more about her current relationship with him. There are many examples of these types of metaphors that helped affirm to me how nature plays different roles in our lives. In all, this experience solidified my commitment to incorporating the natural world into my own life and helping others connect to nature as well. I look forward to incorporating ecotherapy with all my future clients.

CHAPTER 11

Becoming an Ecotherapist

MEGAN E. DELANEY

Figure 11.1 Kristen in her favorite tree.

> This place, this tree is so magical! It was a place of healing and refuge for me as a wayward teenager, just down the path from our property. I must have spent hundreds of hours hanging out here pondering my place in the family of things.

The tree sits on the edge of a meadow of Mima mounds, another fascinating part of the landscape here. They are natural mounds thought to be formed by glacial melting, or earthquakes or expanding clay. The true origins are still unknown which makes them pretty magical too. Across the field, but part of the same property is a Wolf Sanctuary. On this day the wolves harmoniously lifted their voices to howl while we meandered around the branches and awed at the fascinating and impossible ways the Grandfather tree grows. And there was one black Raven on the dead tippy top as we arrived and two cuddling Ravens up there on our departure. This, being in nature, is the best kind of medicine.
—Kristen Huber, MA, LPC, Jersey Shore Ecotherapy

I met Kristen by just Googling "ecotherapy in New Jersey," and her website Jersey Shore Ecotherapy popped up first. I called her immediately. We discovered that she is a graduate of Monmouth University, the program where I teach. We picked a date to meet for coffee. I felt the pull of a kindred spirit the moment she walked in the door. We spoke at long length about our shared passion of the natural world and the miracles of her healing power. She told me story after story of revelations, therapeutic breakthrough moments, powerful metaphors, and lives changed by doing what she calls "thinking outside the couch." Kristen found ecotherapy by doing her own research. Through intuition and her own love of the outdoors, she decided one day to ask a client if she wanted to try a session outside. Immediately, she saw a difference. Her client relaxed, smiled, found respite, and, most importantly, opened up freely and easily. From here, Kristen moved her practice onto paddleboards. She knew the power and peace she gained from paddling on her local lakes and wanted to share that with her clients. Her practice started with one paddleboard and built up over time. Now she has over eight paddleboards (so she can do groups). You might spot her trucking around the Jersey Shore with her big red pickup filled with paddleboards! You will read her own voice in her vignette in this chapter.Kristen found ecotherapy through insight. I found ecotherapy through the classroom. Regardless of how you got here, I hope you are feeling inspired. Nevertheless, setting up your ecotherapy practice is not as simple as just lacing up your hiking boots and taking your clients outside; there are several factors that must be taken into consideration. The following are some practical and ethical considerations for starting your ecotherapy practice. They include solidifying your own relationship with nature, thinking about the practical and insurance aspects, updating your intake forms and initial interviews, ways to redesign your indoor space, and ways to get up off the couch and get outside. In addition to these practical steps, there are some ethical codes and standards to consider. The American Counseling

Association (ACA) standards are addressed in this text, but consult your own professional standards if you are in another category of professional helpers. Let's start with you.Solidify Your Own Identity

As emphasized throughout this book, having a strong relationship of your own with the natural world is a critical piece. As with all relationships, this can be a work in progress but nonetheless strong and solid. A strong nature identity enables you to easily identify yourself in Reese's (2016) "Seven Factors of EcoWellness":

1. Physical Access is the ability to physically interact in or with what the individual considers to be nature.
2. Sensory Access is the ability to touch, smell, see, or hear nature in the absence of physical nature contact.
3. Connection comprises pleasant cognitions and emotions elicited by one's relationship with nature.
4. Protection (also termed nature self-efficacy) is feeling effective when navigating natural settings and having a sense for what might contribute to one's survival and enjoyment when in or with nature.
5. Preservation (also referred to as environmental agency) is acting on behalf of or advocating for the natural world, whether that means recycling or supporting an environmental cause.
6. Spirituality is feeling connected with one's conception of a higher power and/or life-guiding principles elicited through one's connection with nature.
7. Community Connectedness is feeling connected with others in nature. (p. 347)

In designing your ecotherapy practice, be thoughtful and mindful of each of these categories. It is also important to think and talk about these tenets with your clients. Feeling comfortable and aware of your own ecowellness allows you to guide the journey for others.

One easy way to start your process is in your office. Research on biophilic design or the "greening" of indoor spaces to represent colors, textures, and patterns found in nature has shown to improve productivity and overall mood (Ryan, Browning, Clancy, Andrews, & Kallianpurkar, 2014). Look around your office. How natural does it feel? Do you have windows with views of nature? It might be worth opening the blinds to let in the natural light and views of outdoors. Rearrange your couches and chairs so that you and your clients can see out the window. If you do not have a view of nature from your window, you could add pictures of natural places, such as pictures of trees, vistas, or windows overlooking a beautiful coastline, for example. Check the lighting in your office—is it the glaring overhead florescent kind? Try turning those off and add lamps or change lightbulbs for more subdued and natural lighting. Take stock of the colors in your office; are they soothing and peaceful? Interior designers who use a biophilic approach state that blue, green, and whites promote motivation; blue, green, and yellows stimulate productivity; and yellow, green, and white are inspirational (Grinde & Patil, 2009). If you are not able to paint, add color with pillows, throws, and pieces of art. Of course, adding plants to your office will definitely green the space.

Including plants in indoor places, especially windowless places, improves mood and reduces blood pressure (Field, 2000; Lohr, Pearson-Mims, & Goodwin, 1996). If you are unsure about your green thumb, start with a low-maintenance plant like a succulent. Golden pothos vines and spider plants are also fairly easy to maintain and will vine/produce offsets that hang over window ledges or bookshelves. Dracaena plants are also hardy in many different conditions and produce big, beautiful green leaves with yellow stems. Of course, there is the ever-popular lucky bamboo that seems to survive even in the most inhospitable of office conditions. Another option for adding plants is using artificial plants. I am a self-confessed houseplant addict and prefer the live variety but understand that not everyone is the same. There are many beautiful and authentic-looking artificial plants available in almost every home store. They have even fooled me at times and, of course, take little effort except for the occasional dusting. Now that you have greened up your indoor office, let us talk about next steps in taking your work outside.

INTAKE FORMS AND INITIAL INTERVIEWS

Above and beyond the typical information collected in intake forms, I add additional questions and add specific information. For example, I ask a few simple questions:

> Do you enjoy spending time outside?
> If so, where and when do you go outside?
> Would you be comfortable having counseling sessions outdoors?
> Do you have any medical or physical considerations that are important to consider?

These questions become good starting points in the intake interview. I also include information on my informed consent. The following is an example. Discuss what to include with your insurance carrier and/or attorney if necessary.

A large part of my practice encompasses ecotherapy, which broadly defined is how our connection to nature and the natural world influences our mental and physical health. As an ecotherapist, I may suggest that our sessions take place in an outdoor environment such as a park, nature trail, beach, etc. We will discuss in advance best places to meet in the outdoors. There may be some risks (tripping, insect bites, etc.) that are regular occurrences when being outdoors. If you have physical concerns, allergies, or other considerations that may affect your experience being outside, please be sure to inform me before we go outside. By initialing below, I (or on behalf of my child), understand and take responsibilities for those risks.

If you work at an agency or organization, be sure to discuss with the administration and your supervisor what to include on intake forms.

During the initial interviews, I begin to explore the client's relationship and previous experiences with nature. These discussions include a conversation about when, where, and how often the client goes outside. Other questions include childhood interactions with nature as well as family and cultural traditions involving nature. Early in the therapeutic process, I begin to talk about the healing power of nature and our deep connection to the natural world. I use the questions in the intake interview as well as responses in the initial interview to start the dialogue. More often than not, clients seek me out because of ecotherapy. I discuss my approach to counseling as well as my focus on ecotherapy both on my Psychology Today profile as well as on my personal website. In addition, referrals come to me through referrals, either by past clients or friends/colleagues who know about my work. One further note: If you work with children, be sure to have very specific conversations with parents/guardians about how, where, and why you do your work. Make sure you know about any experiences and/or medical conditions that the child may have that may affect your work. Be specific about where you are meeting and what you will be doing. One of the greatest ethical considerations for counselors is to do no harm. Being, thoughtful, prepared, and considerate protects yourself and your clients.

MOVING OFF THE COUCH

Moving off the couch and into nature will look very different for every counselor and client. First, give your insurance company a call and talk to them about what additional considerations, if any, you might need to make. If you work with an attorney, you may also like to talk about what language to include on your forms and paperwork. After working out those logistics, consider where and how you will conduct your outside work. Think about what is accessible from your office space. Is there a bench under a tree nearby that you can go and sit together or a walking path through a park? Take first steps that are reasonable before venturing off to bigger or more ambitious places. Before you go, be sure to map out where you are going to go and how long it takes to get there and back from your office. If you hike on a trail, scope it out in advance to see how long it reasonably takes to walk and to ensure you know where you are going. Being prepared is always important when being outside. Carry a charged cell phone with you in case of emergencies. Also, be sure to carry a first aid kit, water, and some snacks, and perhaps a small umbrella and an extra layer. Always be sure that someone, other than the client, knows where you are going and how long you will be gone. Finally, take the client's lead. I recently had a young client who loves the beach. With his parents' approval, we would meet at a local beach for our sessions, not to swim but to collect shells and build in the sand.

A final but important consideration is to talk about confidentiality. There is a chance that while you work with a client outside you may run into someone that either you or they know. Before you go out, be sure to talk with your client about how they want to handle a potential interaction with someone that you may see. Would they prefer to say you are friend, colleague, therapist, or associate? If you work in a small town or rural area, it is likely that folks will know you are a counselor. This is something to consider when thinking about where and when to conduct sessions outside. How comfortable will your client be if seen by others when working with you? You may consider driving further away or finding a more remote site to conduct your work. It is important to talk to your clients about all of these considerations.

ETHICAL CONSIDERATIONS

As counselors, we abide by the ACA (2014) Code of Ethics. If you are a helping professional from another field, consult your appropriate ethical codes. Ethical decision-making is paramount in what we do as therapists. The ACA Code of Ethics states the central doctrines of professional ethical behavior are

- *autonomy*, or fostering the right to control the direction of one's life;
- *nonmaleficence*, or avoiding actions that cause harm;
- *beneficence*, or working for the good of the individual and society by promoting mental health and well-being;

- *justice*, or treating individuals equitably and fostering fairness and equality;
- *fidelity*, or honoring commitments and keeping promises, including fulfilling one's responsibilities of trust in professional relationships; and
- *veracity*, or dealing truthfully with individuals with whom counselors come into professional contact. (p. 3)

Using these principals as a guide, there are several ethical codes I consider important when embarking on an ecotherapy practice.

A.1. Client Welfare

Because the primary responsibility of the counselor is the client's welfare, we must consider it paramount in our ecotherapy practice. As such, we have honest and open conversations with our clients about all aspects of the work we do together.

A.1.c. Counseling Plans

Particular to ecotherapy, we must make distinct plans when we conduct our practice outside. This involves being very thorough in choosing an outdoor location. We must scope it out well before bringing any clients to the site. Being prepared includes having a clear plan for any circumstances that might arise. Being outdoors brings an element of uncertainty, but that is part of the healing aspect of nature as well. In order to be as prepared as we can, we must think about predictable hiccups. These can include sudden changes in weather and having the right clothing and gear to deal with potential change. Know how to access medical personnel if a client or you were to get hurt. It is also important to know if your client has any allergies or medical considerations. It is critical to carry extra water and snacks, a first aid kit, and a working cell phone with you at all times. Also be sure that someone knows where you are at all times. Talk to clients in advance about what they should bring with them, such as a comfortable pair of shoes, extra layers, water, sunscreen, snacks, and medical supplies (if needed). Of course, we cannot plan for everything, but we can be prepared for what we can control.

A.2.a. Informed Consent

As mentioned earlier in this chapter, having a detailed and explicit informed consent is important for ecotherapists. Discuss this with your lawyer in advance, if applicable. Clients have the choice to start and remain in a counseling relationship and need a full understanding of the process, especially those clients who are new to the process. During the initial meeting, we always take the time to read and verbally review the informed consent. This can start your conversation about ecotherapy with the client. Of course, clients can choose whether or not to participate in ecotherapy, but they cannot make an informed decision without a clear explanation of the process of counseling, including the logistics of what the counseling session might look like outside. Having it clearly spelled out in your informed consent will help you as the clinician better explain the concept and the process with your clients.

A.4.a. Avoiding Harm

"Counselors act to avoid harming their clients, trainees, and research participants and to minimize or to remedy unavoidable or unanticipated harm" (ACA, 2014, p. 4). As ecotherapists, when we get out of the relative safety of our offices, we must think about how we best can avoid harm for our clients. Being prepared is of ultimate importance. We must not do anything that is outside of our abilities (and insurance limitations). We must not make our clients do anything completely outside of their abilities and/or may cause them greater harm than good. However, sometimes challenging oneself can be therapeutically important. I had a client who did not feel like she was capable of walking long distances. Instead, we sat at a park. In time, I was able to walk with her for short distances, and then longer distances. Eventually she was walking a full mile with me each time we met, an accomplishment that brought her great pride (plus the added physical health benefits). Therefore, we must make judgments, in consultation with our clients, on what risks might be truly harmful and which might be worth pursuing for the potential benefits. The ACA (n.d.) warns that risk management is very complex. "ACA believes that, whenever questions arise, counselors should consult with a lawyer licensed in the jurisdiction in which they practice."

B.1.c. Respect for Confidentiality

Counselors always respect the confidentiality of current and prospective clients. As we know, there are times where confidentiality must be breached. These exceptions are outlined in depth in the ACA (2014) Ethical Guidelines.

B.3.c. Confidential Settings

As ecotherapists, we are at higher risk for working in settings that may not ensure confidentiality. As mentioned previously, it is important to have these conversations with clients before venturing outside. If we work at parks, beaches, or hiking trails, we will eventually bump into other people. First, be mindful of the sites you choose. A beach on a summer afternoon does not typically allow for confidentiality, nor does a park bench near a popular playground. Be sure to know your outdoor spaces, including how suitable it is at the day and time you are meeting your client. Furthermore, be aware of others while you are working. A client might be emotionally engrossed in a story or a feeling and may not notice others nearby. It is your job to steer the client away from others within earshot. Clients might also run into people they know. You might see people you know. Have this conversation with your client in advance. Be empathic and aware of your client's needs. If a topic feels particularly vulnerable, decide whether it feels safer discussed in the office.

C.2.a. Boundaries of Competence

The ACA (2014) Code of Ethics states that counselors "practice only within the boundaries of their competence, based on their education, training, supervised experience, state and national professional credentials, and appropriate professional experience" (p. 8). Since there is no recognized credential for ecopsychology, you must make a judgment about your level of readiness to incorporate ecotherapy into your practice. Starting small and slowly and working your way to more complex concepts and techniques is important.

There are many terrific books on the subject. Core readings on the topic include:

>
> Roszak, T., Gomes. M. E., Kanner, A. D., & Brown, L. R. (Eds.) (1995). *Ecopsychology: restoring the earth, healing the mind*. Berkeley, CA: The University of California Press.
>
> Buzzell, L., & Chalquist, C. (Eds.).(2009). *Ecotherapy: Healing with nature in mind*. San Francisco, CA: Sierra Club Books.
>
> Clinebell, H. (1996). Ecotherapy: *Healing ourselves, healing the earth*. Minneapolis, MN: Augsburg Fortress Press.
>
> Jordan, M., & Hinds, J. (Eds.) (2016). *Ecotherapy: Theory, research and practice*. London, England: Macmillan International Higher Education.
>
> Louv, R. (2008). *Last child in the woods: Saving our children from nature-deficit disorder*.

Chapel Hill, NC: Algonquin Books of Chapel Hill.

Louv, R. (2012). *The nature principle: Reconnecting with life in a virtual age*. Chapel Hill, NC: Algonquin Books of Chapel Hill.

Nichols, W. J. (2014). *Blue mind: The surprising science that shows how being near, in, on, or under water can make you happier, healthier, more connected, and better at what you do*. London, United Kingdom: Little, Brown.

Kahn, P. H., & Hasbach, P. H. (2013). *The rediscovery of the wild*. Cambridge, MA: MIT Press.

Kahn, P. H., & Hasbach, P. H. (Eds.). (2012). *Ecopsychology: Science, totems, and the technological species*. Cambridge, MA: MIT Press.

McGeeney, A. (2016). *With nature in mind: The ecotherapy manual for mental health professionals*. Philadelphia, PA: Jessica Kingsley.

Florence Williams, *The Nature Fix*.

Williams, F. (2017). *The Nature Fix: Why nature makes us happier, healthier and more creative*. New York, NY: W.W. Norton and Co.

Another resource is the journal *Ecopsychology*, the only peer-reviewed publication that contributes work exclusively on the topic. The quarterly editions include the latest research on topics including biophilia; ecotherapy; the psychology of environmental destruction; science, technology, and the depth of experience with nature; the rediscovery of the wild; urban sustainability; indigenous cultures; responsibility for protecting natural places and other species; and human–animal interaction. Another helpful resource is the Children and Nature Network (CN&N), a nonprofit organization started by journalist Richard Louv that brings together scholars, activists, health professionals, journalists, and leaders all around the world on the collective cause of granting children safe and easy access to nature. The CN&N website is full of resources as well as links to the latest research on the topic. If you desire hands-on and immersive training, there are places throughout the world that offer extensive training in ecopsychology and ecotherapy. Do some due diligence before participating in these trainings. Check the credibility of the organization and the credentials of the speakers. Check to see if the speakers practice and/or publish on the topic.

ETHICS OF EARTH KEEPING

In addition to counseling ethical considerations, as ecotherapists we go beyond to think deeply about how we, as inhabitants on Earth, ethically treat our planet. I am always mindful of what I know from my training and experiences with the National Outdoor Leadership School (NOLS) and

Outward Bound, and I use in my practice as a wilderness therapist the concept of "leave no trace." Leave No Trace is a set of outdoor ethics that help to protect and encourage conservation of the outdoors. It consists of seven principles:

1. Be prepared and plan ahead.
2. Travel in the wilderness on durable surfaces in order to leave as little impact from your footsteps.
3. Dispose of all waste properly, which includes carrying out all items that are not native to the ecosystem.
4. Leave behind what you find—never take anything out of the ecosystem.
5. Minimize the impact of fires by using provide fire pit (if available), if not by keeping fires small, extinguishing fires entirely, cleaning all fire pits to look as if they were not there, spreading ashes very widely.
6. Respect wildlife by making your best effort to not disturb any natural habits and being respectful of their living space.
7. Be considerate of any other visitors. (REI Co-op, n.d.)

I teach these principles to my students and clients before we start any lessons or sessions outside. In many ways, these principles can easily be adapted to everyday living. These ethical tenets are engrained in my daily

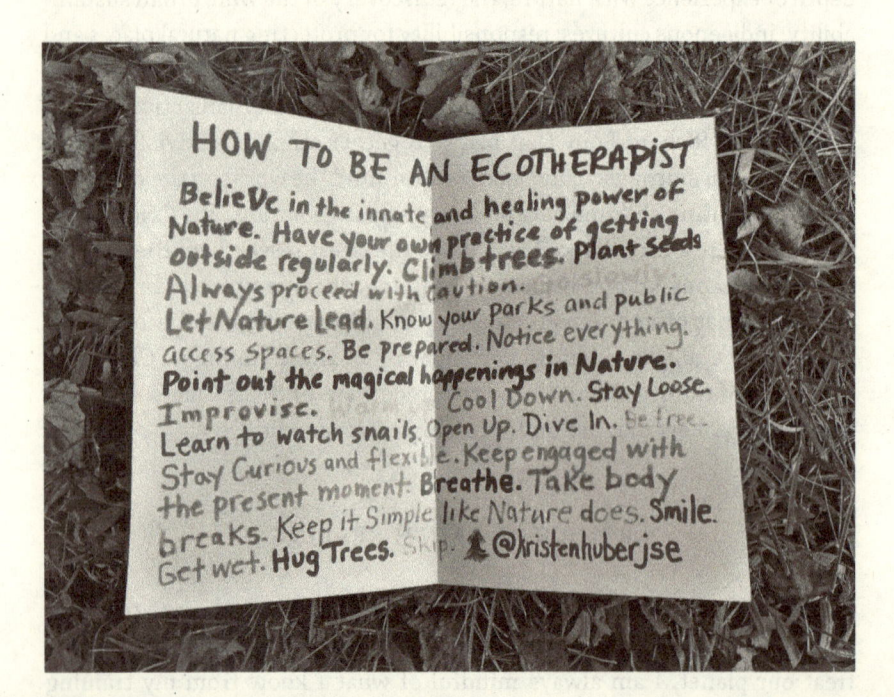

Figure 11.2 Kristen's guidelines for Ecotherapy.

behaviors and guide my ethical decision-making about how I interact with the natural world.

I also try to live as minimally as possible, thinking about the footprint I leave behind with my choices. This is especially difficult with children who seem to explode stuff in every room they enter, but still I try. For example, I think about my purchases and try to use as little packaging as possible. I recycle, of course, but also try to reuse and sometimes repurpose things rather than throw them out. I eat organic and support local farmers and local businesses. Yet I am conscious that these decisions are easier for me to make than others. I have the financial means to buy organic foods and to support local farmers markets and businesses, which often cost more than chain grocery stores. I live near natural places that are free, accessible, and safe. I have access to public transportation, a car, a bicycle, and an able body that can get me to the places I want and need to go. Explore equity with your clients. Take the time to be aware of and have conversations with our clients about their relationship with and access to natural spaces. Without judgment, we may have to guide our clients and educate them on best ways to care for our planet, especially ways that work best for their emotional and financial abilities.

BE CREATIVE

I only went out for a walk and finally concluded to stay out till sundown
   for going out, I found, was really going in.

—John Muir

A final note is: Be creative. Natures presents itself with endless creativity and inspiration. Let what you see, feel, smell, and experience in the natural world inspire you to think *outside the office*. Just as nature is for everyone, I believe ecotherapy is too. We all have the capacity, even in small ways, to green our practice. Take what you do best and think about how you might be able to incorporate the tenets of ecotherapy. Introduce the concept to another, and inspire someone to step outside and reconnect, or try something new.

I promise you, you will feel better for it.

REFERENCES

American Counseling Association. (2014). *American Counseling Association Code of Ethics 2014*. Retrieved from http://www.counseling.org/resources/aca-code-of-ethics.pdf.

American Counseling Association. (n.d). Risk management. Retrieved from https://www.counseling.org/knowledge-center/ethics/risk-management

Field, T. (2000). The effect of interior planting on health and discomfort among workers and school children. *HortTechnology, 10*(1), 46–52.

Grinde, B., & Patil, G. (2009). Biophilia: Does visual contact with nature impact on health and well-being? *International Journal of Environmental Research and Public Health, 6*(9), 2332–2343.

Lohr, V. I., Pearson-Mims, C. H., & Goodwin, G. K. (1996). Interior plants may improve worker productivity and reduce stress in a windowless environment. *Journal of Environmental Horticulture, 14*(2), 97–100.

Reese, R. F. (2016). EcoWellness and guiding principles for the ethical integration of nature into counseling. *International Journal for the Advancement of Counselling, 38*, 345–357. https://www.doi.org/10.1007/s10447-016-9276-5

REI Co-op. (n.d). Leave no trace principles. Retrieved from https://www.rei.com/learn/expert-advice/leave-no-trace.html

Ryan, C. O., Browning, W. D., Clancy, J. O., Andrews, S. L., & Kallianpurkar, N. B. (2014). Biophilic design patterns: Emerging nature-based parameters for health and well-being in the built environment. *International Journal of Architectural Research, 8*(2), 62–76. https://www.doi.org/10.26687/archnet-ijar.v8i2.436

CHAPTER 11A

ON BEING AN ECOTHERAPIST

Kristen Huber

It doesn't happen all at once. You become. Kind of like how the Velveteen Rabbit became real. By the time you are an ecotherapist, you're weathered with sun and wind and you know the sound and feel of crunchy earthy things. That's where I begin, the place where I started to become. I am a first-generation Saltwater Piney, local to the New Jersey Pine Barrens. My maternal grandparents eventually moved to their shore house from Philadelphia, and I was raised in that same home, practically a stone's throw from a national treasure, Barnegat Bay. My father, born in Georgia, was also raised here at the New Jersey Shore. My siblings and I are all native to this land, Ocean County, a quiet, rural place where the scrubby pines simmer down to meet and greet and soak in the saltwater sea. The bay was in my every breath. Life was a constant utilitarian opting outside: bringing in firewood, shucking fresh crab, clamming, blueberry picking, lightning-bug chasing, tree climbing, canoe paddling, barefoot toes in the dirt and grass, garden growing, and love sewing way of life. Things kind of made sense outside in a way that made life on the inside more bearable. It was my own trauma that turned the nurture of nature into my medicine, and that is where it all began.

Nature, especially in my childhood, was constantly binding me to the present moment, making something real of the thoughts and feelings in my body while at the same time gently washing away the difficult stuff. To further ignite my fire, the Pacific Northwest became my home away from home as a wayward teenager. I fell in love and was in awe of "vast, calm, measureless mountain days, inciting at once to work and rest!" (Muir, *John of the Mountains*, 1938). I lived in Olympia through a bachelor of arts in psychology and a hearty start to my professional counseling career. Nearly a decade was spent exploring the Olympic, North Cascades, and Mount Rainier national parks and tons of wild spaces in between. It was as a clinician in an inpatient dual-diagnosis chemical dependency center that gave me my first professional ecotherapy experience. On campus, they had a small ropes course tucked neatly on the back corner of the property. It was there, and on the basketball court playing four square, that I observed the potent outdoor medicine at work. It was also there, outside, where I felt the most capable and connected in my new role as a counselor.

It feels appropriate, however, to give an honorable mention to my yearlong experience at a Native American school, Chief Leschi, in the Tacoma area. I was only there once a week, but that was enough to cultivate another cornerstone of my practice of the wild. At first, I struggled to connect with the staff and students. When seeking advice from a colleague he simply stated, "You must be very busy; we all see you walking quickly from place to place." The feedback helped me realize my fast-paced Jersey undertones were creating the obstacle. As I slowed down, adopting the pace of nature as Ralph Waldo Emerson suggests, I started to see the opportunities all around me, as the sun finds the morning dewdrops on the fresh green grass. Before long, I was invited into a girls group facilitated by the Native American women, the teachers and mothers and keepers of the children. In the group, cultural and ceremonial traditions of craft making were passed on. They used natural elements to create prayers and gifts, all while honoring their ancestors and Mother Earth and giving the youth a safe place to talk and share. The intertwined teaching of practical and useful skills, with spiritual underpinnings, had a profound impact on me both personally and professionally. This interplay of community and culture engendered an already familiar feeling, that which I now think of as eco-interconnectedness. Sadly, the black smoke in the sky from 9-11 called my heart home, and in 2002 I moved back to New Jersey. When I left Washington State to return home, I took with me the core value of environmental stewardship, that sense of responsibility for the ground below my feet wherever I am standing. It is a value that Native Americans effortlessly embody, and I believe it is the essence of ecotherapy.

Returning to New Jersey crystallized the final element of my becoming an ecotherapist: formal practice. Being home at the shore had an innate grounding effect. I was delighted to get back to the forests and creeks of my childhood. It felt more than ever like I knew who I was and how I wanted to evolve as a counselor. In every direction I wandered, nature grabbed hold of my heart and kept a little piece for its own survival. It reminded me over and over again of a simple truth: I am. Here, in the now, undeniably connected to this wild place I call home. In short order Monmouth University became my academic home as I pursued my master's degree in professional counseling. Feeling so inspired and prepared upon graduation, I gifted myself a month-long yoga teacher training program on the magical Paradise Island. I braved the Bahamian winter while deepening my connection to my own body, living, practicing, and being exclusively outside. Yoga as a complimentary medicine became a great companion to my ecotherapy aspirations. It was the catalyst for the implementation of a summer program with at-risk youth back in New Jersey, the start of dabbling with outdoor individual and group sessions. The year was 2006, the infancy of my formal ecotherapy practice. I remained in my role as a pregnancy prevention counselor until joyously and ironically leaving to give birth to my first son.

Motherhood was the dawn of a new season and led me to undiscovered insights about the power of nature, especially in regard to being prepared for the elements. I learned to travel with a tote in my trunk with preparations for all kinds of on-the-go adventures and weather: wet feet and first aid, snacks and water, with a spare set of everything. I found the joy in watching my son connect with nature and the ease it brought to developmental milestones like learning to walk in the soft lush lawn and potty training anywhere and everywhere! It was during this time that I endlessly explored my local open spaces: Wells Mills, Double Trouble, Jakes Branch, Cattus Island, Island Beach State Parks, and more. I made it my mission to hike every trail, find every little hidden treasure, and know the best resting places nestled near bodies of water. I became so familiar with my parks that they became my place of refuge and restoration. Again, nature was my medicine, dispelling all the anxieties and tribulations of motherhood and inciting hope and wonder with every step. After a couple years as a stay-at-home mom, I gingerly returned to counseling, this time working for the community YMCA. In-home counselor was my next role, and I was assigned to youth and families all across my community. The job afforded me a new kind of flexibility for formal ecotherapy practice. I was trained to be aware of dogs, bedbugs, and unclean, unkempt homes. These potential hazards only solidified my resolve to just go outside, and so I did. From then forward, I regularly engaged nature as my cofacilitator, kicking around mindfully with clients on all the trails I had come to know so well.

Although the in-home model offered the freedom to practice psychotherapy in my own way, the work was also intense. Eventually, I reached my expiration point with another due date looming, and I retreated to motherhood and my own personal practice of the wild once again, this time with two little boys in tow. When I was ready to return to work, I transitioned into an outpatient office setting at Ocean Mental Health. Those four bland, windowless walls, cold and frozen with buzzing florescent lights and long sterile hallways, saw me through the remainder of my required clinical hours. It was surprisingly tolerable, even fun sometimes, and I enjoyed the comfort of having other therapists to consult with and debrief the more difficult sessions of the day. Full licensure was like the sun rising out of the ocean at daybreak; it was bright and warm and held all the promise of a new way. I did what any caged bird would do when the door suddenly swings ajar: I took off and flew right into the great wide open of private practice.

Jersey Shore Ecotherapy was born on March 1, 2014. This was the season of my professional life where I grew into my craft. That first summer, I bought two stand-up paddleboards and spent a total of 10 hours

Figure 11a.1 A young client on her paddle board.

on the water with individual clients, not to mention probably five times that paddling on my own or with friends. It was exhilarating! I felt more accomplished and determined than ever as I watched clients open up, dive in (literally sometimes), and be free, finding the growth and healing they were seeking.

By my second season, I owned four sup boards, then five, and so it went. I started a side project called Peace in the Pines with a friend, and we began to host Sup-Yoga and Pedal-Yoga retreats using them as a way to explore mindfulness and self-care. What has been constant throughout is my enthusiasm for getting outside and my gentle invitation for clients to try it too, to see how it feels when you think outside the couch, to see how it feels when you sit still like a frog, wash off the day in the creek, let your worries blow away with the wind, spend 5 minutes practicing following your breath, stretching your spine, or just dropping into your body. Does the dancing glimmer of the sun on the water make them feel hopeful or peaceful or more alive? It's always fun for me to see what creatures or happening will emerge as an exclamation point on the session.

Figure 11a.2 Kristen getting a little wind and water therapy!

Every fall, with the first crisp breeze, I stow away my boards and return to the sanctuary of the trails; by then I'm ripe for the slower pace of the forest. My summers are bustling now with over 100 hours on the water with clients (thank goodness for my yearly intern!). There are teen groups and afternoons full of individual session after session. In the last two years I have introduced sailing workshops, cleverly coined Wind Therapy.

I do have a couch in a lovely and inviting office space, where I diffuse essential oils and prefer to spend as little time working as possible. It is there for rainy days and blistering cold days, for menstrual days and not feeling so good days, for days when the sun is too hot or for any old day at all. It is important that no explanation is needed for a client to choose an office session. It is also there for clients who aren't appropriate, prepared, or interested in ecotherapy sessions. Over and over again nature presents the metaphors needed to help clients along on their journey. I believe it is through the outdoor mind-body experience that we all find eco-interconnectedness. I work deliberately to cultivate this feeling in clients in many ways. One pillar of that is a simple campaign out of Australia, Take Three for the Sea (#takethreeforthesea). I practice and model taking three or more pieces of litter anytime I visit any waterway or wild space with them. My most edifying moments are when my clients begin to do the same. This action reflects their tie to the sacred places where they are brave and safe and working toward their goals. Nature becomes their resource, and, it is my hope, they will become its keeper.

INDEX

For the benefit of digital users, indexed terms that span two pages (e.g., 52–53) may, on occasion, appear on only one of those pages.

Note: Figures are indicated by *f* following the page number

adulthood, the state of, 52–54
adventure-based counseling, 73–75, 76
adventure-based therapy, 183, 216–17
adventure immersion, 5–6, 222–23. *See also* adventure-based therapy
American Counseling Association (ACA) Code of Ethics, 237–41
   boundaries of competence, 240
   central doctrines of professional ethical behavior, 237–38
   client welfare, 238
     avoiding harm, 239
     counseling plans, 238
     informed consent, 238
   confidentiality, 239–40
animal-assisted therapies (AATs), 150–51, 202–3. *See also* equine-assisted therapy
   animal-assisted example, 139–44
   Level 2 AAT, 23
   overview, 137–38, 185–86
   policy trends, 138–39
   use in groups, 87–89
   for veterans, 125–26
animals, 38, 105*f*, 157. *See also* dogs; horses; totem poles art therapy; *specific topics*
   the human–animal connection, 201–5
   nurturing, 185–86
anthropocentrism, 9
art therapy, 38–39
   in nature, 38–41
   nature-based, 218, 220*f*

audition, 68–69
autonomy, fostering, 237

barefoot on the ground, walking/running, 63, 245
beneficence (ethics), 237
Bible, 160–61
biophilia, 24–25
   defined, 8, 24–25
   origin of the term, 8
biophilia hypothesis, 8
biophilic design, 63–65, 234–35
biophobia, 9–10
Buddhism, 161
built environments, 63–64
Buzzell, Linda, 20–21, 22–23, 123

cases, 67. *See also* mindfulness-based ecotherapy group for college students
   Brian and his family, 128–37
   David, 151–53
   Han and Major, 139–44
   JD, 107–10
   Joseph, 50–52, 65
   Mark, 169–73
children. *See also specific topics*
   case of Jeffrey, 41–44
   heavy work, 38
Children and Nature Network (CN&N), 12, 241
Christianity, 158–59, 160–61, 170
Circle of Reciprocal Healing, 23. *See also* ecotherapy: Level 2

classrooms, 103
  outdoor, 4, 32, 102f (see also teaching: outside)
climate change, 9–10
Clinebell, Howard, 7, 20, 21, 22, 35
collective unconscious, 159–60
confidentiality, respect for, 239
confidential settings, 240
conflict, good, 54–55
Conn, S., 19
connection, 234
counseling, professional, 12–13. See also specific topics
  defined, 13
counselor education, integrating ecotherapy into, 206–8. See also Ecotherapy: Applied Ecopsychology
  adding nature to every class, 208–12
counselor education settings, applying nature to, 207–8
counselor educators, 73–74
creativity, 243–44

Darwin, Charles, 154–55, 156, 159
death, natural cycle of life and, 157–58
Delaware River, 176, 179
depression, 11–12, 72, 101, 103, 181–83, 184. See also cases: Han and Major
developmental, individual-differences, and relationship-based approach. See DIR-floortime approach
DIR-floortime approach, 42–43
dogs, 137
  Boots (Beagle mix), 201–2
  service, 138, 185–86
  therapy, 185–86, 203–5
  Yankee (Goldendoodle), 203–5, 203f, 204f

earthing. See barefoot on the ground; grounding exercises; hugging a tree
eating disorders. See horticultural intervention for clients with eating disorders

ecofeminists, 20
ecological circle, 20
ecological spirituality, 20. See also ecospirituality; ecotherapy
Ecological Wellness Checkup, 22
ecopsychological theory, 24–25
ecopsychologists, 21
ecopsychology, 18–19
  applied (see ecotherapy)
  books and other resources on, 240–41
  credentials in, 226–28, 240
  defined, 22–23
  goal of, 18
  nature of, 21
  origin of the term, 18
  origins, 17–20
  tenets, 24–25
  writings on, 20
Ecopsychology (journal), 241
Ecopsychology (Roszak), 18
ecospiritual consciousness and the human experience, 162–63
ecospiritual intervention. See also ecospirituality: clinical applications
  goal of, 173
ecospirituality, 219. See also ecological spirituality
  clinical applications of, 163
    altars to alter, 164–65
    case studies, 169–73
    figure-ground with the environment, 167–69
    finding a sacred spot, 166–67, 168f
    going with the floating, 169
    one with tree meditation, 165–66, 167f
    prayer flags to create personal energy, 165
  counseling, nature, and, 154–56
  definition and nature of, 27, 154, 155–56
  early concepts of, 156–58
  in ecotherapy, 162–63
  goals of, 162–63
ecotherapist
  becoming an, 232–34
  solidifying one's identity, 234–35

being an, 245–50
how to be an, 242f
ecotherapy
  books and other resources on, 240–41
  combining theories, 54–57
  counseling and, 25–27
  deeper, 22–23
  defined, 225
  dimensions within, 20
  ethical considerations (*see* American Counseling Association (ACA) Code of Ethics; ethics)
  intake forms and initial interviews, 235–36
  is good for children in any season, 37f
  Level 1, 12–13, 126
  Level 2, 12–13
  overview, 20–22
  training in, 225–31
Ecotherapy: Applied Ecopsychology (course), 21, 212–19
  assignments, 220
  books used, 214
  class topics and activities, 215
  course description, 213
  learning objectives, 214
Ecotherapy: Help With Nature (Buzzell and Chalquist), 20–21
Ecotherapy (Clinebell), 20
ecotherapy techniques for children, 35
  sensory play, 36–38
  taking the office outdoors, 36
ecowellness, 26, 215
  Seven Factors of EcoWellness, 234
ego vs. spirit, 161–62
empathic failures, repairing, 54–55
environmental agency/preservation, 234
environmental generational amnesia, 24–25
equine-assisted group therapy, 88–89, 90f
equine-assisted therapy, 150–51, 152f, 186–87, 217–18. *See also* horses
  bond between equine therapist and horse, 152f
  for veterans, 138–39
    case of Han, 140–41, 144

ethics. *See also* American Counseling Association (ACA) Code of Ethics
  of Earth keeping, 241–43
evolution, 154–55, 156, 159

felt meaning (Gendlin), 163, 170–71
feminism, 54. *See also* ecofeminists
fidelity (ethics), 238
figure-ground with the environment (context of consciousness), 167–69
floating in water, 169
  opportunities for, 169
flower garden, 61f
flowering plants and bees, relationship between, 58
flowers, 59–60, 117, 164, 191–92. *See also* horticultural intervention for clients with eating disorders
forest bathing, 67–68, 183–85, 215, 216f
forming–storming–norming–performing–adjourning model of group development, 77–78
Freud, Sigmund, 158–59
From Combat to Calm (program), 217–18

Ganges River, India, 176–77, 178, 179, 179f
garden. *See also* flower garden
  cycle of the, 195–200
  tending to a, 104–5
gardening, 89–90, 190–92. *See also* horticulture therapy/horticultural therapy
  mindfulness in, 190–91
green exercise, 182–84
  defined, 182
greenhouse, 89
greening
  of indoor spaces, 234–35 (*see also* biophilic design)
  of psychology, 18
"green rehabilitation program," 183
grounding, 88. *See also* barefoot on the ground; hugging a tree
grounding exercises, 37–38, 81–82, 84, 91f, 106f, 228

group counseling
  case example (*see* mindfulness-based ecotherapy group for college students)
  overview of, 75–76
  tenets of, 76
    group stages, 77–78
    therapeutic factors, 76–77
group development, Tuckman's stages of, 77–78
group settings, nature-based interventions in, 73–75
group work, ecotherapy, 74*f*
growth-fostering relationships, 54–55
  "Five Good Things" that occur in, 55
guilt, 97–98
gustation, 70–71

Hasbach, Patricia H., 24–25
health benefits of nature, 11–12
hiking group, joining a, 60–61
homework, nature as, 40–41
horses, 87–88, 219*f*, *See also* equine-assisted therapy
horticultural intervention for clients with eating disorders, 188–89
  instructions, 190–91
  length of activity, 190
  materials, 190
  rationale, 189
horticulture therapy/horticultural therapy, 23, 89–90, 127, 181–82, 218–19
Huber, Kristen, 226–28, 229–30, 232–34, 249*f*
  guidelines for ecotherapy, 242*f*
  in her favorite tree, 232*f*, 232–33
  paddleboarding and, 225–28, 233
  use of paddleboards in ecotherapy practice, 216, 225–26
hugging a tree, 34*f*, 39
human-centered nature therapy, 22–23. *See also* ecotherapy: Level 1
Human Development courses, 207, 211

immersive experiences. *See* adventure-based therapy; adventure immersion
India, 69, 161, 175–79. *See also* Ganges River

individual differences. *See* DIR-floortime approach
industrialization, 9–10
informed consent, 80, 238
inreach (ecotherapy), 20

Jersey Shore Ecotherapy, 225–26, 231, 233, 248–49
Jesus Christ, 161
Jung, Carl Gustav
  nature and, 17–18, 159–60, 163
  on religion and spirituality, 159–60
  on the solar system, 161–62
justice, 238

Kahn, Peter H., 24–25
Kenya, 4–5

Leave No Trace, 241–42
  principles of, 241–43
Louv, Richard, 10, 12, 33–34, 108–9, 241

masks in art therapy, 39, 218, 220*f*
materialistic disorder, 19
McCauley, Emmi, 226*f*
meaning, search for
  Freud, Jung, and the, 158–60
meditation. *See also* mindfulness
  one with tree, 165–66, 167*f*
mental health benefits of nature, 10, 11–12, 33–34, 101–3. *See also* cases
mental health issues. *See also* depression
  military-specific, 124–25
  in students, 100–3
metaphors
  client- vs. counselor-driven, 57–58
  defined, 57–58
  use of nature metaphors, 53–54, 57–58, 89–90, 116–17, 172, 191–92
middle school ecotherapy groups, 114–15, 118
  ecotherapy activities, 115
    indoors, 117
    that foster resilience, 117
  incorporating mindfulness, 116
  the joy of exploration, 118
  use of nature metaphors, 116–17
military culture, 120–21
  children, 123

service members/veterans, 121–22
spouses, 122–23
military families, a horticulture approach to working with, 127
horticultural case application, 128
military-specific mental health issues, 124–25
military/veteran populations
animal-assisted therapy, 137–38
animal-assisted example, 139–44
policy trends, 138–39
counseling using nature-based interventions, 125–27 (*see also* military families)
deployment, 120, 123 (*see also* cases: Han and Major)
equine-assisted therapy for, 138–39, 140–41, 144
moving nature-based therapy forward with, 145–46
mindfulness
in gardening, 190–91
incorporating, 116
in schools, 105–6
mindfulness-based ecotherapy group for college students, 79
informed consent, 80
promoting the group and screening, 79–80
week one: introduction, 80–81
week two: practicing mindfulness, 81–83
week three: letting go, 83–84
week four: acceptance, 84–86
week five: living in the present, 86–87
week six: animal-assisted healing, 87–89
week seven: horticultural therapy, 89–90
mindfulness exercises, 82, 84, 106, 116, 151, 229–30
Mother Earth, 20, 154–55, 156–57, 158–59
and the cycle of life and death, 157–58
and her creatures, 157
Mother Earth Day, 154
motherhood, 247–48
"Mother" nature, 163
Mount Kenya, 4–5, 5*f*

mucking, 217–18, 218*f*
Myers, J. E., 26

National Outdoor Leadership School (NOLS), 4
Native Americans. *See* Navajo
nature. *See also specific topics*
access to, 234
bringing it indoors, 107
capacity to connect with (*see* biophilia)
early introduction to, 3–7
humans' relationship with, 8–10
research on beneficial effects of, 11–14
nature-based therapies, 125, 126, 145. *See also* ecotherapy; military/veteran populations; *specific topics*
nature breaks, 63
taking mini-breaks and mini-solos, 63
nature-deficit disorder, 10, 108–9
nature self-efficacy, 10, 12, 24–25, 33–34, 234
Navajo, 195–200
Nietzsche, Friedrich, 163
9/11 terrorist attacks, 169–72, 246
nonmaleficence (ethics), 237
nurtured by nature, being, 20, 55–56, 73–74, 77–78, 82–83, 84, 225, 228, 245
defined, 35
nurturing
animals, 185–86
connections to the natural world, 118
the earth, 154–55, 228
importance of, 189–90
nature, 77–78, 82–83, 84, 228
one's relationship with nature, 73–74
plants, 39, 182, 189–90
sowing as, 70

ocean, 85*f*
dipping toes in, 208–9, 209*f*
ocean floating, 169
olfaction, 68
one with tree (meditation), 165–66, 167*f*
outdoors, humans spending less time, 10–11
outreach (ecotherapy), 20
Outward Bound, 187–88

paddleboarding, 216, 217f, 225–28, 248f, 248–49
  Kristen Huber and, 225–28, 233
patch, planting a, 59–60
Peace in the Pines, 249
physical access to nature, 234
picnic, family
Pierce, Gloria, 7
play
  ecotherapy and, 35
  nature and, 32–35
preservation/environmental agency, 234
protection. *See* nature self-efficacy
psychoeducation groups, 76

reciprocity, 58
  of nature, 26–27
  of our relationship with nature, 20, 21, 57
Reese, Ryan F., 26, 234
Reese EcoWellness Inventory, 26. *See also* ecowellness
relational–cultural theory (RCT), 54–57
relational expectations, altering, 54–55
relationship-based approach. *See* DIR-floortime approach
relationships. *See* growth-fostering relationships
religion, 158–59, 160
  animals as integral part of, 157
  earliest form of, 157
  Freud on, 158–59, 160
  history, 156–59
  spirituality and, 155, 178–79
  world religions and nature, 160–62
resilience, ecotherapy activities that foster, 117
rewilding, 24–25, 215
  of the human species, 24–25
rock climbing, 217
ropes courses, 86–87, 216–17
Roszak, Theodore, 7, 18–19, 20

sailing workshops, 250
sand play, 38
schools. *See also* classrooms; middle school ecotherapy groups
  case study, 107–10
  integrating the therapeutic benefits of nature in, 103–7

  student mental health and learning, 100–1
  using nature to treat mental health disorders in, 101–3
Self–Earth Care Plan, 22
Self-Exploration (class), 176–77
sensory access to nature, 234
September 11 attacks (9/11), 169–72, 246
Serenity Stables, 150–51, 217–18
shinrin-yoku, 67–68, 215. *See also* forest bathing
somatosensation, 70
spiritual awareness, 20
spirituality, 155, 234
  counseling, nature, and, 154–56
  definitions and nature of, 155, 234
  dimensions of, 155
  early concepts of, 156–58
  Jung and, 159–60
spiritual values and beliefs, 173

teaching, outside, 211. *See also* classrooms: outside
tents (child ecotherapy), 38
totem poles art therapy, 39–40
transcendence
  defined, 26
  and ecowellness, 26
trees, 210f, 212f
  hugging, 34f, 39
trust, 127. *See also* animal-assisted therapies: animal-assisted example
  animal-assisted therapy and, 137–38, 141–43, 185, 186
trust fall (ropes course), 87
trust walks, 141–42, 211–12, 213f
tunnels (child ecotherapy), 38

upreach (ecotherapy), 20
"Using Nature as a Therapeutic Partner" (Phillips), 12–13

veracity (ethics), 238
veterans. *See* military/veteran populations
vision, 69–70

walking during the schoolday, 103–4
water, 175–77. *See also* Delaware River; Ganges River; ocean

wilderness, 24–25. *See also specific topics*
wilderness experiences, immersive. *See* adventure immersion
wilderness therapy, 187–88, 241–42
  defining, 187
Williams, Florence, 183–84, 188, 214, 222–23
Wind Therapy, 250

wood as mother symbol, 164
woods, 11, 42f, 101
  walking in the, 171–72 (*see also* forest bathing)

Yalom, Irving D., 76, 155
yoga, 96, 246–47, 249
  restorative, 219